CHARLESTON

The Bloomsbury Muse

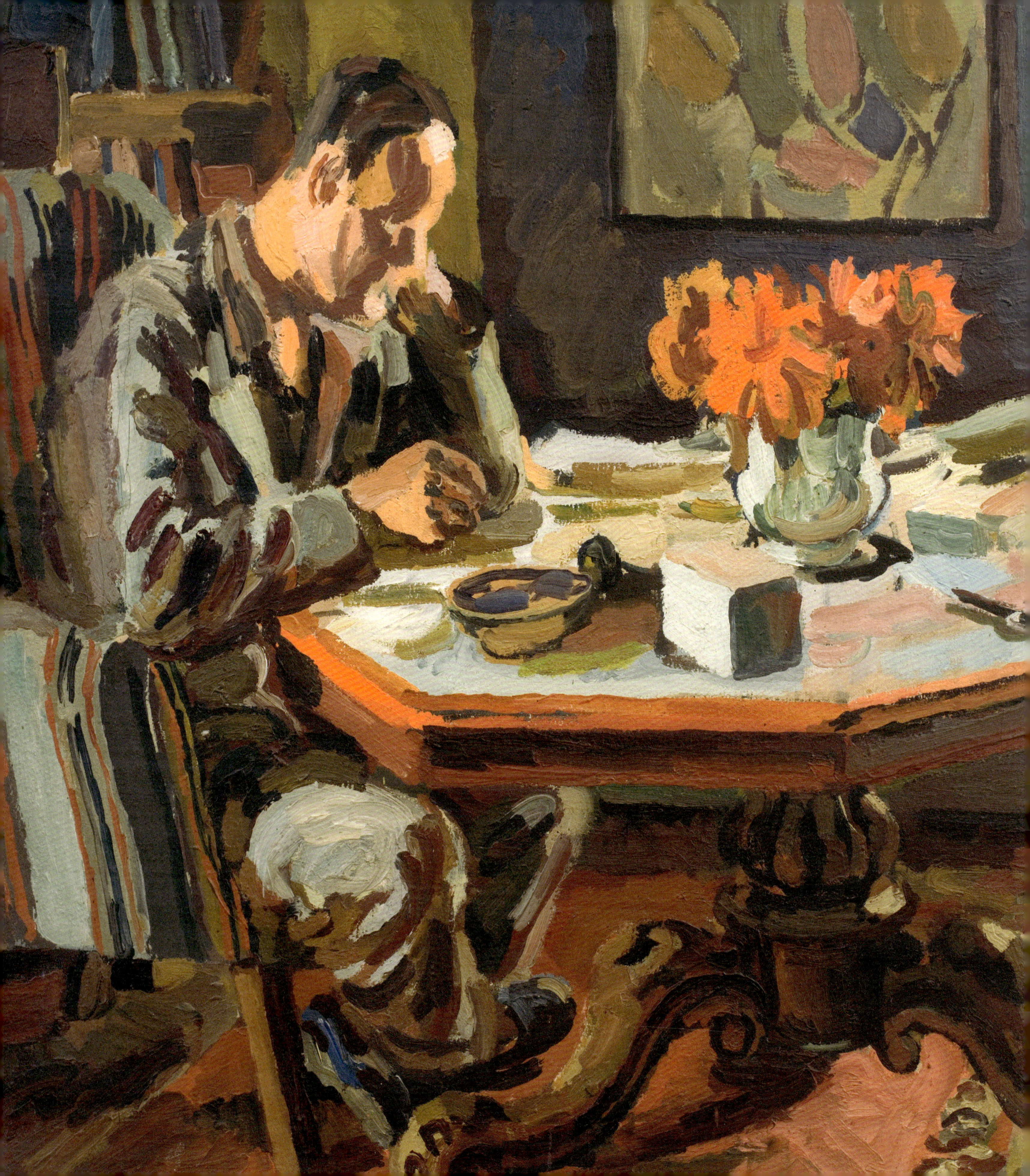

CHARLESTON
The Bloomsbury Muse

EDITED BY
LAWRENCE HENDRA AND ELLIE SMITH

with essays and contributions by
DARREN CLARKE, DEBORAH GAGE,
RICHARD SHONE AND MATTHEW HOLLIDAY

PHILIP MOULD & COMPANY
2021

First published on the occasion of the exhibition
Charleston: The Bloomsbury Muse at

PHILIP MOULD
& COMPANY

14 September 2021 – 10 November 2021

ISBN 978-1-913645-18-2

British Library Cataloguing in Publication Data

A catalogue record for this book is available from the British Library

PRODUCED BY
Paul Holberton Publishing
89 Borough High Street, London SE1 1NL
paulholberton.com

Designed by Laura Parker
Printing by Gomer Press, Llanysul

Front cover: Duncan Grant, *The Hammock, Charleston*, (cat. 12)
Frontispiece: Duncan Grant, *Angus Davidson at Charleston* (cat. 13), detail
Opposite: Vanessa Bell, *The Pond, Charleston* (cat. 4), detail
Overleaf: Duncan Grant, *Still Life with Gourd in a Blue Bowl* (cat. 8), detail

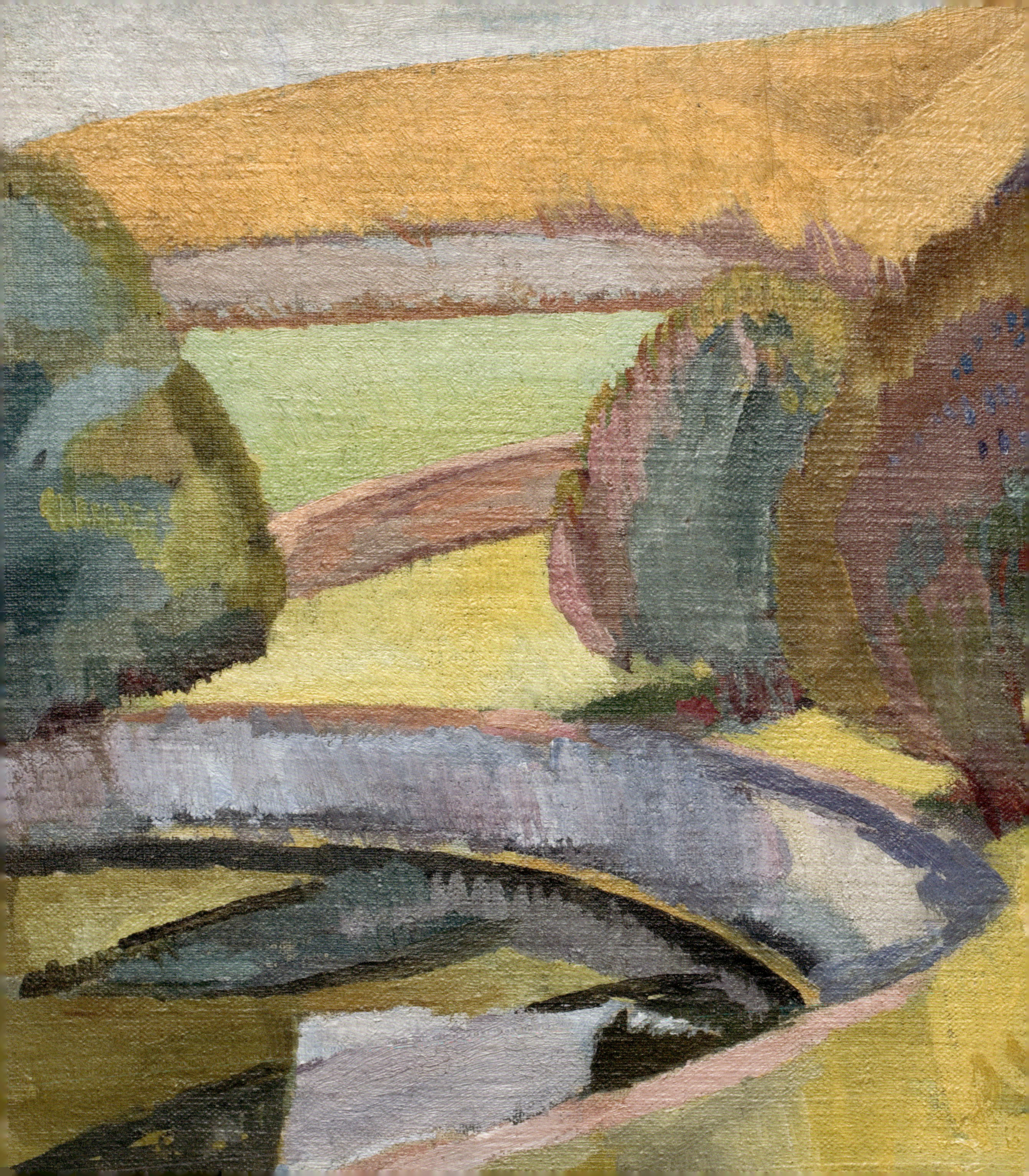

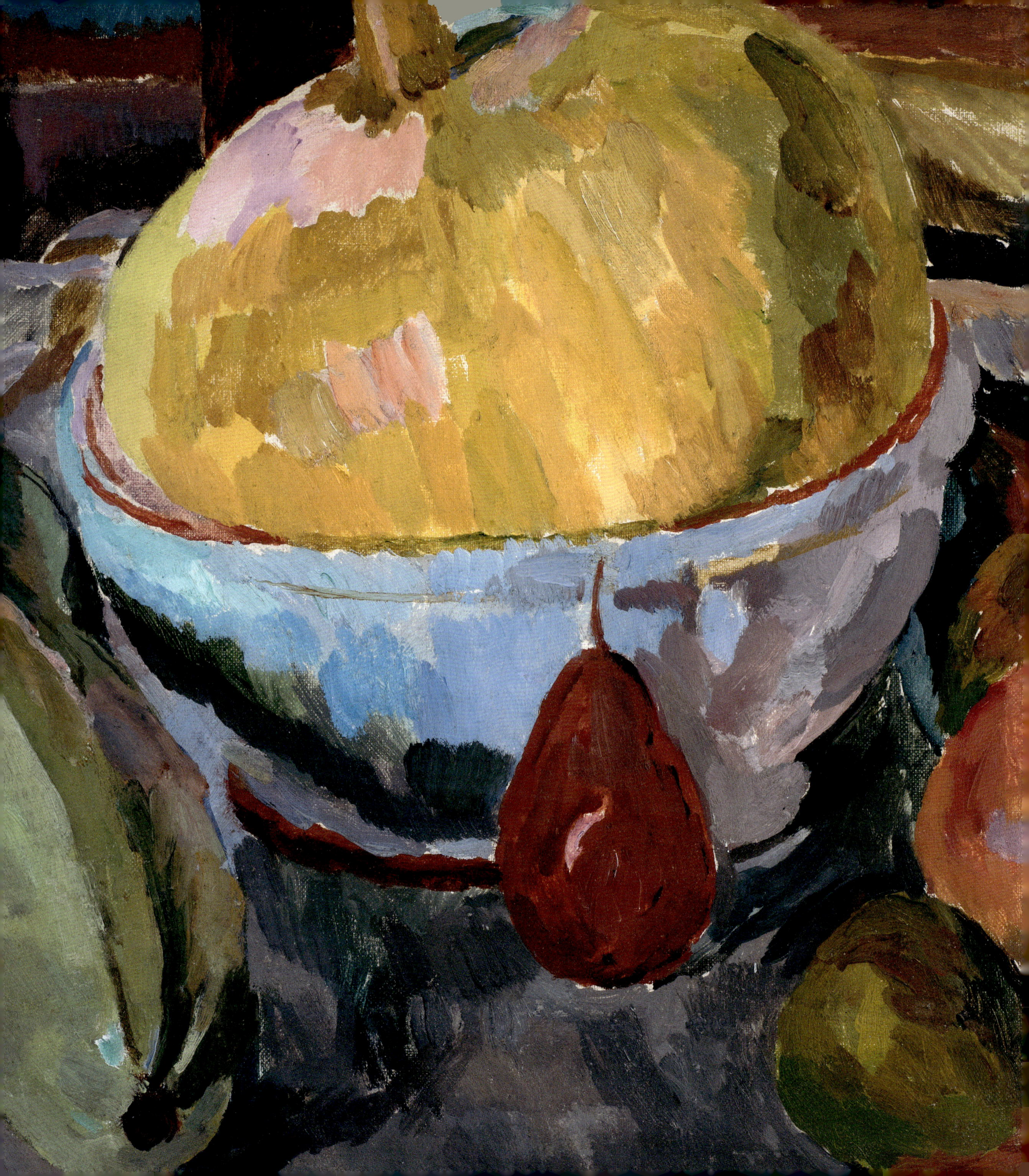

Contents

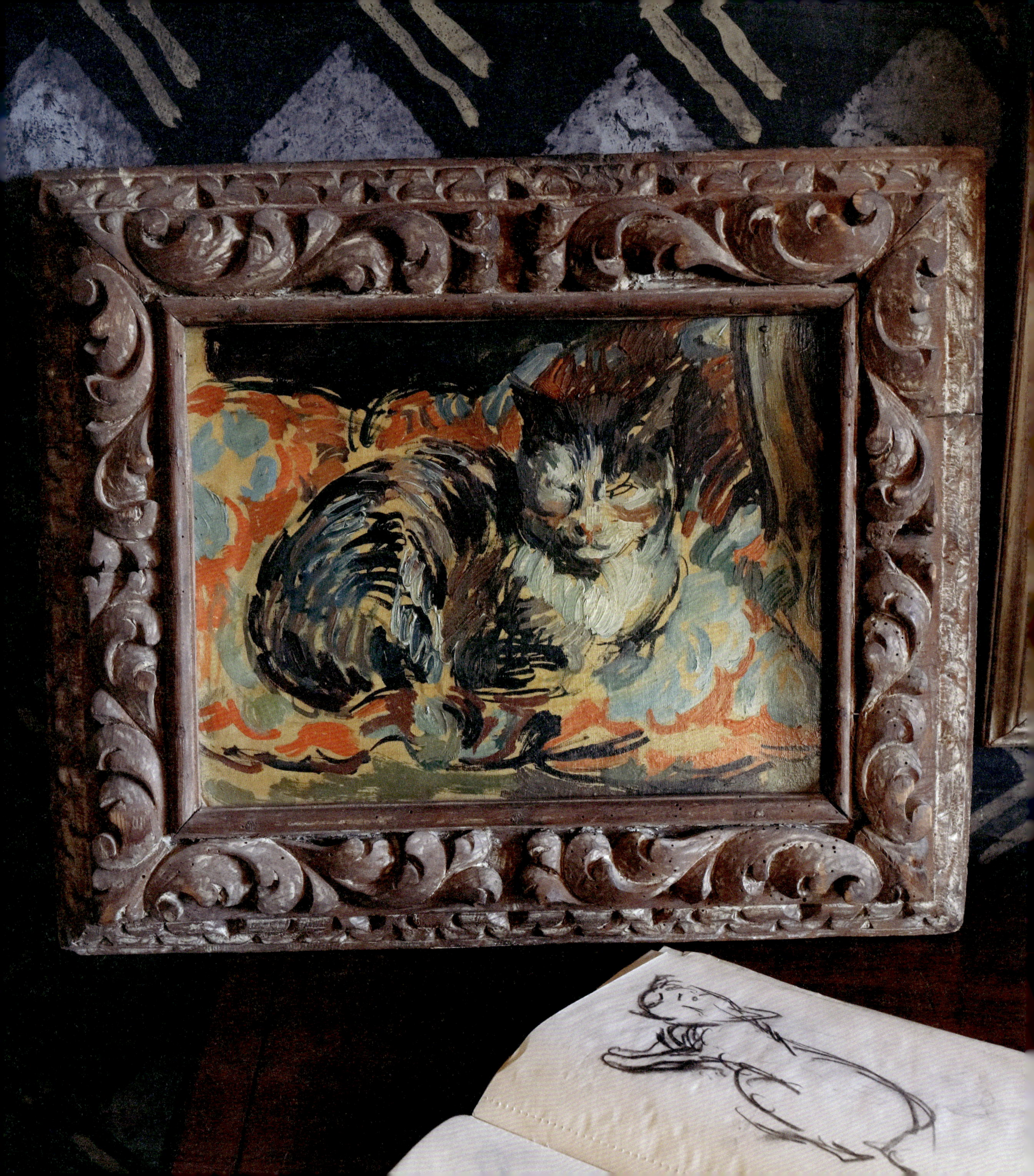

Introduction

PHILIP MOULD

As a deep admirer of twentieth-century British art, and having an equally strong attachment to our native rural history, I felt that Charleston – the Bloomsbury Group's Sussex retreat as well as a home – was the perfect theme for an exhibition.

Lockdown in my own home in the Cotswolds heightened this urge, and, surrounded as I am by ancient barns and a pond (as is Charleston), together with the knowledge that during the Second World War Charleston's own occupants were to a degree locked down, not to say fearful, the idea gained more resonance. This feeling culminated at the point – now mercifully passed – when The Charleston Trust and all it had achieved appeared in peril due to the economic strictures as a result of these pandemic times. Thanks to the adept response of Nathaniel Hepburn and his trustees, for now this terrible spectre has been seen on its way. This exhibition and catalogue are a means of celebrating – in the broadest sense – a place and phenomenon that deserve forever to prosper.

As always, apart from the artists, it is the people who make things happen whom I wish to thank. I list them all below (I hope without omission), but at its point of embarkation this exhibition would have been inconceivable without the generosity and collaboration of The Charleston Trust and its staff. Many items from their exquisite collection fill these pages. Darren Clarke, Head of Collections, Research and Exhibitions, has also written an evocative and lyrical essay about Charleston's history between and including the two wars.

As well as the other private lenders, without whom this exhibition could not have happened, I would also like to thank Debo Gage, who applied some of the same zeal and goodness of spirit as she did in founding The Charleston Trust, to help us with ideas and introductions, and who has delightfully added an essay about how her campaign to save Charleston came about in 1979.

A doyen of the subject of art and Charleston, it was a great pleasure to us all when Richard Shone offered to be interviewed by Matthew Holliday about his part in the Bloomsbury story. We are also extremely grateful to him for acting as a consultant when asked on art historical conundrums.

Our gallery staff have been dedicated and unstinting with their time to make this happen. Such a project would be inconceivable without them. I am indebted to my co-director Lawrence Hendra and researcher Ellie Smith for writing the catalogue entries and to the rest of the team – Catherine Mould, Emma Rutherford, Laura Edmundson, Selina Fischer and Rosalind Sutcliffe – for their enduring commitment throughout this challenging and unpredictable time. I would also like to thank and acknowledge: Jason Badrock, Sophie Bradford, Mark Dalton, Natalie Duff, Emily Hill, Tracy Jones, Robert and Matthew Travers, and the team at Paul Holberton Publishing.

1. *The Cat, Opussyquinusque* (cat. 17) by Duncan Grant, and Vanessa Bell's sketchbook in the Dining Room, Charleston
The Charleston Trust

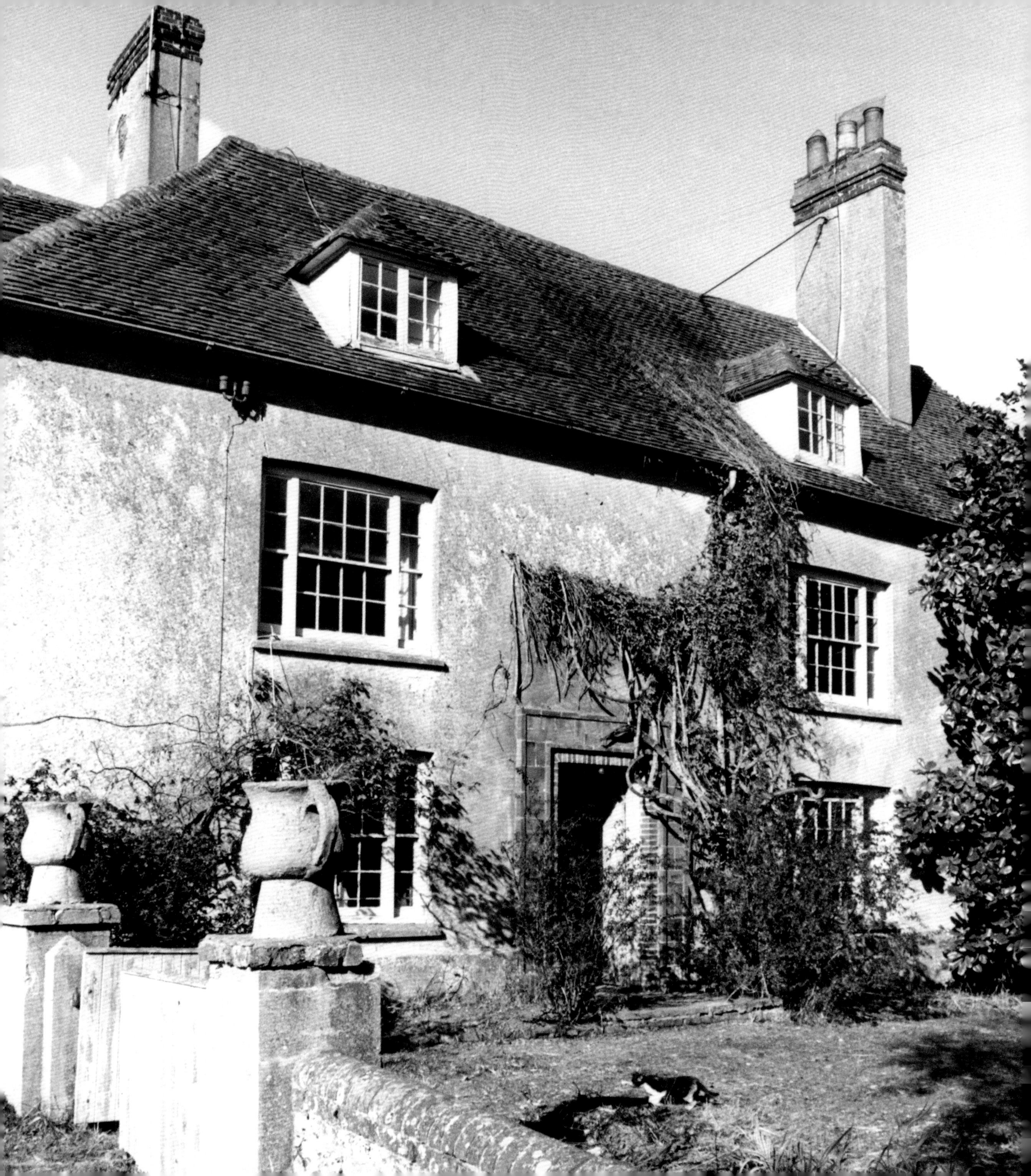

Charleston as Muse

DARREN CLARKE

Dr Darren Clarke is the Rausing Head of Collections, Research and Exhibitions for The Charleston Trust. He has curated several exhibitions, including Orlando at the Present Time *(2018),* Post-Impressionist Living: The Omega Workshops *(2019) and* Duncan Grant: 1920 *(2021)*

2. Charleston, late 1970s
Tate Archive

Charleston is an old farmhouse that sits at the foot of the South Downs, a range of hills so high that clouds sometimes get stuck on them. It was built in the seventeenth century where the Downs meet the Weald, the flat, fertile land that stretches northwards. Geographically it is halfway between Brighton and Eastbourne near the south coast of England but feels a million miles away from the hustle and bustle of these seaside towns. Off a long, winding track, past field after field, the house sits opposite a cluster of farm buildings of flint and brick.

The scars of Charleston's evolution, its wooden frame, the changes and the additions made over the centuries, are hidden under a unifying layer of render, climbing vines, roses and clematis. It sits square to the lane, simple, quite plain, and deceptive in its size. Frances Partridge described it as 'a comfortable hen' protecting its young and letting them thrive.[1] In 1916 it gave protection to a new family, one that had been driven from London, political refugees, moving to the countryside to work the land, to prove themselves pacifist but not idle, not without conviction.

The Great War had been raging for over a year when conscription was introduced for all single men under forty. The artist and designer Duncan Grant, like many of his friends, was a conscientious objector. He and his then lover, the writer David Garnett, were eventually given exemption from conscription on the condition that they did work of National Importance; this included farm labouring.

In September 1916 fellow artist Vanessa Bell came down to the county town of Lewes, secured employment on a nearby farm for Grant and Garnett and arranged to sublet Charleston. She knew the area quite well, for Charleston was only five miles from the site where Asheham once stood – the house that Bell and her sister, Virginia, took in 1912 and where Virginia and Leonard Woolf would continue to live until they moved to Monk's House in the nearby village of Rodmell after the war.

In October 1916 this unconventional family moved in: Duncan Grant, David Garnett and Vanessa Bell, together with her two sons, Julian, aged eight, and Quentin, aged six, from her marriage with the art critic Clive Bell. There were also the children's nurses, a maid and a dog, an Irish lurcher called Henry. The economist John Maynard Keynes (cat. 7) had a room, visiting at weekends from his job at the Treasury.

Bell, Grant, Keynes and Garnett were part of the Bloomsbury group, an informal collection of friends, some related by blood, many connected by love, who valued truth, honesty and the pursuit of pleasure and personal freedoms above all things. Coming of age as the old century and the old queen died, they wanted to escape the hypocritical pomposity of their Victorian youth and make a new world. Unbeknownst to anyone at the time, Charleston would play an important role in this personal ambition.

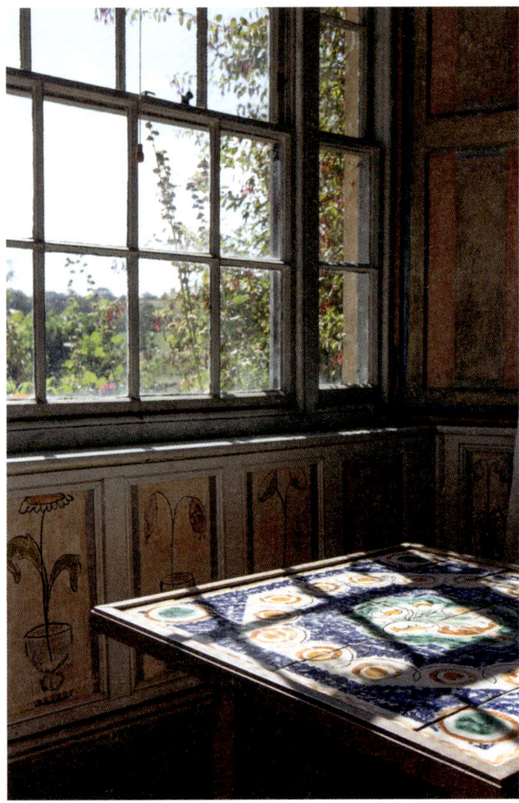

3. Clive Bell's Study, Charleston

4. The Library, Charleston

For many years previously Charleston had been a guest house. Postcards exist showing the elegant if rustic building, rising above a pond, with a well-maintained and manicured front garden. The proud chatelaine stands in front of the house, while guests manoeuvre a boat across the pond.

This previous life clung to the walls of the building, with floral and embossed wallpapers lining most of the rooms. Virginia Woolf described them as 'awful'.[2] Bell agreed and wrote to Grant, explaining that 'unfortunately nearly all the rooms were papered with rather horrid but quite new papers'.[3] Permission was given by the landlord to paint the rooms, and a decorator was employed. He used distemper, binding chalk with sizing that was probably made from boiled-up rabbit skin. Charleston is surrounded by chalk. On an early visit Bell described the landscape: 'The colour is too amazing now – all very warm, most lovely browns & warm greys & reds & with the chalk everywhere giving that odd kind of softness'.[4] Bell and Grant brought these colours inside, mixing Indian red and cobalt blue pigments into the white chalk of the distemper, making a soft-grey covering for the rooms. While Bell was in London sorting out things to send down, Grant wrote to her, telling her that the freshly painted Garden Room was 'lovely', but that, in a violent act for a pacifist household, Henry had bitten the decorator's leg.[5]

On to this blank canvas of a house designs began to take form. Under the window in the children's schoolroom (later Clive Bell's Study) Bell painted delicate, long-stemmed blooms, defying gravity as they balance in transparent glass tumblers and rummers (fig. 3). On the back of the door Grant painted a still life – a vibrantly decorated jug filled with artificial flowers from the Omega Workshops. A project originated by Roger Fry, with Bell and Grant as co-directors, the Omega was an attempt to bring the aesthetics and excitement of Post-Impressionist painting into the design of household goods. Textiles, carpets, clothes, ceramics, furniture, children's toys: there was little to which the artists and designers at the Omega in Fitzroy Square would not turn their hand. Charleston was to become the living embodiment of the Omega's ethos.

The influence of the Omega is seen in Bell's first bedroom, now the Library (fig. 4), with its black and Pompeiian-red walls. Grant brought light and wit to the room, painting a cockerel above the window to wake Bell up in the morning and the irascible Henry below it, to protect her at night. On the back of the door are figures and motifs similar to those in his painting *The Lemon Gatherers*, an oil study that Bell had bought after it was exhibited in a Friday Club exhibition in 1910, though the figures at Charleston are gathering more temperate fruit – apples and pears.

In February 1917 Bell decorated the fireplace and the two doors on either side in Grant's bedroom. She stated that she was 'not doing

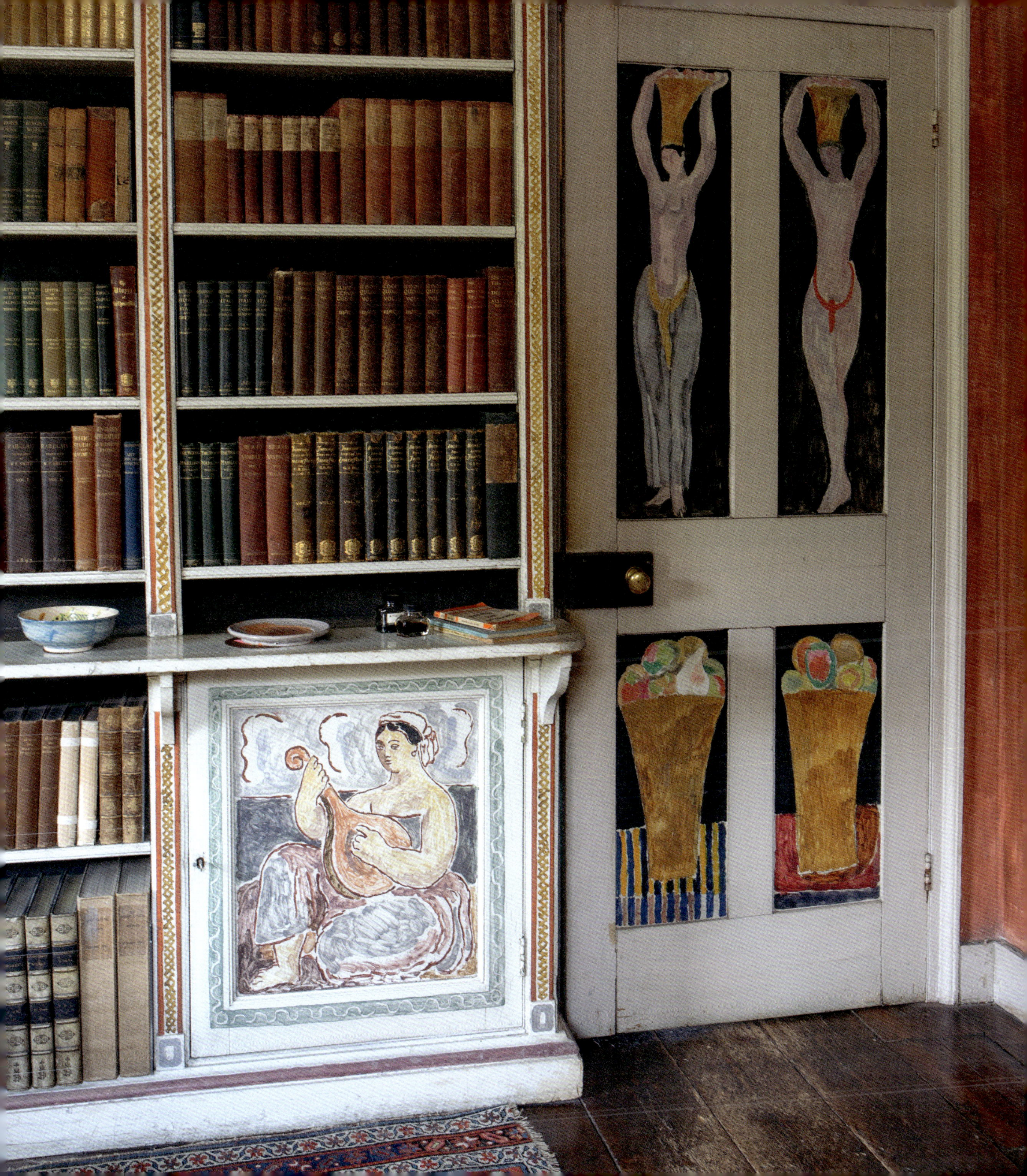

anything very startling – only pots of flowers and marbled circles'.[6] But Bell's designs still hold the energy of over a century ago, with the wonderful curves and twisting shapes of the flowers and jugs, which contrast with the rigid grid of lines that bound them (fig. 5). So many colours, contrasting and clashing, their vibrancy emphasised against the softness of the white walls.

The act of iconoclasm, painting over the previous occupants' taste in wall decoration, became the artists' first creative act in the house. But, for Bell, Charleston was a continuation of a project started in London in 1904 when, after the death of her father, she moved herself and her siblings out of the gloomy and oppresive house in Hyde Park Gate to disreputable Bloomsbury and into 46 Gordon Square. Here she expressed her independence in the way that she decorated and furnished her home. If she was going to run the household, it would be on her terms. She painted the walls light colours and only had a few pieces of furniture, clearing the air, clearing the rooms, making space for new conversations, new guests, new ideas and new endeavours.

She later wrote: 'It was exhilarating to have left the house in which there had been so much gloom and depression, to have come to these white walls, large windows opening onto trees and lawns, to have one's own rooms, be master of one's own time'.[7] Virginia Woolf recalled how they 'were full of experiments and reforms', that 'everything was going to be new, everything was going to be different, everything was on trial'.[8]

Charleston would house experiments in relationships as well as design and domesticity, investigating new ways of living and of loving. Vanessa Bell had married the art critic Clive Bell in 1907, but by the move to Charleston they were no longer living as a married couple, though he often visited, bringing his partner, Mary Hutchinson (cat. 2). A triangular relationship existed at Charleston, with Duncan Grant being shared like wartime rations between Vanessa Bell and David Garnett. Grant usually had male lovers but had a sexual relationship with Bell over two or three years. During this time he also had a sexual relationship with David Garnett, who usually had female lovers but had fallen for Duncan Grant, though he still saw his girlfriends in London. Experiments are not easy; sometimes they fail. There were many jealousies and arguments. These passions, illegal in law and immoral in the wider society, had to be kept hidden from staff and children. Even honesty and openness had boundaries.

There were domestic challenges. Charleston was not an easy house to run. There was no electricity and no telephone. Water came from underground springs and had to be pumped daily. Bell had help: Mabel and Flossie Selwood, nurses to Bell's two sons, and Jessie the maid had accompanied her to Sussex. Another maid, Blanche Payne, also came to

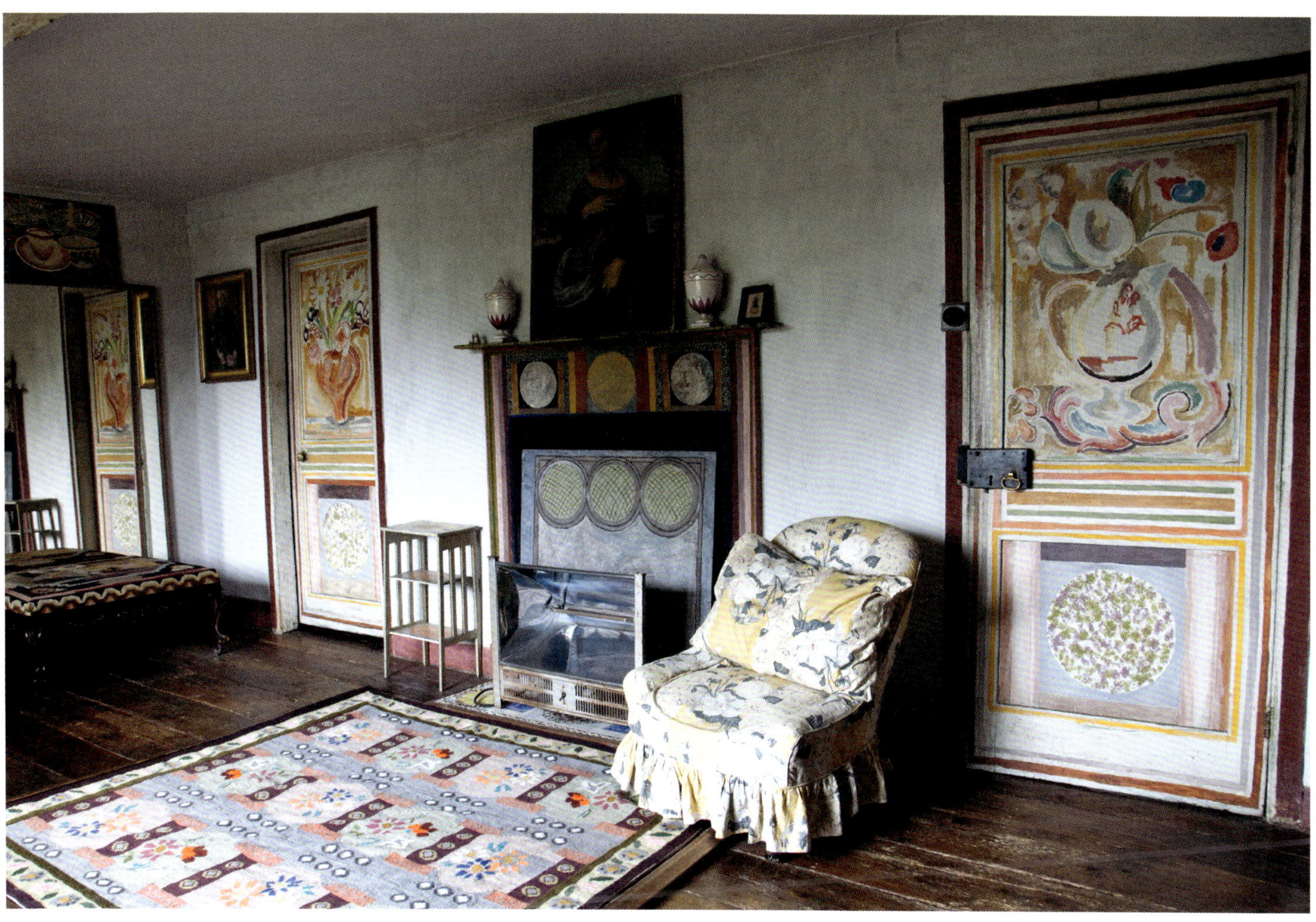

5. Duncan Grant's bedroom, Charleston

Charleston but soon fled to town. Bell described herself as 'overwhelmed by domestic difficulties'.[9]

It could also be a physically challenging environment in which to live. When seen in summer, when it gently hums with heat and colour, Charleston is Edenic and welcoming, but the winters bring a harshness that is sometimes unbearable. That first winter was one of the hardest. Quentin Bell recalled that 'the snow was thicker and the frost deeper than we were ever to see it again until 1940'.[10] The water supply to the house froze up and water had to be collected from a spring in a nearby field. Guests were warned to 'bring an extra blanket and of course your hot-water bottles'.[11] What is thought to be Bell's first painting made at Charleston shows her new garden in winter: yellowing grass, ice-blue sky, a fractured grey surface on the pond, the shapes as crisp as a bright winter's day. It still hangs at Charleston – a small, concentrated square of luminosity (cat. 4).

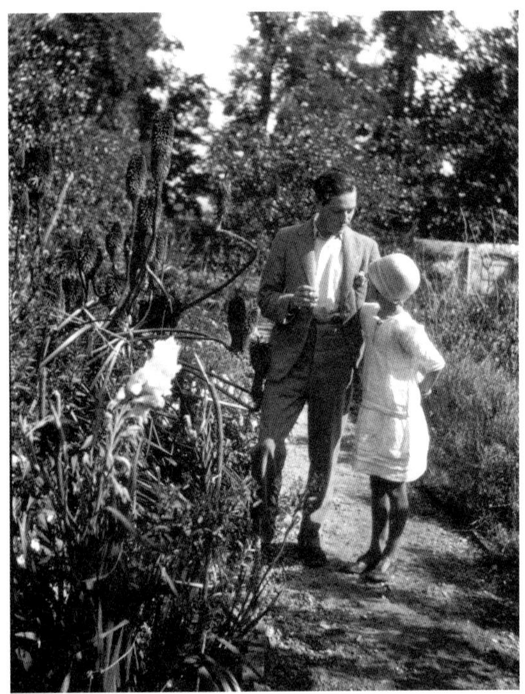

6. Duncan Grant and Angelica Bell in the garden at Charleston, 1927
Tate Archive

In an attempt to hold back the cold, Roger Fry (cat. 10), the true harbinger of innovation, designed an extension to the mean grates and fireplaces – an arrangement of iron braces and fire bricks intended to extend the fireplace and bring as much heat as possible into the room. Temporary solutions often became permanent fixtures, and these constructions remain in place today. At Charleston utility was turned into treasure; cheap and simply constructed bits of furniture were transformed into bright, colourful and humorous works of art. By one of Fry's fireplace constructions in the Garden Room sits a wooden box to keep firewood. Hardly a piece of furniture at all, five rough squares of wood, crudely nailed together. On four sides Duncan Grant painted figures – musicians and dancers. They connect Charleston with the avant garde of London, with the radicalism of the Ballets Russes, with the sensuousness of the naked body.

Grant also painted a linen chest (cat. 6). The wood is unvarnished, quite rough, the edges unfinished; nails and splinters lay in wait to snag unsuspecting fingers, but Grant has poured magic on this simple crate with wonderful colours and designs. A swimmer moves through waves of green water on the front panel, while still lifes and brightly painted and marbled designs of circles and patterns cover the ends and the back. Hidden under the lid is Leda and the Duck, undermining the masculine aggressiveness of the classical narrative. It is a piece of furniture for a new way of living, turning adversity into poetry – playful, joyful, intelligent and beautiful.

It is this eclectic accumulation of designs, furniture, textiles and ceramics that makes Charleston a home. There was no great project, no plan. Things were decorated, changed over time as and when they were needed. It was not a house for show; it was a house to be lived in, but it was still a house that had a visual and aesthetic discipline and philosophy.

Art and innovation rubbed alongside the pressures of duty and domesticity. Grant became ill from farm work, losing weight and developing arthritis in his joints, but there were still commissions to be carried out for costumes and set designs. He painted when he could, capturing still lifes of this new world.

Garnett wrote his first novel, *Dope Darling: a story of cocaine*, that was published under the pseudonym Leda Burke. The prewar life of bohemian London and bohemian figures was remembered in the oil lamp-lit evenings at Charleston.

Garnett also kept bees, and there were plans to add to the household income by selling Charleston honey. Dora Carrington designed the labels. The artists briefly planned to have flamingos on the pond, disrupting the Sussex landscape with their pink presence.

7. Simon Bussy, Vanessa Bell and Duncan Grant
Photograph by Lady Ottoline Morrell, 1922
National Portrait Gallery Photographs Collection

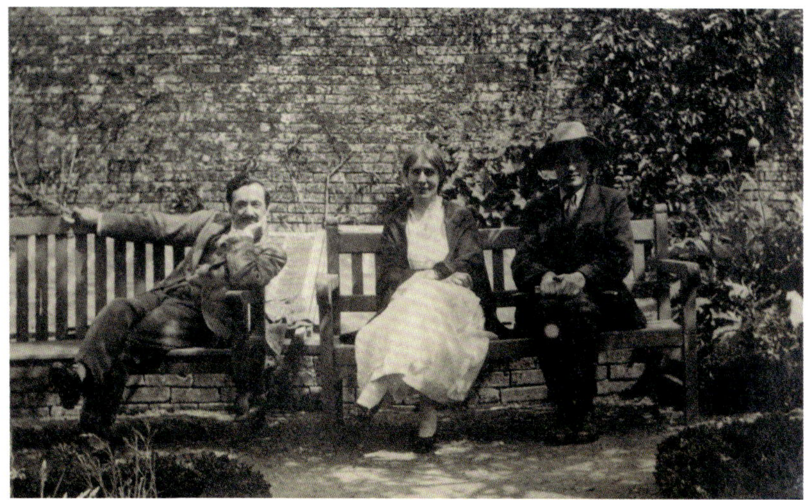

Vanessa Bell had wanted another child for some time. She wanted one with Duncan Grant's looks and talents and personality. When peace was finally declared on 11 November 1918 she was eight months pregnant, staying at Charleston as Grant and Garnett travelled to London to join the celebrating crowds.

Angelica Vanessa Bell (fig. 6, cat. 22) was born at 2am on Christmas Day 1918. She would be raised as the daughter of Clive Bell, not told of her true parentage until she was almost an adult. After she was born she became very ill, losing weight. Dr Moralt came down from London for a while, and she put things right.

This wartime family stayed at Charleston for the first part of 1919, but as Angelica thrived and the freedoms of peace beckoned, a new chapter began. Garnett left the household, the passion in his relationship with Grant replaced with a deep, life-long friendship. Bell and Grant continued their companionship, friendship and love – continued their experimental forms of domesticity and creativity.

After the end of the Great War the artists were able to resume their urban lives in the high-ceilinged drawing rooms and studios of Bloomsbury and Fitzrovia. Visits to Europe included long stays in Rome and Paris. Winters were spent in the South of France, the artists eventually renting a villa of their own in Cassis, following the light and avoiding the cold of England. All this took precedence over time spent in Sussex. But Charleston was kept on, and each summer the family returned. The shutters were opened wide, flooding the painted interiors with sun-drenched serenity.

Picture Charleston, and it is bathed in the glow of a Sussex summer. The rooms become places of cool, shaded refuge from the glare of

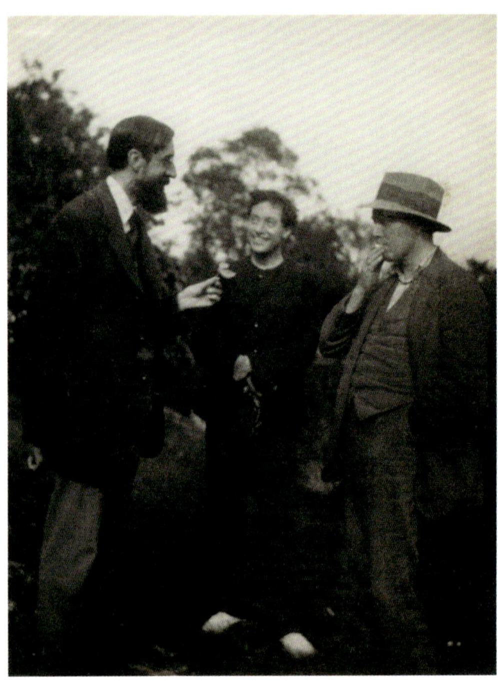

8. Lytton Strachey, Duncan Grant and Clive Bell
Photograph by Vanessa Bell, 1922
National Portrait Gallery Photographs Collection

the sun – the garden lush with tall plants, the freshness of the green foliage mixed with what Virginia Woolf described as 'the pink light of the giant hollyhock'.[12] Vanessa Bell peppers her letters with descriptions of the delights in her summer garden – that it was a 'medley of apples, hollyhocks, plums, zinnias. Dahlias, all mixed up together',[13] and 'a mass of flowers & as gay as possible – tobaccos & stocks smell strong in the evening. I often wander about in it at odd moments for the pleasure of the sights and smells'.[14]

In the summer of 1920 this serenity was broken when John Maynard Keynes introduced Charleston Time. Set an hour earlier than the rest of the country it ignored British Summer Time, which had been introduced in 1916. Virginia Woolf complained of having to have an 'inconvenient early tea'[15] and Lytton Strachey (fig. 8), visiting in September, explained to Dora Carrington the impossible situation, and how Vanessa Bell was 'too feeble to put him [Keynes] down', how Clive Bell ignored it and stuck to 'normal time ... too tetchy to grin and bear it' and how the housekeeper had 'let the kitchen clock run down, so that the servants have no time'. Strachey described it all as 'extremely Tchekhofesque. But luckily the atmosphere is entirely comic, instead of being fundamentally tragic as in Tchekhof. Everyone laughs and screams and passes on.'[16] Charleston Time was not repeated.

For a brief moment in 1923 Charleston was in danger of being lost. The land agent from whom Bell was renting it wanted the house back. Bell began looking for a new house in the country. She sent an update to Grant, who was in London, describing 'a Georgian house in Essex ... it really sounded almost too good to be true, to be sold for £750 with central heating & 2 bathrooms & 8 bedrooms'.[17] But disappointment arrived in the second post. Thankfully, Bell was able to negotiate a long lease and keep Charleston. 'I don't think the house in Essex would have suited', as she wrote: it was in a village street, and she very much valued her privacy.

With the security of a long lease the artists could start making some major changes to Charleston. For a studio they had been using an army hut in the garden called Les Misérables, but decided to construct a large purpose-built space. Roger Fry designed it, incorporating the old chicken run and earth closet at the north side of the house. The original walls were built up, and an inexpensive roof thrown across, with a bank of windows and double doors facing north, into the walled garden. By the summer the artists were ensconced in their new workplace, with Bell writing: 'I get to like the studio more & more. I think the colour is different from any other place I have painted in & one may be able to get quite new effects'.[18] It was decorated by Grant, the walls washed with a brown size. The large, long mantlepiece, home for a foliage of cards and cuttings, pots and tiles, and a

9. The Studio, Charleston

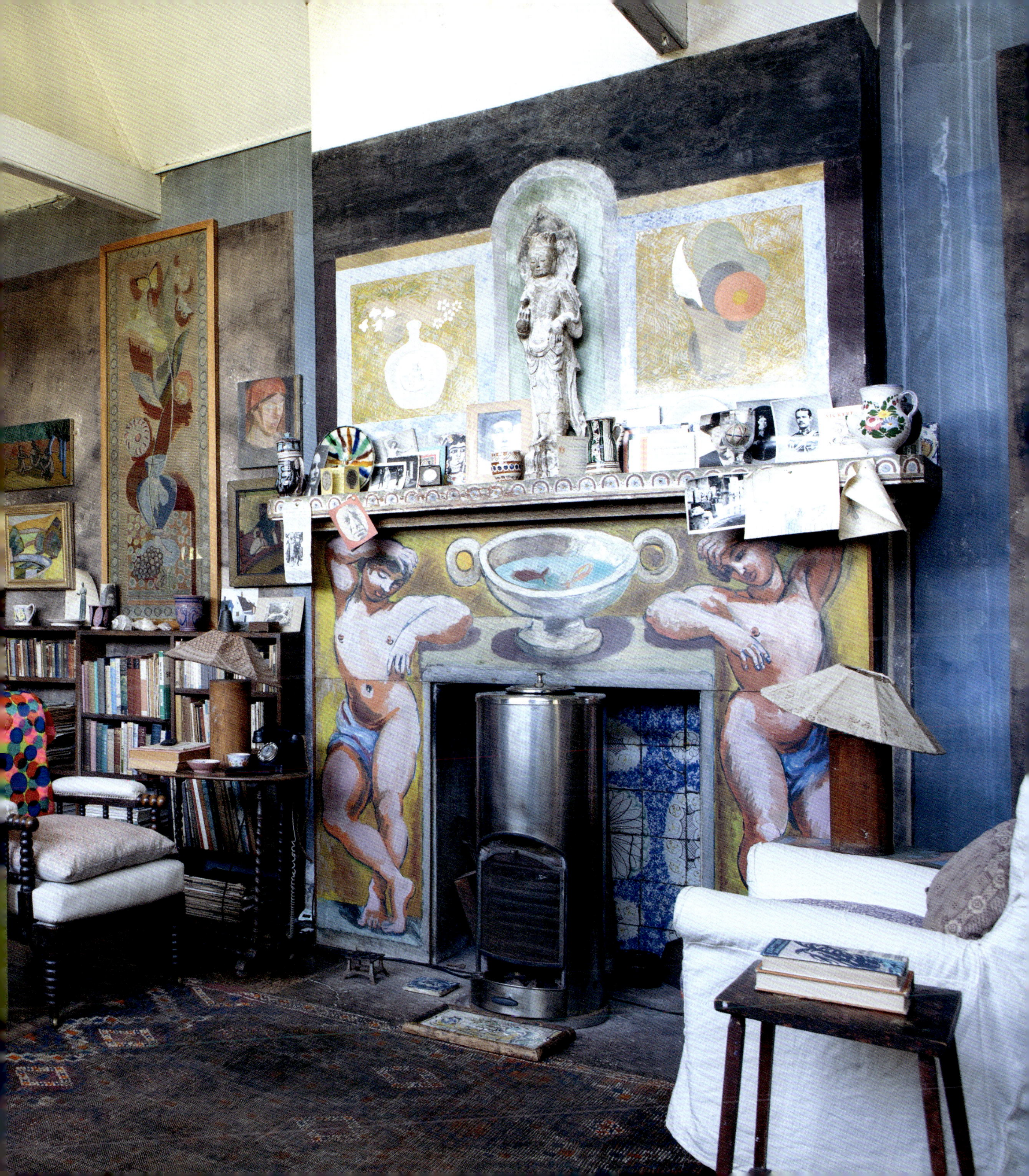

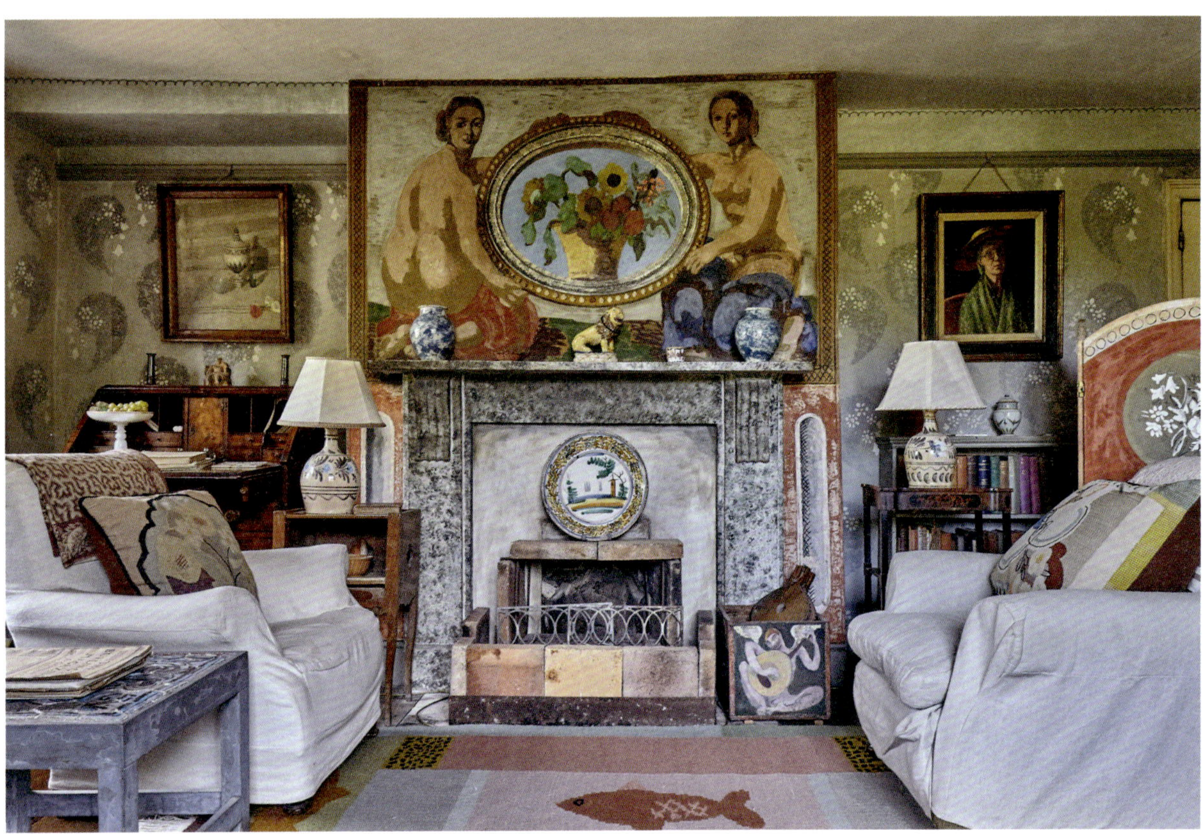

10. The Garden Room, Charleston

11. Clive Bell's Study, Charleston

plaster copy of a sixth-century figure of Kuan Yin, the Chinese Goddess of Mercy, is supported by two caryatids painted on board (fig. 9).

Other decorations were carried out in the house: Grant's elegant and monumental women holding a mirror to the walled garden over the fireplace in the Garden Room (fig. 10), Bell's simple arrangements of circles and cross hatching in what would become Clive Bell's Study (fig. 11). Window embrasures were painted, the Spare Room being given a complete decoration in 1936. The artists' commercial work began to be used in the house: textile designs for Alan Walton, ceramic designs for Clarice Cliffe and Foley – all from the early 1930s.

The 1920s and 1930s are considered the golden years of Charleston – long summer days, parties in the garden, young friends and hijinks. Angelica Bell was given a 'sham birthday' in the summer to make up for being born on Christmas Day and Quentin Bell's birthday was 19 August. A large party was thrown for him in 1936. Duncan Grant dressed as a Spanish dancer; Vanessa Bell described the costume to her son Julian: 'I have never seen anything quite so indecent. He has made himself a figure in cardboard of a nude female, which is none too securely attached

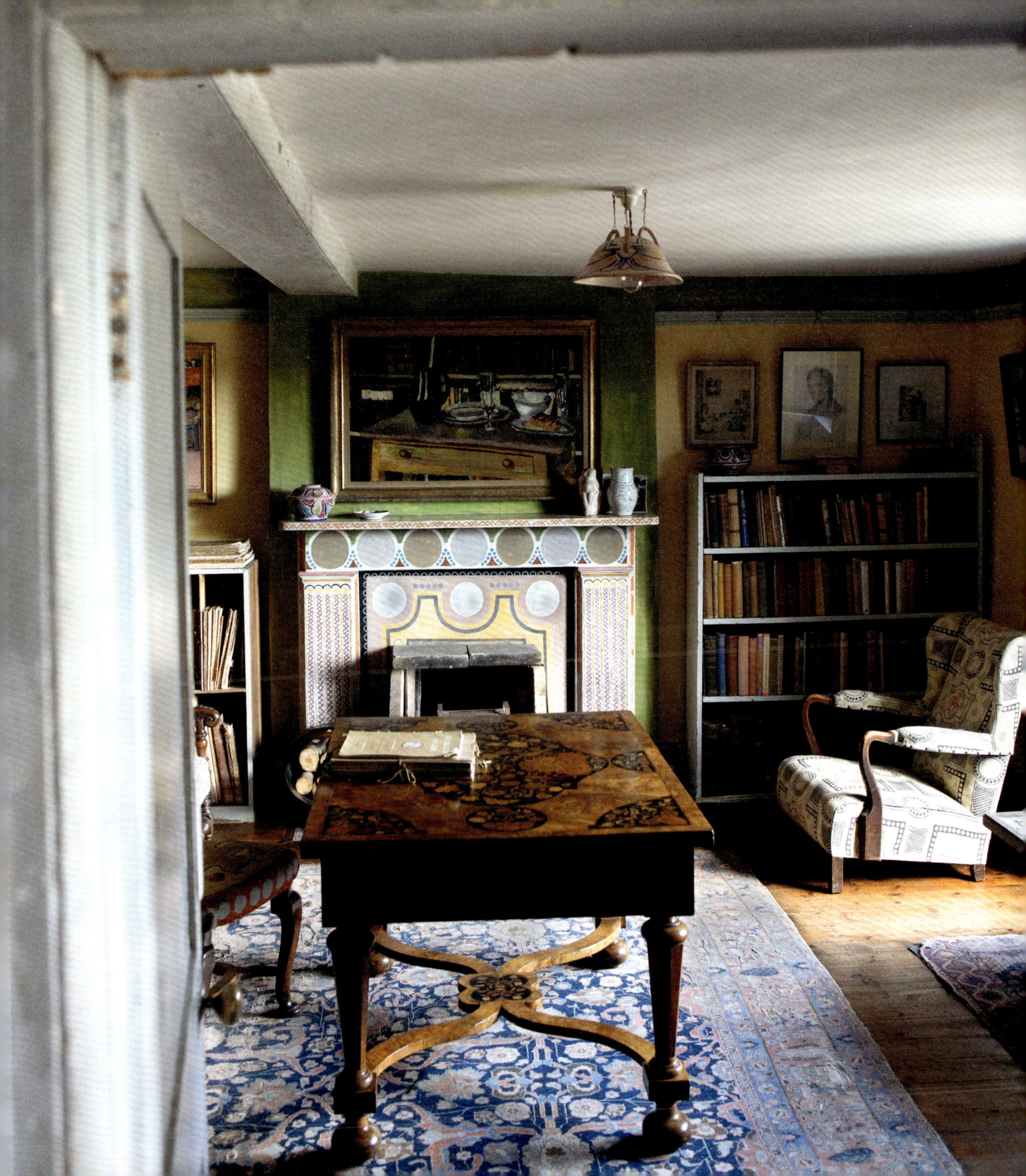

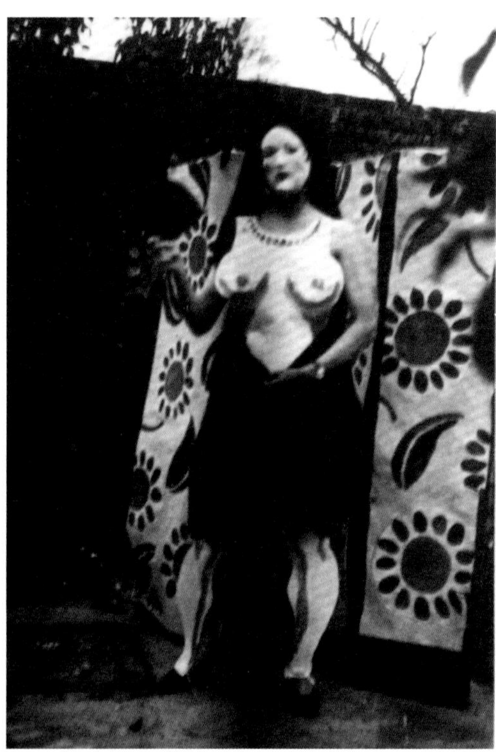

12. Duncan Grant, 1936
The Charleston Trust

by tapes to his own figure, and then he wears a simpering mask, a black wig and Spanish comb and mantilla, which partly conceals and reveals the obscene figure, while a Spanish air is played on the gramophone and Duncan flirts gracefully with a fan. I can't imagine what the audience will think of it' (fig. 12).[19]

Quentin Bell was also in drag for a sketch his father had written in which he played an American tourist visiting Charleston in the future when it had become a museum – the play *A Hundred Years After or Ladies and Gentlemen*. Vanessa kept a large cupboard that was full of pieces of textile that she and Grant would use for the backings to still lifes, for dressing up or as costumes in amateur dramatics.

Music from the gramophone drifted around the place, though, as Frances Partridge noted, 'they use very old wooden needles in the gramophone, so that everything sounds like the distant wailing of gnats'.[20] A guest at Angelica's twenty-first birthday party drove his car into the pond; and one year, at the annual fireworks display for Quentin's birthday, Grant knocked over a bucket of petrol, setting fire to the water's surface.

But it was always a delight for Bell to see her garden become a haven for her children and their friends. She wrote in 1936: 'I must say it has been rather amazing here this week .... The house seems full of young people in very high spirits, laughing a great deal at their own jokes, lying about in the garden which is simply a dithering blaze of flowers and butterflies and apples.'[21]

But the 1930s were also a period of loss. Lytton Strachey died in 1932, Dora Carrington shortly afterwards. Roger Fry died in 1934, and in 1937 Bell's eldest son, Julian, who had travelled to Spain to drive an ambulance during the civil war, was killed. Vanessa Bell received the news in London and, racked with shock and grief, was brought down to Charleston where she was cared for by her sister Virginia Woolf. Quentin Bell recalled: 'On one of the few days when she could not come over to Charleston, Virginia sent her sister a note. I found Vanessa quietly crying over it in the garden. "Another love letter from Virginia," she smiled very faintly.'[22]

Vanessa Bell began to value the isolation that Charleston offered and with the advent of the Second World War the house once again secured itself as the centre of the artists' world, promoted from a seasonal home to their primary residence, which it would remain for the rest of their lives.

Architects and builders were employed, plans submitted. New spaces were created, old spaces opened up, walls removed, windows added (fig. 13). Vanessa Bell had a new studio space created in the attic (fig. 14) with a long window looking north, and a new ground-floor bedroom made out of a larder and storeroom with a bath in the corner and large, metal-framed French doors opening out on to the garden. Clive Bell became a permanent resident, turning Vanessa's old bedroom into his

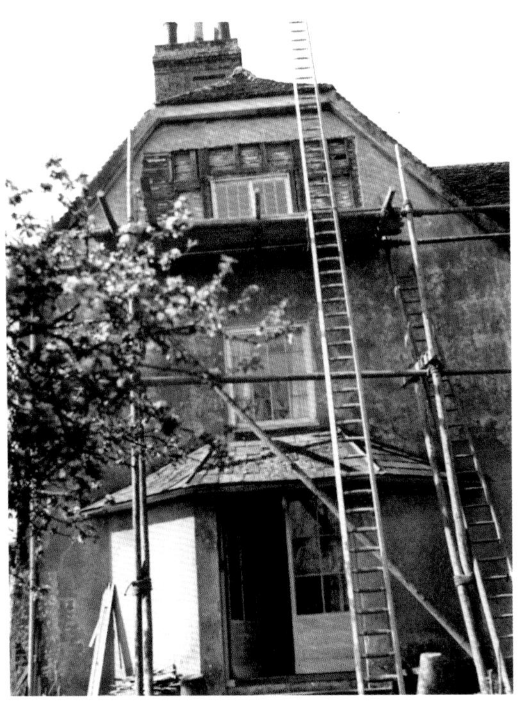

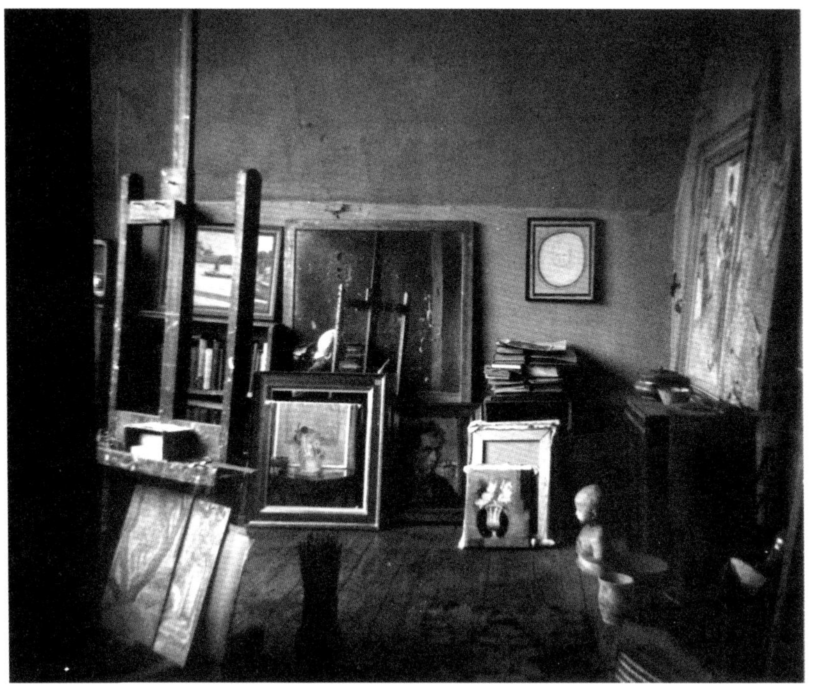

13. Charleston, c. 1939
The Charleston Trust

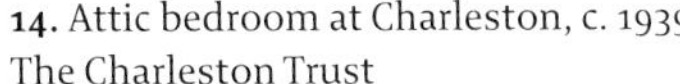

14. Attic bedroom at Charleston, c. 1939
The Charleston Trust

Library. A telephone was installed in the Dining Room, though Bell was reluctant to give out the number.

The artists' large neighbouring studios at 8 Fitzroy Street in London were sublet, and a great number of works that were stored there were brought to Charleston, filling its spaces, its outbuildings and attics. In July 1939 the work of the artists filled Charleston, evacuees from the city. Bell wrote to Grant describing their arrival: 'The first van ... began to give forth paintings at an alarming rate which we stacked in the yard ... nude followed nude of every sex & colour'.[23]

The best paintings, removed from the walls of London homes, were hung at Charleston: works by Picasso, Juan Gris and Matisse, Sickert, Vlaminck and Rouault – a modernist exhibition in a farmhouse in Sussex.

There are striking similarities between life at Charleston in the First and Second World Wars: correspondence from both eras is concerned with the bringing together of furniture, the allocation of space, the provision of amenities and the production of food. Woolf noted this when in February 1941 she described the activities at Charleston to Mary Hutchinson: 'We take tea at Charleston: Clive is digging a trench; Nessa feeding fowls; Duncan painting Christ; Quentin driving a tractor – all as it was in 1917.'[24]

The Dining Room was decorated in the winter of 1939, during what was known as the Phoney War – a period of relative calm before the conflict began. Black distemper lightly clings to the surface, with a pattern of

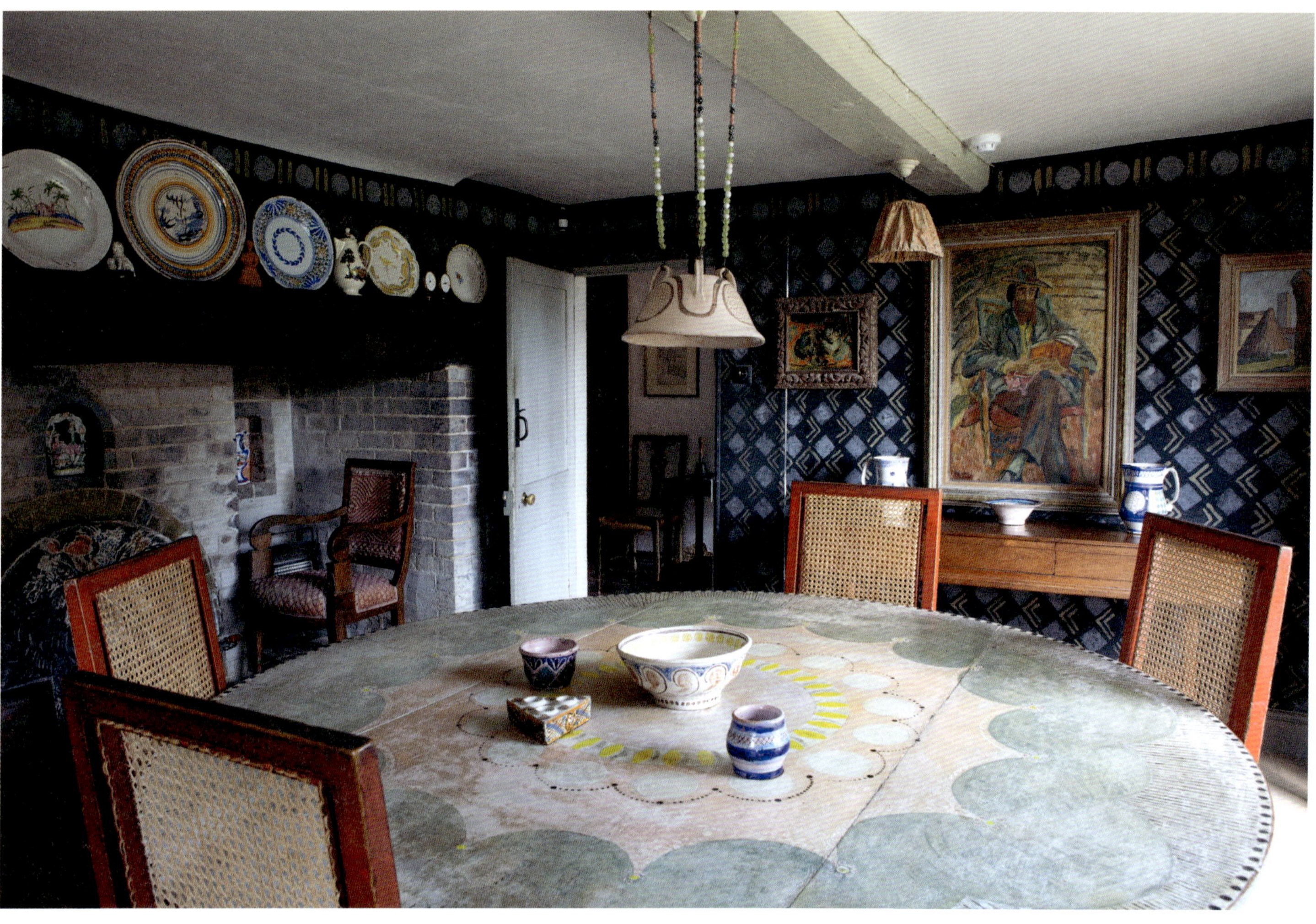

15. The Dining Room, Charleston

sponged diamonds and handpainted chevrons that stretch around the room and drip down the wall (fig. 15). At night the lamp over the round, pink and yellow dining table makes a concentrated pool of light, but in the day, especially when the sun is rising in the east and pouring through the windows, the decorations seem to shine.

For Grant the Second World War provided a different experience from the First when, as a conscientious objector, the demands on his time by the authorities and the ill health he suffered from working on the land restricted the opportunities that he had to paint. By 1939 it was as an artist that his contribution to the war effort was most appreciated, although he had joined the Home Guard, along with Clive and Quentin Bell, and in an interview in 1976 he claimed that had he been young enough he would have joined the arm services to defend the country and fight the threat to democracy.[25]

In 1940 Grant became an official war artist, employed on a short-term contract by the War Artists Advisory Committee, which had been set up in November 1939 and was chaired by Sir Kenneth Clark. Grant spent two weeks in May 1940 in Plymouth making studies of a gunnery lesson.

During his absence from Charleston, Bell and Grant corresponded by post. Bell's letters reveal her anxieties at a time when invasion was a very real threat. For Grant it was a chance to see the naval preparations and experience the bureaucracy of war. There is a palpable sense of loss, anguish and impotence in Bell's letters. She wrote to Grant on the effect of the advancing German armies, 'How can anyone or anything one cares for survive such ruthlessness?'.[26] Later she wrote, 'Clive & Quentin have both returned to bed evidently in the depths of depression. They have both joined the para shooters, at least Quentin has given his name & Clive says he is going to give his. I see there's no hope for it for if Parachutes did come here I suppose no one could keep out of it'.[27]

Charleston, like other places within ten miles of the vulnerable south coast, was declared a 'restricted area'. Roadblocks were set up and incomers checked. Vanessa Bell found some solace in the effects of these wartime measures. Being in a restricted zone to a degree satisfied her increasing need and quest for isolation. Graham Sutherland and his wife had been invited for the weekend but Bell was relieved when they were forced to cancel. Another benefit of being in a 'danger zone' was, as she wrote to Grant, that 'at any rate I think we are safe from refugees'. The countryside, which for many was a place of safety, of refuge, for Bell and her household and neighbours was now a place of danger with the imminent threat of invasion and possible extinction.

But the restricted zone brought its own local invaders to Charleston as Bell explained in a letter to Grant. 'Clive has now been made something in the nature of liaison officer .... Apparently they are trying to arrange that two patrollers should watch every night from points all along the country, each person doing it one night a week .... This house is a place to which they can come to telephone or change if wet etc. I wonder if there's any sense in it, but I suppose something of the sort must be done.'[28] Bell's offer to assist the men of Charleston in their war work was refused, as she explained in a letter to Jane Bussy, who was living in France. She wrote, 'As I gather that their principal job will be to rush back and telephone and as female eyes are as good as male ones I can't see why there should be this sex barrier. But they say the presence of females on the Downs at night would lead to extra difficulties, though Clive is all for it. So far little has happened.'[29]

On 7 September the Blitz began. Both Bell and her sister Virginia Woolf heard and often saw the planes flying over Sussex, heavy-laden with their bombs, on their way to destroy London. There were air battles overhead as the RAF intercepted the German bombers along the coast. Woolf's diary

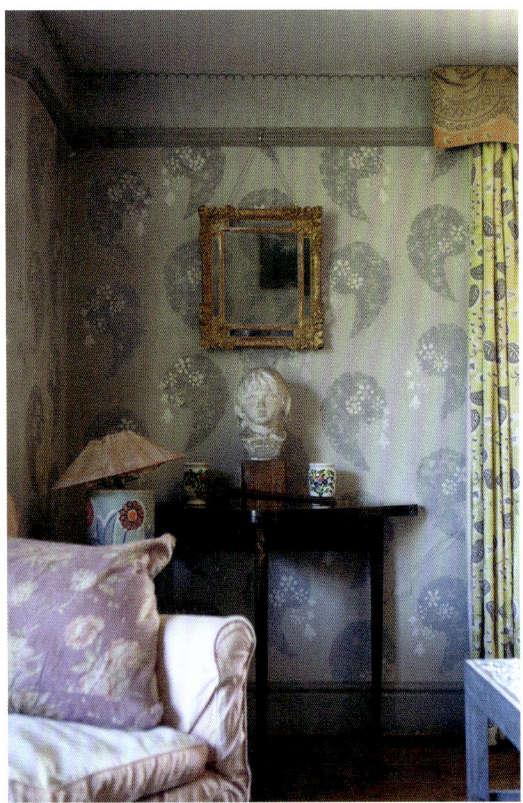

16. The Garden Room, Charleston

for this period provides a vivid portrait of Sussex in wartime and captures both her and her sister's engagement and detachment from the conflict around them.

Grant's and Bell's neighbouring studios at 8 Fitzroy Street were destroyed in late September 1940 by an incendiary bomb. Grant wrote to his mother on the subject, 'Vanessa takes it very philosophically and says she can always paint more pictures'.[30] For Bell it appeared on the surface to be another opportunity to stay at Charleston, writing that while it is inconvenient not having a place in London, 'I find that in my old age, even if there were no war I think, I really prefer a country life'.[31]

A greater loss came the following spring when Virginia Woolf drowned herself on 28 March 1941. Bell's cover for her last book, *Between the Acts*, published posthumously in July of the same year, shows a closed curtain, a private space, edged with garden flowers.

It was this uncertainty, this sense of threat to creativity, to the landscape and to all that was familiar that formed the emotional backdrop against which the Berwick murals (cat. 27) were conceived and executed. Bell and Grant's work fills the small church in the nearby village. Grant's *Christ in Glory* sits high above the chancel arch surrounded by four angels. The familiar landscape of the South Downs unfolds across the murals. Three local servicemen kneel in prayer; Charleston's walled garden is the setting for Bell's *Annunciation* and a local barn for the *Nativity*. Schoolboys and local characters populate the scenes.

The murals are often seen as a turning inwards by the artists, mainly because of their relatively remote, rural location and their religious subject matter, but these murals sit happily and centrally in their wartime oeuvre. Rather than being introspective they demonstrate part of a project of looking outwards, the pinnacle of a series of schemes that engages in a zeitgeist of public art – an art rooted in public display and performance, in community and theatre.

In 1940 the Committee for Encouragement of Music and the Arts (CEMA) was formed with Keynes becoming its chair. Bell and Grant worked on many CEMA projects and exhibitions. They were commissioned to decorate a primary school in Tottenham and curated an exhibition of designs for a small theatre and arts centre that could be built in every small town once the war was over. In 1941 Grant had a second commission from the War Artists Advisory Committee, to paint St Paul's Cathedral rising up out of the remains of the bombed buildings that surrounded it.

When the war finally ended there were parties, but for Bell the best part was returning to Charleston, where they were able to turn on all the outside lights for the first time since 1939, and where 'the garden was simply fairy land – with nightingales – yes, we were sure of it, singing loudly. We walked about on the lawn and did our best to realise we were at peace.'[32] The Garden Room was painted at the end of the war, the calming grey walls decorated with a large paisley pattern – a room to enjoy this new-found peace (fig. 16).

Peacetime also brought a return to London, and trips abroad, but Charleston remained at the centre of the artists' lives. The gardens were occasionally filled with life, visits from grandchildren, from young friends, but a quiet calm rested across the high roof and chimney stacks. Vanessa Bell died in her bedroom in 1961; Clive died in 1964. Duncan Grant continued to live until 1978, surrounded by loyal supporters and visitors, his good friend Paul Roche and his family – a young generation of art historians eager to hear first-hand about the birth of British Modernism, Charleston protecting them all.

Notes

1 *Charleston and Bloomsbury* (c. 1995), directed by Jamie Muir [Film]. Sussex: The Charleston Trust.

2 Woolf, V. 14 May 1916, *Letter to Vanessa Bell* in Nicholson, N. and Trautmann, J. (eds.) (1978) *The Letters of Virginia Woolf, Volume Two*, 1912–1922. New York: Harcourt Brace Jovanovich, p. 95.

3 Bell, V. September 1916, *Letter to Duncan Grant*, Tate Archive.

4 Bell, V. 18 September 1916, *Letter to Duncan Grant*. Quoted in Spalding, F. (2006), *Vanessa Bell*. Stroud: Tempus Publishing, p. 154.

5 Grant, D. October 1916, *Letter to Vanessa Bell*, Tate Archive, TGA 8010/5/1132.

6 Bell, V. 22 February 1917, *Letter to Roger Fry*. Quoted in Bell, Q. and Nicholson, V. (2004), *Charleston: A Bloomsbury House and Garden*. London: Frances Lincoln, p. 112.

7 *Vanessa Bell: Notes on Bloomsbury* in Rosenbaum, S.P. (ed.) (1975), *The Bloomsbury Group: A Collection of Memoirs, Commentary and Criticism*. Toronto and Buffalo: University of Toronto Press, p. 74.

8 Woolf, V. 'Old Bloomsbury,' in Schulkind, J. (ed.) (1976), *Moments of Being*. Sussex: Sussex University Press, p. 47.

9 Bell, V. 19 January 1917, *Letter to Saxon Sydney-Turner* in Marler, R. (ed.) (1993), *Selected Letters of Vanessa Bell*. London: Bloomsbury Publishing Limited, p. 202.

10 Bell, Q. (1987), 'Charleston Garden: A Memory of Childhood' in *Charleston: Past and Present*. London: Hogarth Press, p. 87.

11 Bell, V. 19 January 1917, *Letter to Saxon Sydney-Turner* in Marler, R. (ed.) (1993), *Selected Letters of Vanessa Bell*. London: Bloomsbury Publishing, p. 202.

12 Woolf, V. 12 August 1928, in Bell, A.O (ed.) (1980), *The Diary of Virginia Woolf, Volume Three*: 1925–1930. New York: Harcourt Brace Jovanovich, p. 190.

13 Bell, V. 15 August 1930, *Letter to Roger Fry*. Quoted in Bell, Q. and Nicholson, V. (2004), *Charleston: A Bloomsbury House and Garden*. London: Frances Lincoln, p. 134.

14 Bell, V. 15 August 1936. *Letter to Julian Bell*. Quoted in Bell, Q. Garnett, A., Garnett, H. and Shone, R. (ed.) (1987), *Charleston: Past and Present*. London: The Hogarth Press, p. 138.

15 Woolf, V. 26 September 1920, in Bell, A.O (ed.) (1978), *The Diary of Virginia Woolf, Volume Two*: 1920–1924. New York: Harcourt Brace Jovanovich, p. 69.

16 Strachey, L. 4 September 1920, *Letter to Dora Carrington*. Quoted in Bell, Q., Garnett, A., Garnett, H. and Shone, R. (ed.) (1987), *Charleston: Past and Present*. London: The Hogarth Press, p. 138.

17 Bell, V. April 1923, *Letter to Duncan Grant*. Tate Archives.

18 Bell, V. 26 August 1925, *Letter to Duncan Grant*. Tate Archives.

19 Bell, V. 29 August 1936, *Letter to Julian Bell* in Marler, R. (ed.) (1993), *Selected Letters of Vanessa Bell*. London, Bloomsbury Publishing, p. 419.

20 Partridge, F. (1999), *Memories*. London: Phoenix, p. 163.

21 Bell, V. 29 August 1936, *Letter to Julian Bell* in Marler, R. (ed.) (1993), Selected Letters of Vanessa Bell. London, Bloomsbury Publishing, p. 420.

22 Bell, Q., and Nicholson, V. (2004), *Charleston: A Bloomsbury House and Garden*. London: Frances Lincoln, p. 147.

23 Bell, V. 23 July 1939, *Letter to Duncan Grant*, Tate Archive: TGA 20078/1/44/211.

24 Woolf, V. February 1941, *Letter to Mary Hutchinson*, in Nicholson, N. (ed.) (1980), *Leave the Letters Till We're Dead: The Letters of Virginia Woolf, Volume Six*, 1936–1941. London: The Hogarth Press, p. 472.

25 Duncan Grant talking to Robert McDonald of Canadian Broadcasting, Charleston, 31 December 1976, Tate Archives.

26 Bell, V. May 1940, *Letter to Duncan Grant*, Tate Archives.

27 Bell, V. May 1940, *Letter to Duncan Grant*, Tate Archives.

28 Bell, V. 29 May 1940, *Letter to Duncan Grant*, Tate Archive, TGA 20078/1/44/214.

29 Bell, V. 6 June 1940, *Letter to Jane Bussy* in Marler, R. (1993), *Selected Letters of Vanessa Bell*. London: Bloomsbury Publishing, p. 469.

30 Grant, D. 26 September 1940, *Letter to Ethel Grant*. Quoted in Spalding, F. (2006), *Vanessa Bell*. Stroud: Tempus Publishing, p. 297.

31 Bell, V. 13 January 1941, *Letter to Jane Bussy* in Marler, R. (1993), *Selected Letters of Vanessa Bell*. London: Bloomsbury Publishing, p. 473.

32 Bell, V. 12 May 1945, *Letter to Angelica Garnett* in Marler, R. (1993), *Selected Letters of Vanessa Bell*. London: Bloomsbury Publishing, p. 497.

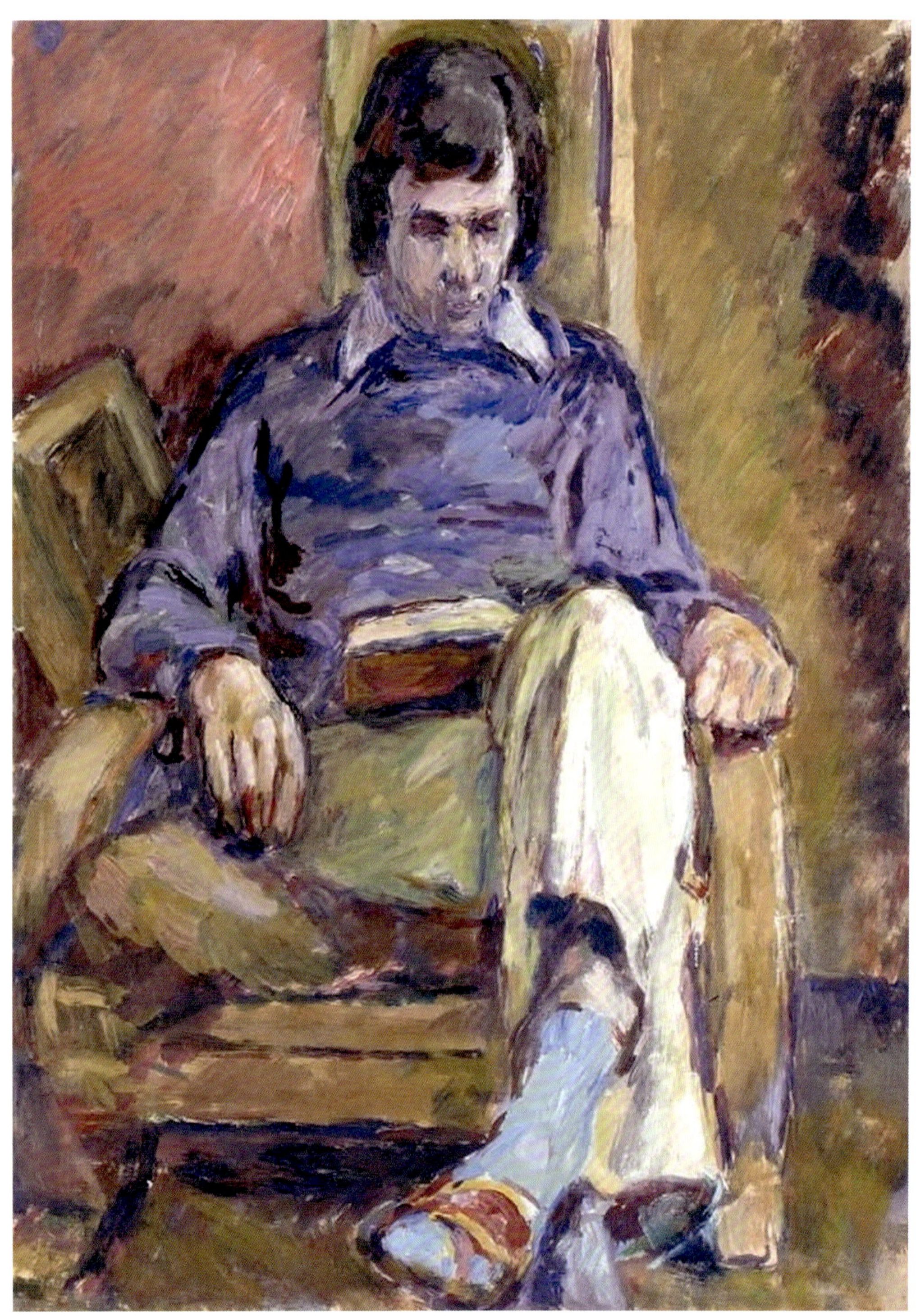

17. Duncan Grant
Portrait of Richard Shone, c. 1969
Oil on paper laid on board
23 × 16½ in. (58.5 × 42 cm)
Private collection

Charleston Recalled

RICHARD SHONE *with* MATTHEW HOLLIDAY

Richard Shone (fig. 17) was still a schoolboy when he first met Duncan Grant. He contributed three decorations to Charleston, most notably the reclining nude figure in Clive Bell's bathroom. While at Charleston, Shone wrote part of Bloomsbury Portraits *(1976), described by one critic as 'the standard visual history' of the group. He has written several more books and catalogues on modern British art, French art, and the YBA Movement. Shone was Editor of* The Burlington Magazine *from 2003 to 2015.*

MH Richard, can you tell me how you became friends with Duncan Grant and the background to your first visit to Charleston?

RS Don't forget I was a schoolboy. I was away at school; I wasn't living with my family for the term time. And I was already aware of, and interested in, Bloomsbury. And then one day, in 1964, I read a review of an exhibition of works by Duncan Grant at Wildenstein's on Bond Street to celebrate his eightieth birthday, and I thought heavens, he's alive! – and there are recent works in this show! So I wrote to the gallery for a catalogue and said 'I will pay for this out of my pocket money', but no, it came *with compliments, Wildenstein*, and I read it and was fascinated by it; and so I thought, well, why not? I'll write to him and say 'I'm hoping to see your exhibition'. And fairly soon afterwards a very nice, very modest, one-page letter came back. He said: 'I'm glad you got the catalogue, and I wonder what you're doing at school, and what you might be doing *after* school'. That's when the correspondence started, and it was with fantastic pleasure I would receive a letter every two or three weeks – nothing sensational – lovely descriptions of Charleston life.

MH And how long did that correspondence last before you visited Charleston?

RS Several months until the summer [1965], when I suggested to my parents that I might go for a visit, and they didn't know anything about it at all. They were (probably quite rightly) a little bit worried that I was going off by myself at that tender age to see this painter.

MH Did you have a track record for going on jaunts about the country?

RS No, no [laughter]. Anyway, they decided to go to London, and they wanted to go for a holiday somewhere, so they put me on a train, and I went to Lewes, and Duncan met me at Lewes station. That was followed by a hair-raising drive in his little green Morris to Charleston in time for a drink before supper.

MH Were there some nerves on your part about actually meeting him?

RS I've thought about that so often, and I don't think I was nervous; I thought it was an adventure.

MH So you pull in, on to the famously bumpy track. Was it sunny?

RS No, it was evening – a summer evening. I think it was late August, but I don't remember much about it until dinner that evening at eight o'clock, summoned by a bell rung by Grace [Higgens]. That was the terrible moment I was faced with an artichoke, which I'd never seen before, let alone eaten!

MH I wonder if you could speak about the atmosphere of the house itself?

RS Clive Bell had only been dead about ten months before I went, so it was very full of the atmosphere of Clive – his tin trunks and boxes with his name 'C. Bell' and his guns in the porch, and his rather smart old overcoats hanging there too; and on the table in his writing room great wads of manuscripts in his beautiful clear hand. You felt that writing had been going on there until the last moment. There was also a great wealth of art that had belonged to him still on the walls but which was sold or went to the Bell family soon afterwards – Sickerts, Picasso etchings for example. Some of the generosity of the house was due to Clive: the drink from the Wine Society – he was the one who had originally ordered that. But also you felt – or I began to feel – a certain austerity that came from Vanessa [Bell].

MH That made itself known later?

RS It became apparent to me within a couple of years, yes; the way everything was ordered in her bureau in her bedroom, letters tied up in ribbon and put into the little pigeon holes, and her work basket in the sitting room with its wonderful coloured wools and so on.

MH And what about the studio? You've described elsewhere sitting for Duncan Grant on the first morning of your visit. Were you aware that this was a space of activity, of past performances?

RS Only as a painting activity. I didn't know about any other kind – whether Leonard or Virginia [Woolf] had sat there, or Maynard [Keynes]. I didn't know about that.

MH What about the sense of creative freedom and spontaneity that the house is celebrated for; was that palpable?

RS I only became aware of it by doing it, really. There wasn't some sort of tradition that you had to paint something.

MH 'Welcome, paint the walls …'.

RS [Laughter] Exactly. And I was thinking this morning: did I ask Duncan if I could paint the bath, paint that chair, paint that box ….

MH Which of your decorations came first? Do you remember?

RS I think it was the chair in the studio with a plate of mushrooms on the seat. And then on one rainy afternoon, I think in 1970, I painted the side of the bath upstairs in Clive's bathroom – that was quite a job (fig. 18). It was a surprise for Duncan. Afterwards he said 'I'm glad you've done that because I wouldn't have wanted to lie on the floor all the time'. He was very pleased, I think.

MH When you painted the chair, were you both in the studio doing your own work?

RS I have an odd feeling that Duncan wasn't in the studio, that I was alone painting. He may have been outside in the garden.

MH So there was a sense of quiet occupation for you?

RS Yes.

MH And did you find your own way about the studio: 'I'll use that box of paint, or a stick of that charcoal'?

RS Yes, he was very good about all that. And he let me use this fantastic, enormous box of pastels – French, top quality – which he'd inherited from Simon Bussy, his semi-informal master and his cousin's [Dorothy Strachey's] husband.

MH That's wonderful.

RS Yes, and Duncan said: 'I've hardly dared use them because they're so good' –

MH 'So you use them'!

RS [Laughter] It was an enormous box with every shade. Of course, Bussy was famous for his pastels.

MH Was Duncan particular about his materials?

RS Not as much as I think he should have been, really. He tried acrylics, which were 'all the go', but he didn't like them very much.

MH And biros for line drawings?

RS Ballpoint for line drawings. He had masses of materials to hand, but some of it wasn't always appropriate to, say, the rather fabulous drawing he'd do on the back of the Sussex telephone book. But you could see the urge he had sometimes: he'd have to go and take any piece of paper and make a drawing, or a carpet design or something.

MH Would he order his materials over the telephone, or was there a shop in Lewes he used?

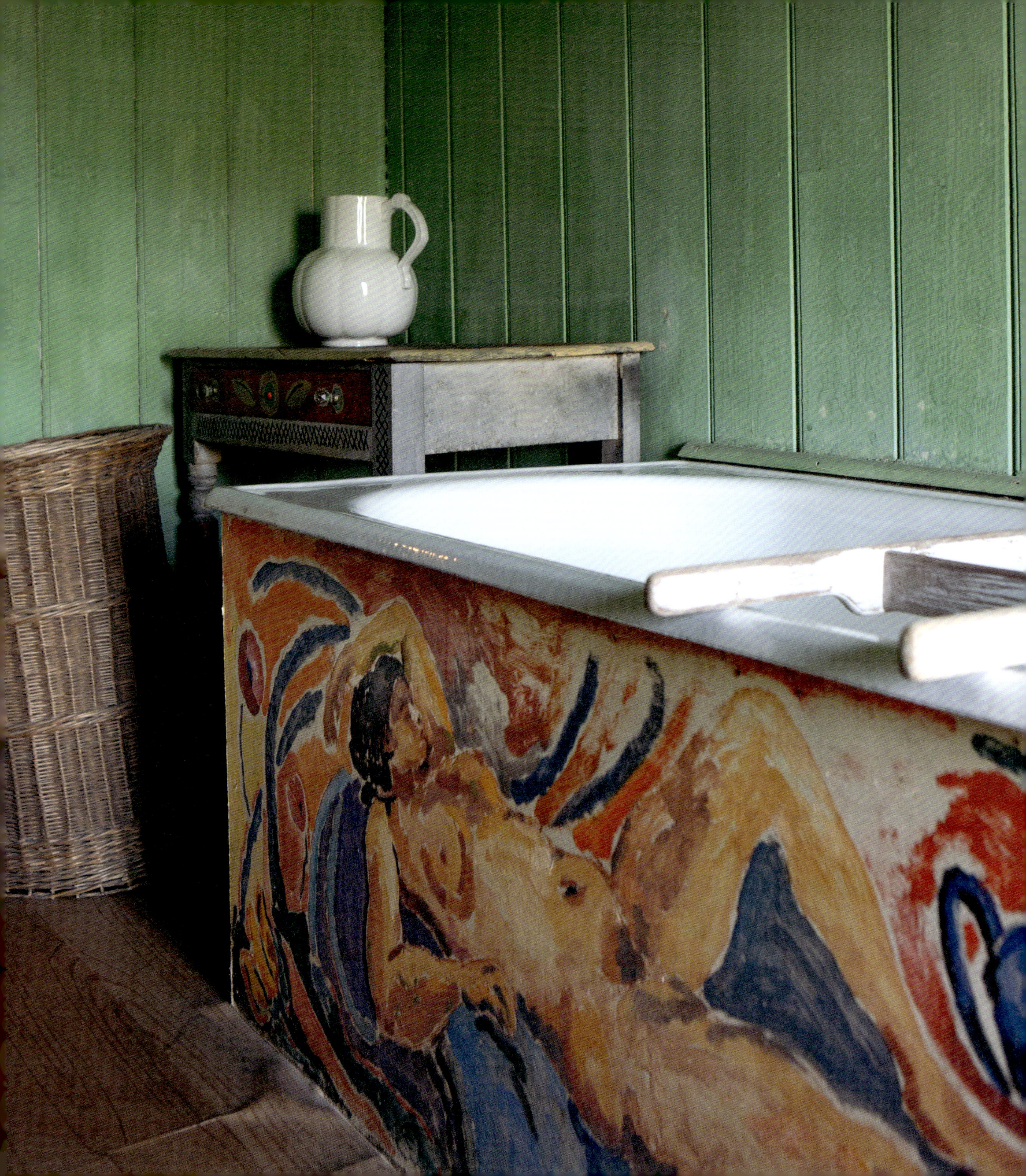

RS There was a shop in London next to his flat in Victoria Square run by the Miss Kemp sisters, and I would sometimes go there before going on to Charleston from Victoria Station across the road. 'Please would you buy me titanium white, burnt umber and two HB pencils?' [Laughter] 'And put them on my account.' 'Oh, it's for Mr Grant? Alright, we'll put that down.' And then in Lewes there was an art shop and a photographer, and he used that a lot for stretched canvases; bunches of six would arrive – rather modest in size, and not the best quality.

MH Going back to your contributions to the house, the most familiar to visitors is probably the upstairs bath. Where did the idea for that scheme come from?

RS The main panel was based on a drawing by Augustus John, which I found in a book of black-and-white reproductions of drawings by early twentieth-century British artists. So I just took the pose of the woman.

MH The panel was plain white before?

RS Yes, absolutely plain. The work took an afternoon and maybe a bit more. And then I did the ends of the bath, which are not good at all – I think I did those on the next visit. Luckily they are rather covered up now.

MH Were you pleased with the figure?

RS Yes, I was [laughter]. I knew it was the best thing I'd ever done, even though I knew it was very Grant and Bell. I had to fit into the house; I wasn't going to paint a Max Ernst or a Magritte or a Jackson Pollock.

MH So it was consciously imitative?

RS Yes. It's how I knew the paint went on; it was how Duncan did it.

MH Even down to the level of finish?

RS Yes. You don't want to finish too much.

MH Before you began had you worked out an idea of the colours you wanted to use?

RS No, you just started out and thought 'let's do a blue vase here, and some yellow and red in the background'.

MH When it came to the restoration of Charleston, because it wasn't by one of the original artists, was there any risk of it being removed?

18. The Green Bathroom, Charleston

RS No. If it was there by the time Duncan died, it was fine. The room was cream coloured, I seem to remember, and we went back to the original green.

The other creative thing I did was paint six cups and saucers for Quentin [Bell] in my own manner. But they've suffered over the years. I remember Lindy Guinness coming down, and she too painted a plate or two that Quentin said, 'here, try this'. He was very good at getting everyone involved and a wonderful presence at the lunch table. He would bring the conversation along. And, of course, he was doing the first work on the Virginia Woolf biography, so he did ask Duncan questions. There were always hoots of laughter – it was nonstop!

Duncan only did one last decoration for the house while I was there (though he restored one or two things): he did a little panel of a fountain – about 1967 – a wooden panel with canvas stuck to it, which went behind the taps of the basin in Vanessa's bedroom. I remember Grace saying, 'have you seen Mr Grant has painted a decoration?' She was very pleased. It was a nice moment.

MH *Bloomsbury Portraits* (1976): let's talk about that. You wrote some of it at Charleston?

RS Yes I did, in Clive's library upstairs, on a little rickety table and with a beautiful view looking down onto the walled garden. I remember two or three long sessions in the house.

MH Were you aware, while you were writing, that, say, Keynes's *The Economic Consequences of the Peace* had been written just across the landing?

RS [Laughter] No. It goes back to the question of creativity. You just did it because you were there.

MH Charleston was an agreeable place to write?

RS Extremely agreeable. It was a good quiet place to be. Duncan would be downstairs in the studio. He was a little suspicious of what I was writing. I never read him any of it.

MH Never?

RS No. Paul Roche read it to him when it came out. I don't know what he thought about it.

MH And when you sat down to write the book were you conscious that you were preparing the first true study of these artists?

RS Yes, very much so, because I couldn't find material anywhere else, except in primary collections – King's College, Cambridge, or The British Library.

MH I suppose you could say that *Bloomsbury Portraits* was the last major work to have been written at Charleston?

RS Part written. Duncan knew I was writing it, and he knew that Anthony d'Offay, his dealer, had been partly responsible for my getting the contract with Phaidon Press to write the book, because d'Offay said, 'I must have a book about the artists I'm dealing in', quite rightly. Originally it was going to be about the whole of Bloomsbury. Anyway, I narrowed it down, with the publishers, to Grant, Bell and Fry.

MH Do you wish you'd included more of Roger Fry?

RS I do now but not then. I think there should have been a little more on Fry's theories.

MH What's your view of *Bloomsbury Portraits* now?

RS I'm so distanced from it I can look at it as a charming account of these people at a time when I could not say a lot of things about them, and that it stands for how things were at that time. I think it was definitely worth doing. Also, I really was the last person to be able to talk to Lydia [Lopokova], Leonard [Woolf], Mary Hutchinson, Teddy Wolfe, Keith Baynes, Robert Medley. They may not have contributed a massive amount of scholarly material, but they contributed to the atmosphere of the times.

MH As, I suppose, did Charleston itself.

RS Yes, you're quite right. There were certain things you couldn't write because you knew you were in this house, and that was how things were; so you couldn't say 'Duncan Grant and Vanessa Bell loved clean walls and bare spaces in their modernist rooms, and their food was so luxurious you felt sick every night' – it wasn't like that. And that's what makes me mad when I read these accounts of Bloomsbury as being snobby, elitist, luxury loving – it wasn't that way at all. Clive brought the touch of luxury, really, which Duncan loved when it was put on a plate in front of him – but not for daily life.

MH He lived off paint.

RS [Laughter] He certainly did, yes!

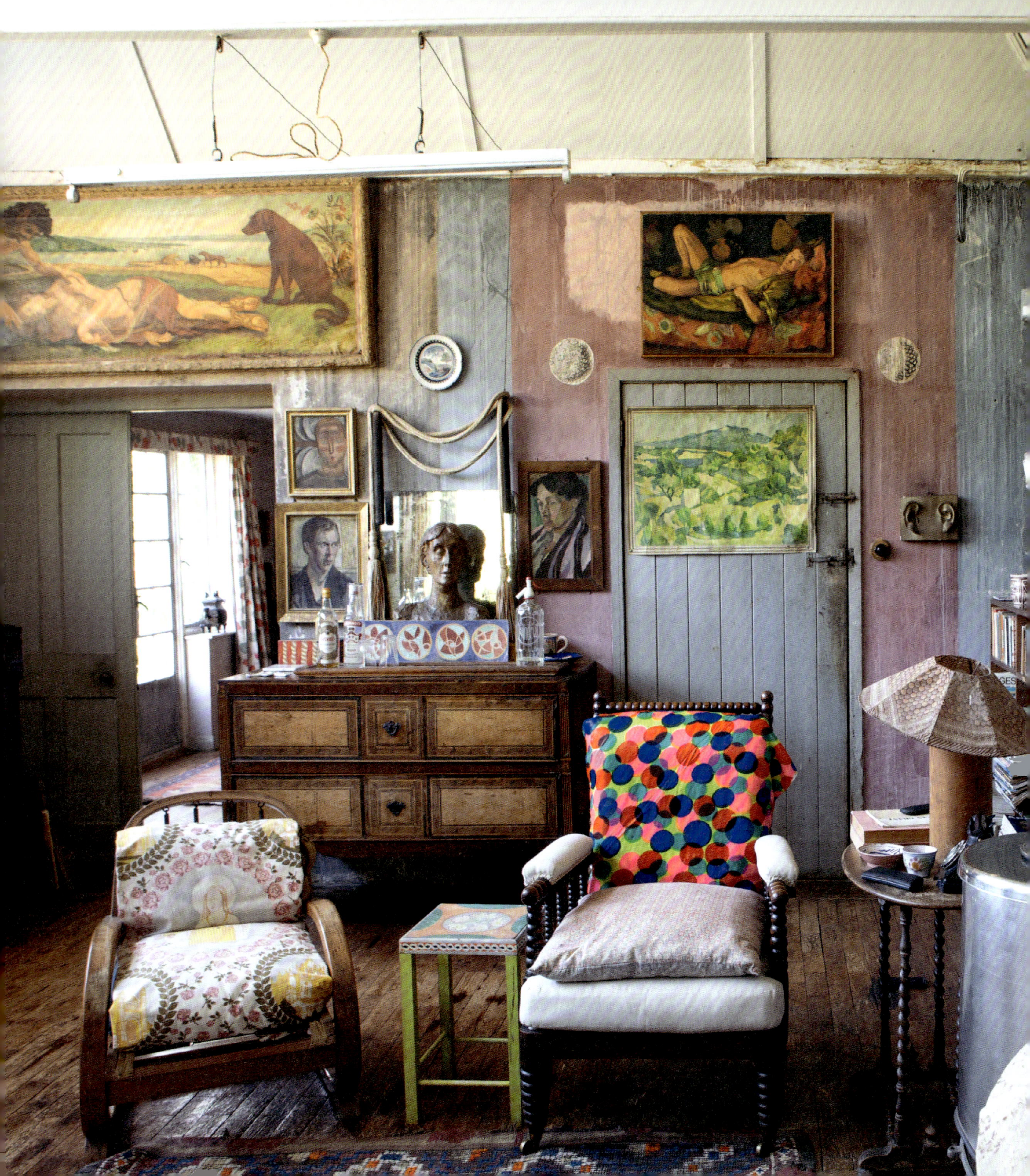

Charleston, Why?

DEBORAH GAGE

Deborah Gage is an international art dealer, who spearheaded the campaign to save Charleston Farmhouse in 1979 and founded The Charleston Trust.

19. The Studio, Charleston

This was the question Philip Mould posed to me when he invited me to write this recollection relating to a place that has been creatively relevant for over a century (2016 marked the centenary of Vanessa Bell's taking the lease of the house and garden from the Firle Estate). Why do we mark time in our society? Why do we need touchstones to inspire, to influence, to guide our aspirations or to leave a trace of our world behind us?

Duncan Grant died in 1978, and a year later I returned from America – where I had lived in New York for the previous nine years – to the lee of the South Downs, where my roots are deeply embedded.

I never met Vanessa, though on occasion I visited Duncan in his studio after her demise. Although Angelica – Duncan's daughter – thought she would take over the lease at Charleston following her father's death, she later changed her mind. Thus, the Firle Estate decided to place the house and garden on the market. As I had missed another house on the estate, I was given a first option to acquire the property. An appointment was made for me to view Charleston.

Angelica was still living there, so, on that Sunday morning in October 1979, I sat chatting with Angelica in her kitchen, surrounded by buckets of slowly rotting apples with their slightly intoxicating smell. We both found ourselves rather bemused. Angelica had overlooked the fact the clocks had moved back at midnight, meaning, from her perspective, that I had arrived an hour too early; and I, because it had been about a decade since my last visit to Charleston and I had forgotten how large it was. It was not exactly the 'week-end cottage' that I had in mind; I felt a tad guilty I was there under false pretences.

When we walked around the house together, with a fresh eye the realisation that Charleston was unique struck me with a jolt. Responding to the bleak surroundings in 1916 when they moved in, the artists' paintbrushes had escaped from their easels, so that, over six decades, layer by layer, the house, its walls (hand-stencilled not wallpapered, which is an entirely different process), doors, window surrounds, mantelpieces and its contents were colourfully and joyfully embellished to become a work of art in their totality; and it was still complete – very much as Vanessa and Duncan had left it. The Firle Estate office were astonished when I telephoned the next day to say that I had no interest in buying Charleston – rather that it should be saved.

I negotiated a year's 'grace' period to give myself the opportunity to raise the funds to purchase and restore the house, contents and garden, and immediately began to air the concept to those I knew. It was not without its detractors. Some of those experienced in the field of heritage and conservation responded with derision, with such sentiments as: Duncan had only died the year before – what justification was there for saving Charleston? Or, had the house and contents been Georgian or Queen Anne, well that would be a different matter ....

Gradually a core group was brought together, and a charitable trust was established to further the cause. A critical tipping point came early on, and quite unexpectedly. My life as an international art dealer means that I regularly cross the Atlantic, and I had been introduced to Pierre Matisse, son of Henri, when I lived in New York. I would stay with Pierre and Tana regularly on my Manhattan visits thereafter and did so shortly after the agreement was made with the Firle Estate. When I told Pierre of this initiative, to my amazement he spontaneously took a Matisse down off the wall of their home and handed it to me with the words: 'Here is your first donation to save Charleston.' I looked at him in disbelief. 'But you have just made the campaign official,' I declared. 'Yes – and get on with it,' he replied.

This was followed by other significant gestures of generosity, including soon afterwards a matching promise for a donation to restore the house and funding for the garden from Lila Aecheson Wallace, co-founder of the *Reader's Digest* magazine, who had also supported the restoration of Monet's garden at Giverny. The Bell family too stepped forward and donated the Charleston Papers, which were sold at auction, and Angelica Garnett gave the contents of the house. This well and truly set us off on the track to save the house, garden and interior at Charleston.

In hindsight I realise that Pierre did more than give us a head start financially. He had become a mentor in my life. As a dealer he represented a cross-section of living international artists in his New York gallery, and through him I had intuitively come to perceive and embrace the intangible necessities that enabled an artist to flourish. So, when Angelica opened the pink front door at Charleston the flash of recognition that I had walked into the home of living artists was immediate.

This was its validity, but why save it?

By training I am an eighteenth-century specialist. The fact of the matter is that if one were to bring together an eighteenth-century interior today, a certain amount would depend upon educated guesswork. However, as a twentieth-century interior, Charleston was a hundred per cent intact.

Significantly it also evokes a sense of place, a haven of peace and tranquillity. The South Downs include some of the most spectacular scenery in southern England and possess an unusual and intangible quality within the vast dramatic space into which the rounded chalk hills rise and fold into one another, under the dome of the sky. It is a landscape that inspired writers such as Belloc, Kipling and Edward Thomas – and of course artists such as Eric Ravilious, as well as Vanessa and Duncan.

Charleston was Vanessa's lair, but it was also a practical and functioning home – a household that revolved around a steady schedule of work which could remain focused and uninterrupted thanks to the presence of a cook (Grace Higgens). It was the hub of a creative synthesis. Family and friends provided conviviality, laughter, and support during moments of sorrow, and through the diversity of visitors they drew inspiration from one another and from the synthesis that Vanessa and Duncan created. Duncan largely confined his homosexual life to London, preferring to keep it apart from his world of domesticity shared with Vanessa at Charleston and the enduring bond between them.

Charleston was one of the first twentieth-century houses complete with its interior to be saved in England. Unwittingly, it was as though we had dropped a pebble into a pond, the ripples of which have since spread, changing attitudes, so that more homes of this period have also been preserved. One of the implications of heritage is that the patterning of the present is always ephemeral, which was a key factor in the case for saving Charleston, in that the clutter and evidence of day-to-day life had survived. Added to this was the advantage that we could draw upon the experience of living family members to ensure accuracy in capturing an immensely personal lifestyle.

When we embarked upon the project in the early 1980s I remember listening to a speech given by Colin Thompson, Director of the National Galleries of Scotland, about the conservation of our cultural heritage. His theme, 'Preservation versus Change – are they Compatible?', struck a profound chord. Here lies the challenge. There is no point to saving a place if it is to be changed in the process. Charleston's validity lies in its quirkiness, its fragility; the essence of the farmhouse was always about experimentation and the engendering of new ideas. The litmus test for the next century will be whether the soul of Charleston remains delicately balanced – its extraordinary resonance and experience is only possible if each visitor's encounter is intimate.

Then our *real* challenge will have been accomplished. Charleston is – and always has been – about experimentation. And the house, grounds and bucolic setting provided Vanessa and Duncan with the perfect canvas to express themselves without inhibition. That is the reason Charleston was saved.

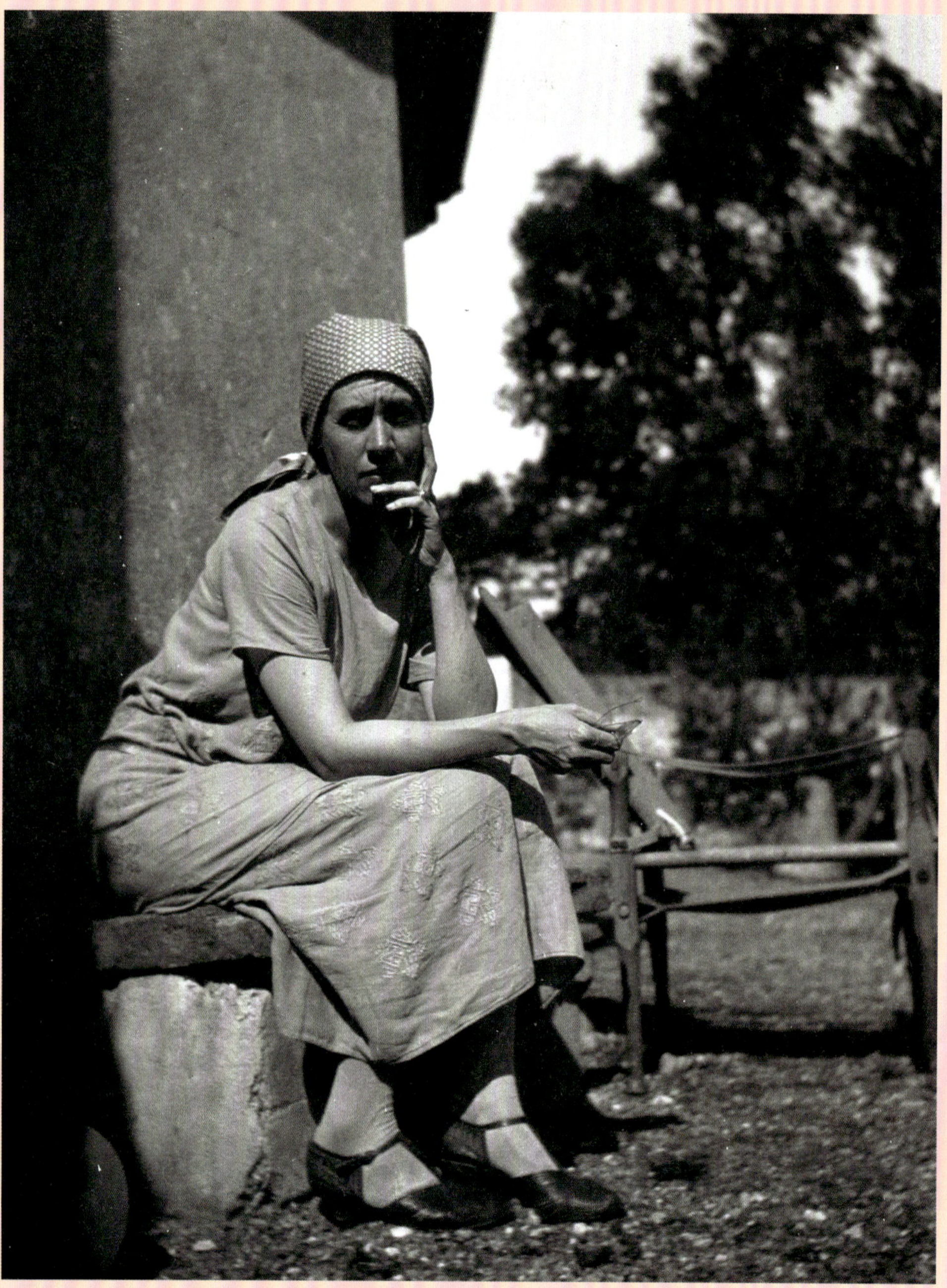

20. Vanessa Bell seated outside the Drawing Room at Charleston, 1926
Tate Archives

I have been seriously considering a plan by which we would give up Gordon Sq and take a house in the Country .... It rather depends upon whether I could find a nice house.

Vanessa Bell, 1915

1

Vanessa Bell
Still Life of Dahlias, Chrysanthemums and Begonias, 1912

Signed *V Bell* upper right
Oil on board laid on panel, 28¾ × 20⅜ in. (73 × 51.7 cm)
Philip Mould & Company

Selected literature Bagenal, B., et al. (1967), *Artists of Bloomsbury: Paintings, Drawings and Watercolours*, 20 June–28 August 1967 (exh. cat.). Rye: Rye Art Gallery, no. 23 (illus.)

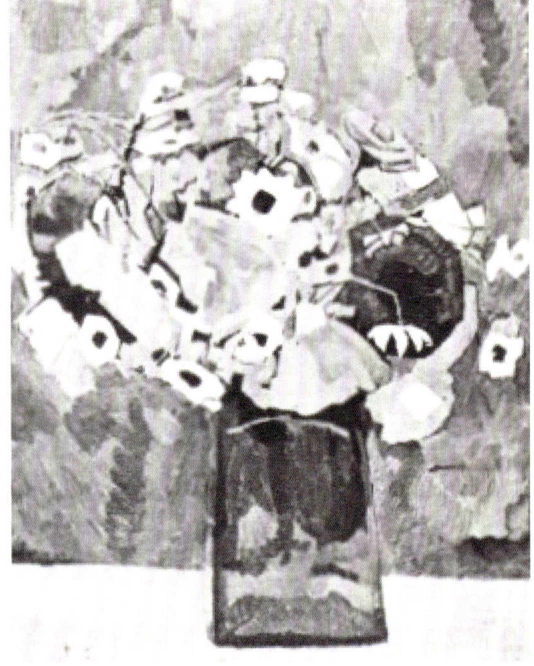

21. Vanessa Bell
Nosegay, 1912
Medium and size unknown
Whereabouts unknown

Although this work was not painted at Charleston – indeed it was painted some four years prior to Vanessa and Duncan moving there – it exemplifies a radical new approach to painting which was central to Vanessa's artistic development in this period. This painting was most likely produced at Asheham House, the weekend retreat of her sister Virginia and her husband, Leonard Woolf, that was located less than four miles away from their own future country home.

Many of Vanessa's early works were lost in 1940 when an air raid destroyed her London studio, and only a small number of paintings produced prior to c. 1910 survive. Those that do show mixed influences from artists of previous generations, including George Frederic Watts and Walter Sickert.

In 1910 Roger Fry opened his seminal exhibition *Manet and the Post-Impressionists* at the Grafton Galleries, and the impact on Vanessa was profound. Her works thereafter were bold – often radical – in their pursuit of colour as a means of describing the mood and character of a person, object or place. One of Vanessa's most accomplished works from this date is *Studland Beach* (c. 1912), which demonstrates her daring combination of strident colour and simplified form and has rightly been described as 'one of the most radical works produced at that time in Britain'.[1]

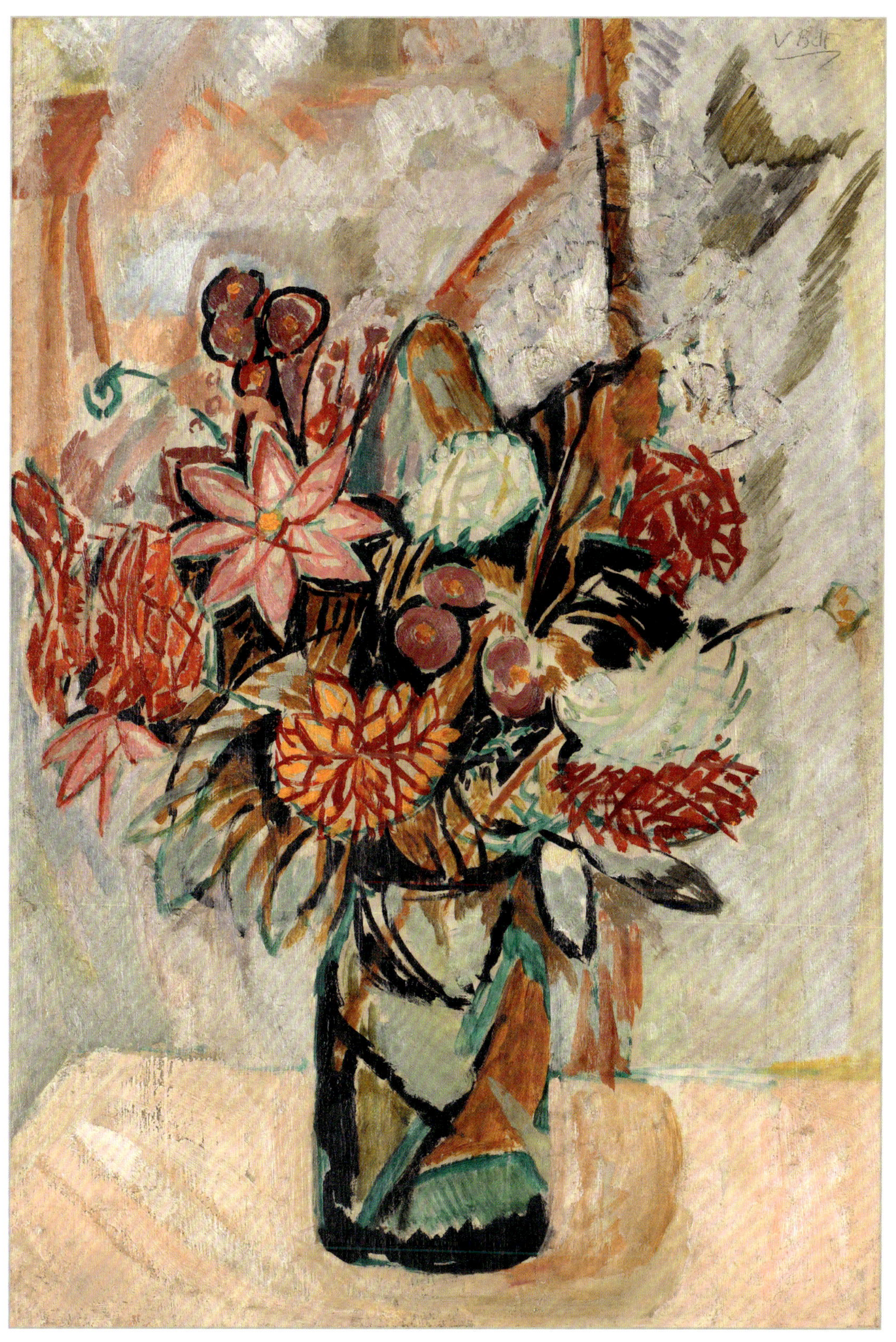

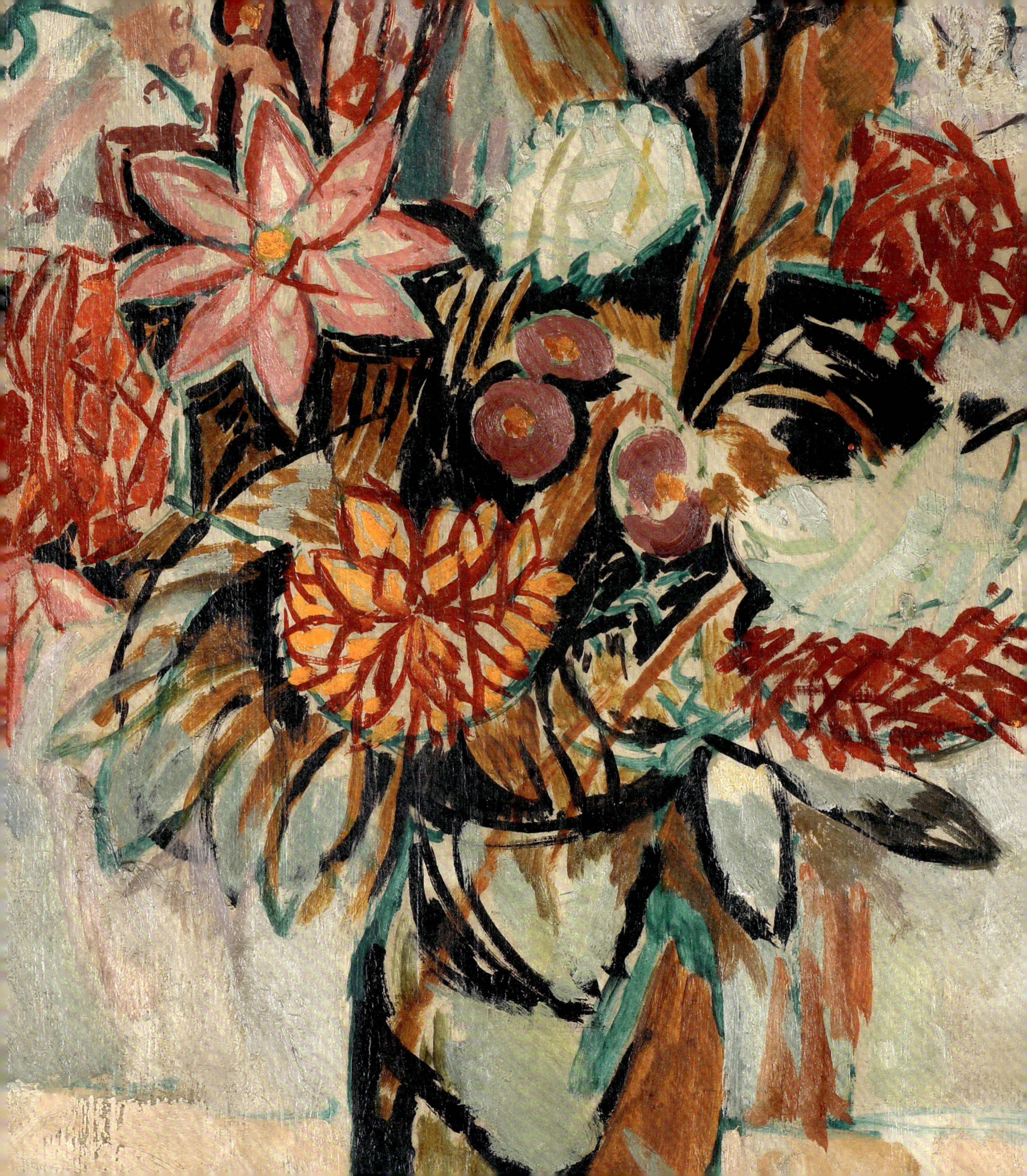

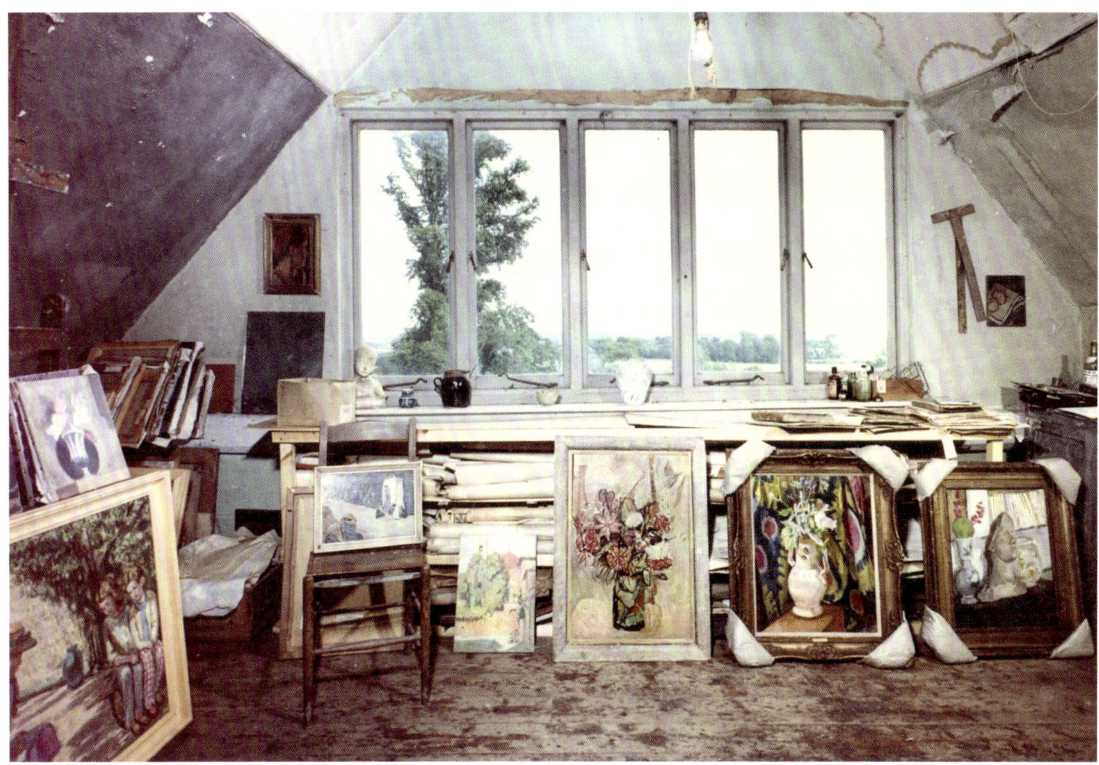

22. Vanessa's studio at Charleston showing the present work, 1970s
The Charleston Trust

Vanessa's exploration of post-impressionist possibilities led to an invitation from Roger Fry to exhibit at the *Second Post-Impressionist Exhibition* at the Grafton Galleries in late 1912. Two of the works she exhibited were painted at Asheham House during a two-month stay from mid-August to mid-October while Virginia and Leonard Woolf were on their honeymoon. Whilst at Asheham, Vanessa worked quickly, painting landscape views, interior scenes, portraits and still lifes. One of her best-known early landscapes, *The Haystack, Asheham*, was painted here and vividly demonstrates the bold new direction in which her work was heading. During the latter half of their stay the weather worsened, and Vanessa and Duncan remained indoors, painting still lifes and interior scenes. One example painted during this time and shown in the 1912 exhibition was *Nosegay* (fig. 21), which, as Richard Shone has pointed out, bears compositional affinities with the present work and may have been painted shortly after it.[2] In this work Vanessa reduces the complex forms of her subject into a series of sharp, geometric shapes whilst using colour to enrich and enliven the composition.
LH

---

1 Shone, R. (1999), *The Art of Bloomsbury*, 4 November 1999 – 30 January 2000 (exh. cat.) London: Tate Gallery, p. 74.

2 See catalogue entry written by Richard Shone: Christie's, London, Modern British Art Day Sale, 2 March 2021, lot 140.

2

Duncan Grant
Portrait of Mary Hutchinson, 1915

Oil on board, 23⅝ × 17⅝ in. (61.4 × 44.8 cm)
Kit Kemp MBE

Selected literature Shone, R. (1973), 'Review of Harvane', *Arts Review*, 10 March 1973, p. 130 (illus.); Shone, R. (1976), *Bloomsbury Portraits*. Oxford: Phaidon, p. 175, pl. 106

This vivid, fauve-inspired portrait of the writer Mary Hutchinson was begun by Duncan Grant in 1915 and possibly finished at Charleston when she came to stay in spring 1917 (fig. 24). It is a startling reminder of Duncan's exploration of colour in his early post-impressionist works.

Mary Hutchinson (née Barnes) was a cousin of Duncan Grant and Lytton Strachey and a prominent patron of the Omega Workshops. Her artistic proclivities are implicitly expressed by Duncan's bold pallet and characterisation. Intelligent, cultured and wealthy, Mary collected paintings by the leading avant-garde artists of the day, including Matisse, who drew her portrait in 1936. She was a renowned hostess and, together with her husband, the barrister and politician St John Hutchinson, she entertained artists, writers and intellectuals at their homes in London and West Sussex.

Soon after her marriage in 1910 Mary was introduced to the Bloomsbury Group. Clive Bell, who was married to Vanessa at the time, was enthralled by Mary and in around 1915 they became lovers, continuing their relationship until the late 1920s. Vanessa was with Duncan by this point, although the relationship between the two women remained frosty. Although they shared an enthusiasm for modern art, Vanessa and Mary differed in their attitudes towards fashion and society expectations: 'Mary I think is made for salons. Her exquisiteness is not lost upon us but it ought really to be seen by the polite world,'[1] Vanessa once remarked, wryly.

Mary is shown seated in front of an abstract work or wall painting at 46 Gordon Square, where Vanessa lived and kept a studio. Mary sat for Duncan and Vanessa simultaneously in February 1915, although the sitting was not a great success. Vanessa wrote to Roger Fry soon after: 'On Friday we painted Mary. Duncan got very desperate and began his again which I think I ought to have done too but I didn't.'[2] Vanessa's portrait of Mary is now in the Tate collection (fig. 23). Four portraits of Mary were begun by Duncan but only the present work was completed and signed and dated, albeit many years later.[3] LH

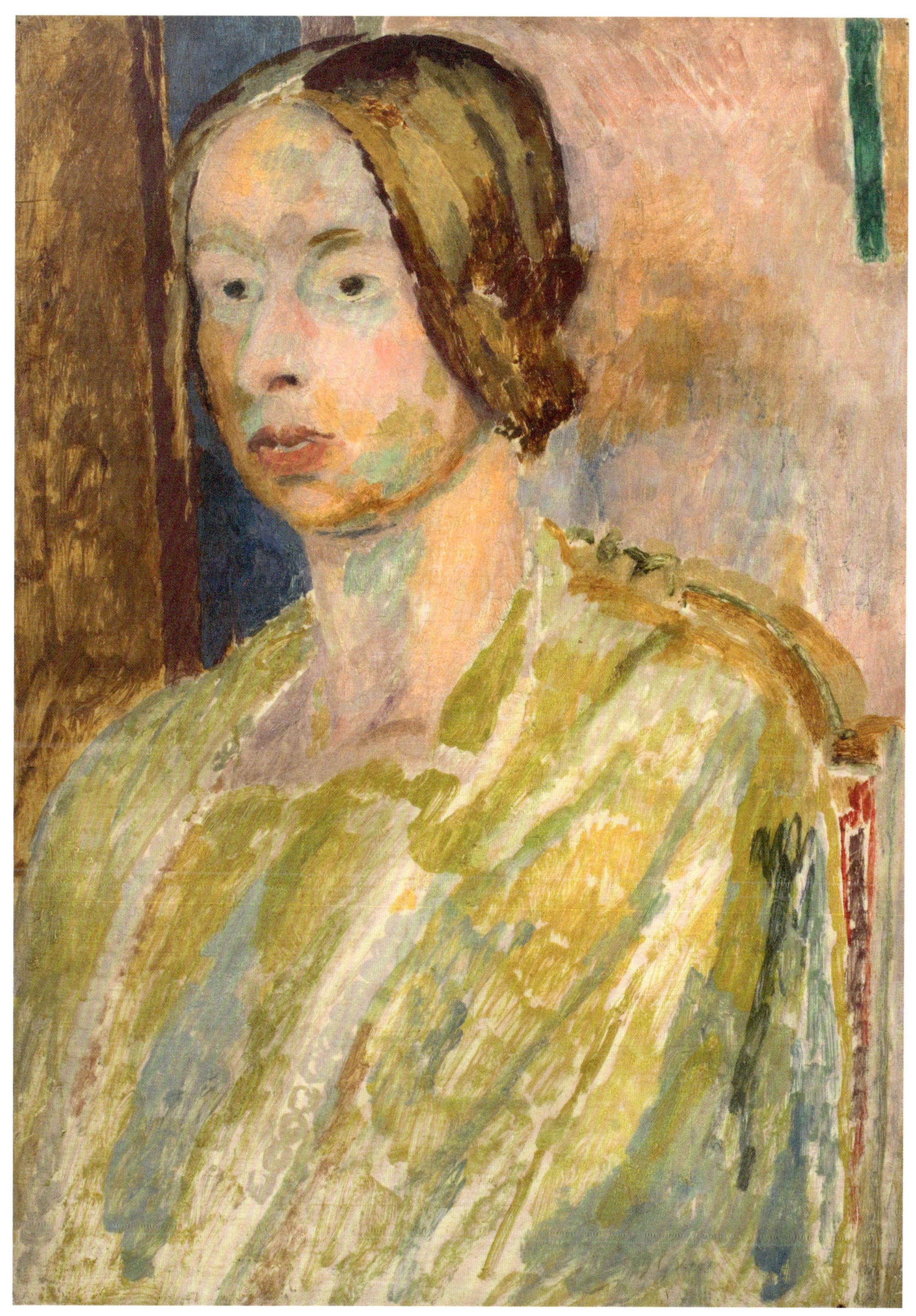

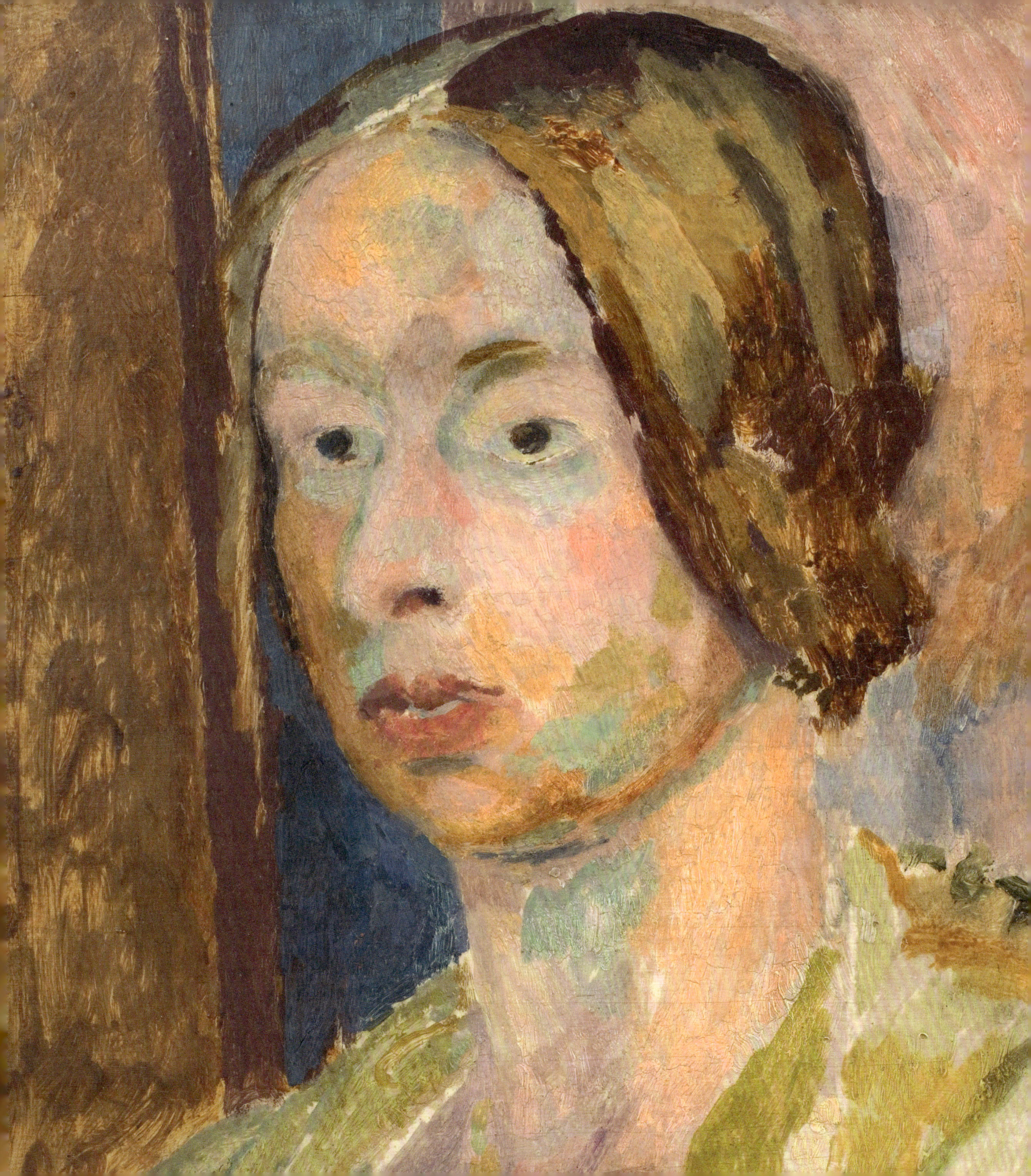

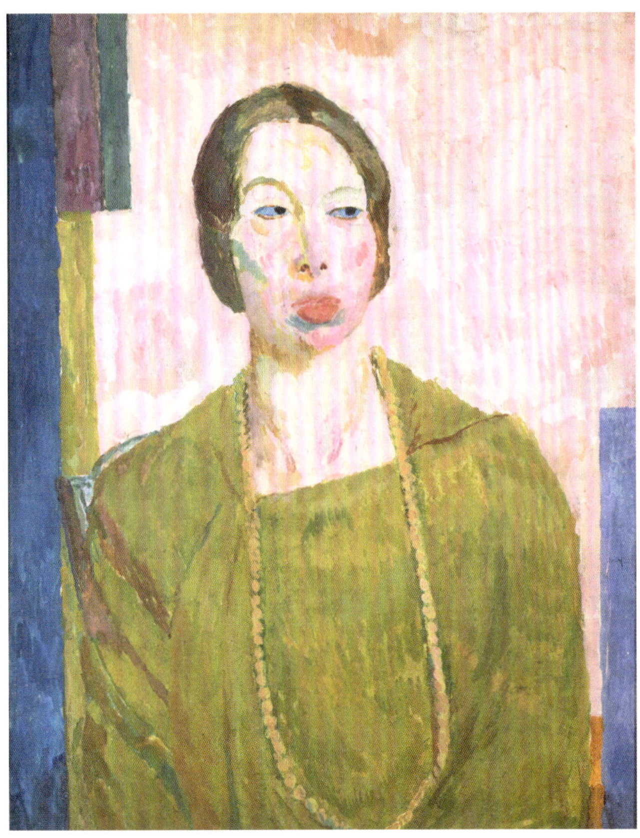

23. Vanessa Bell
Mrs St John Hutchinson, 1915
Oil paint on board,
29 × 22¾ in. (73.7 × 57.87 cm)
Tate

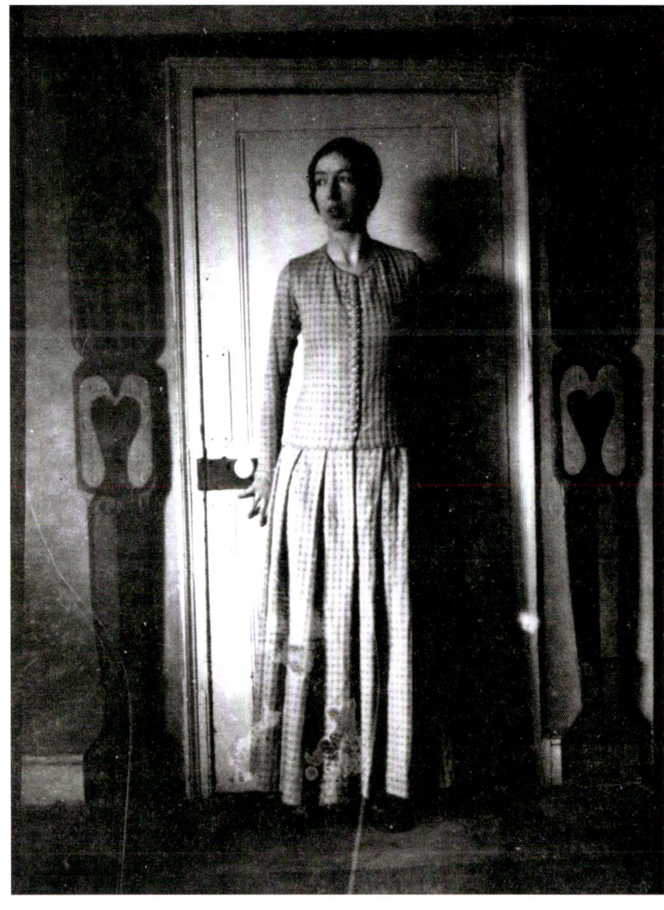

24. Mary Hutchinson at Charleston
Photography by Vanessa Bell, 1917
Private collection

1 Bell, V. 27 April 1916, *Letter to Lytton Strachey*, in Marler, R. (1993), *Selected Letters of Vanessa Bell*, London: Bloomsbury, pp. 194–96.
2 Shone, R. (1976), *Bloomsbury Portraits*. Oxford: Phaidon, p. 175, pl. 106.
3 Shone, R., in Travers, M. (ed.) (2018), *From Omega to Charleston: The Art of Vanessa Bell and Duncan Grant, 1910–1934*, 16 February – 28 April 2018 (exh. cat.). London: Piano Nobile Publications, p. 54.

3

Duncan Grant
Portrait of Vanessa Bell, c. 1915–16

Signed *D. Grant.* upper right
Oil on canvas, 20⅛ × 18⅛ in. (51 × 46 cm)
The Charleston Trust

Selected literature Hitchmough, W. (2020), *The Bloomsbury Look*. New Haven: Yale University Press, pp. 47–48

The year 1915 was decisive in the relationship between Vanessa and Duncan. Despite having met ten years prior, it was in this year that Duncan first became enamoured with the woman who was to become his lifelong partner. In 1915, his friendship with Vanessa developed into a romance which was later solidified when they decided to move with David Garnett to Charleston in 1916.

Duncan's experimental depiction of Vanessa indicates their close relationship; casting aside the constraints of formal portrait commissions, he has explored more radical forms of representation. Bold blocks of colour have been rigorously applied on to the un-primed canvas, referencing techniques employed by such artists as Paul Cézanne and the fauvists. A passage of soft, chalky grey highlights her cheekbone whilst deft flicks of rich maroon add depth to the contours of her profiled nose and chin. The result is an affecting modernist portrayal.

This painting was previously owned by Mabel Selwood, Quentin Bell's nanny before and during the first years at Charleston. Mabel left Charleston when she married and, upon hearing of her engagement, Vanessa invited her to choose a painting as a wedding present.[1] This work was selected and stayed with Mabel until her death. It was then returned to Charleston in the 1990s. ES

OVERLEAF

25. *Portrait of Vanessa Bell* (cat. 3) in the Studio, Charleston

26. *The Pond, Charleston* (cat. 4) in the Studio, Charleston

1 Hitchmough, W. (2020), *The Bloomsbury Look*. New Haven: Yale University Press, p. 47.

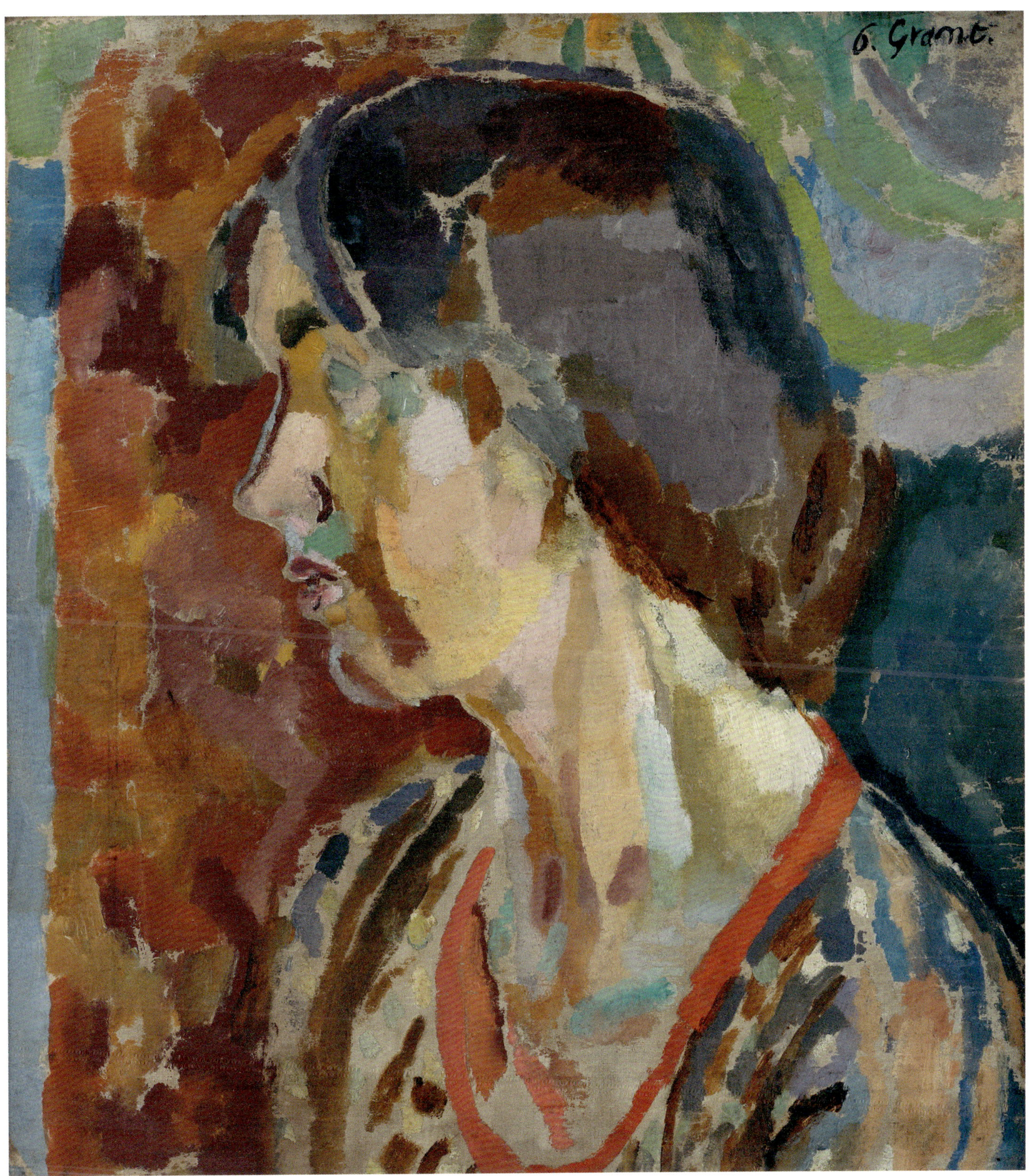
D. Grant.

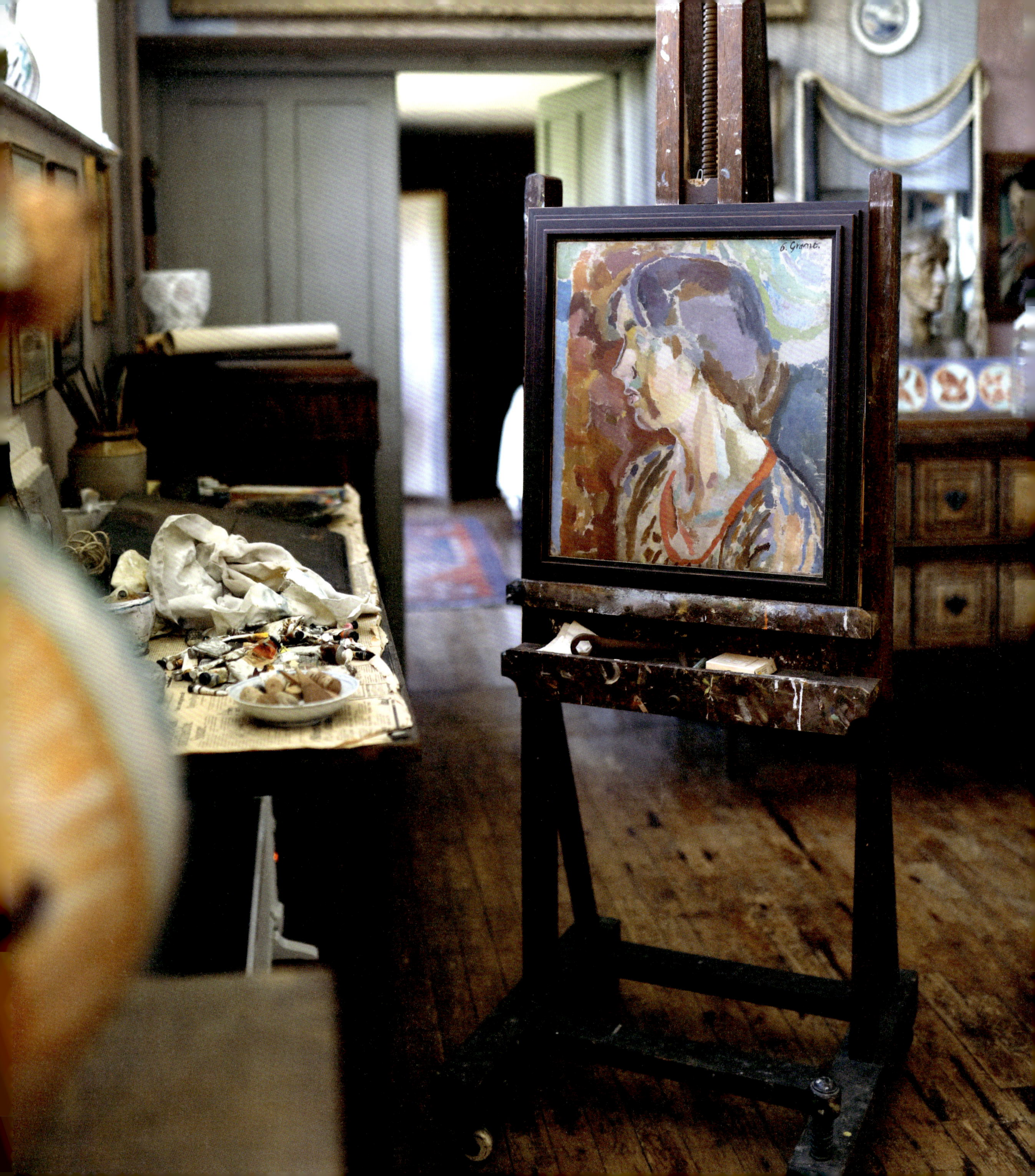
D. Grant.

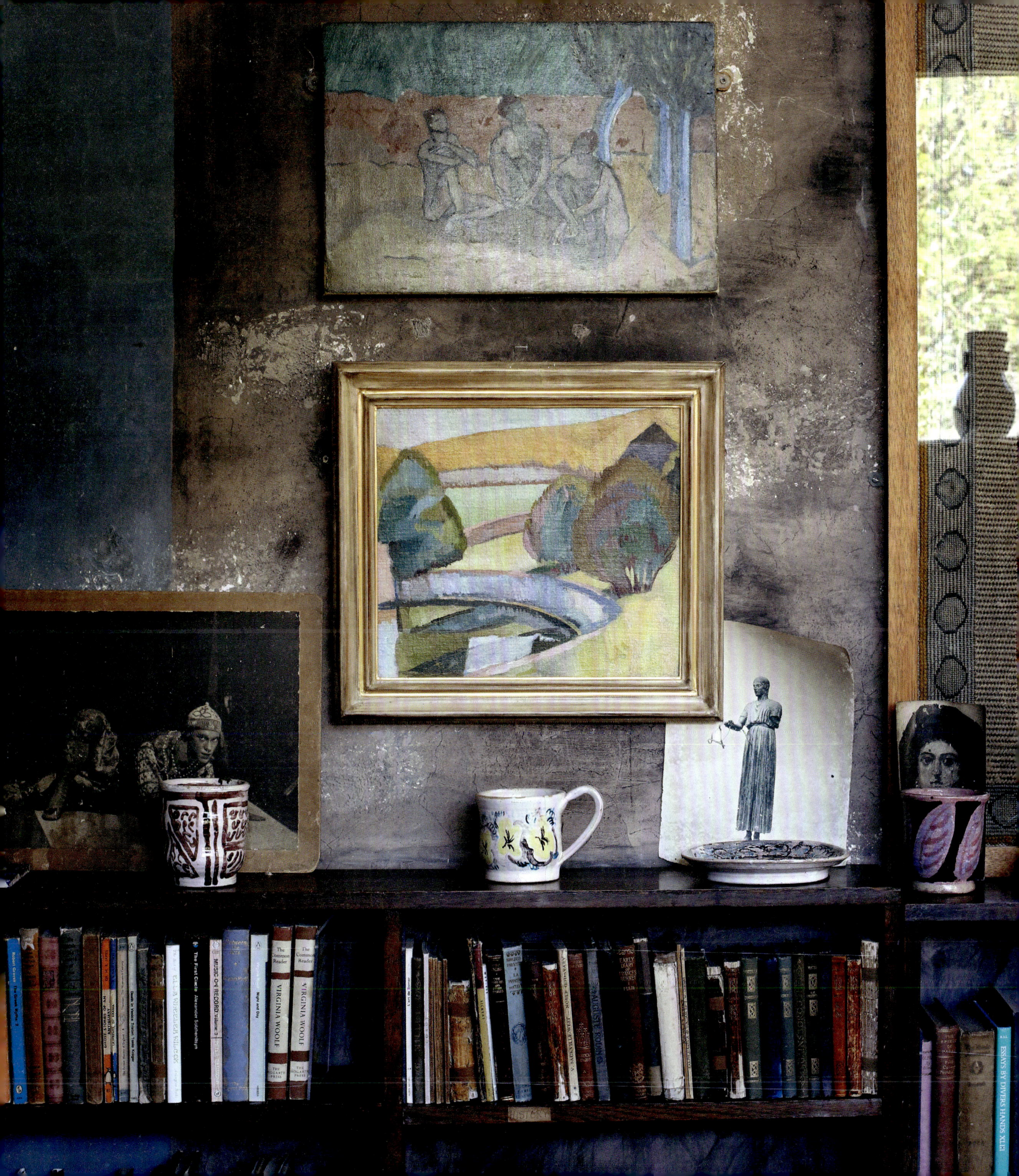
Robert Graves The Greek Myths 2
Death in Venice Tristan Tonio Kroger
ELLA WHEELER WILCOX
The First Circle Alexander Solzhenitsyn
MUSIC ON RECORD Volume 3
Night and Day
The Common Reader
VIRGINIA WOOLF
THE HOGARTH PRESS
The Common Reader
VIRGINIA WOOLF
THE HOGARTH PRESS
ESSAYS BY DIVERS HANDS XLIII

4

Vanessa Bell
The Pond, Charleston, 1916

Oil on canvas, 12⅛ × 14⅛ in. (30.5 × 35.5 cm)
The Charleston Trust

Selected Literature Naylor, G. (ed.) (1990), *Bloomsbury: The Artists, Authors and Designers by Themselves*. London: Octopus, p. 247; Shone, R. (1999), *The Art of Bloomsbury*, 4 November 1999–30 January 2000 (exh. cat.). London: Tate Gallery, no. 109, pp. 185–86

According to Duncan, this was the first work painted by Vanessa Bell after moving to Charleston in 1916. In a letter to Roger Fry penned soon after they moved in, Vanessa described how 'the pond is most beautiful, with a willow at one side and a stone or flint wall edging it all round the garden path, and a little lawn sloping down to it, with formal bushes on it.'[1] The pond was an endless source of artistic inspiration for Vanessa and Duncan and features in numerous works painted at Charleston throughout their lives. It allowed them to play with the varying properties of still water in high summer or frozen winter, as well as providing a lyrical prop in more ambitious compositions such as *The Hammock* (cat. 12).

Stylistically this work can be placed within a series of landscapes painted by Vanessa between 1911 and 1916 showing the influence of European modernism. Like many young British artists, Vanessa was struck by the paintings she encountered at Roger Fry's ground-breaking exhibition *Manet and the Post-Impressionists* staged at the Grafton Galleries between November 1910 and January 1911: 'Here was a sudden pointing to a possible path,' she later recalled, 'a sudden liberation and encouragement to feel for oneself, which were absolutely overwhelming.'[2] Included in this exhibition were twenty-one works by Cézanne, with fauvist landscapes by Matisse, Albert Marquet and Jean Puy. Vanessa's simplification of her subject into a perfect, painterly arrangement of coloured forms echoes the work of these artists, although, unlike that of some of her French peers, her use of colour does not overwhelm the composition. The sweeping wall of the pond and the diagonal field boundary beyond draw the eye up through the composition to Firle Beacon in the distance. Few of Vanessa's early landscapes express so emphatically a sense of place. LH

1 Bell, V. Quoted in Bell, Q. (1997), 'A Vanished World', *Charleston: A Bloomsbury House and Garden*. London: Frances Lincoln, p. 14.
2 Bell, V. in Giachero, L. (ed.) (1997), 'Memories of Roger Fry', *Sketches in Pen and Ink*, p. 130. Quoted in Shone, R. (1999), *The Art of Bloomsbury*, 4 November 1999 – 30 January 2000 (exh. cat.). London: Tate Gallery, p. 73.

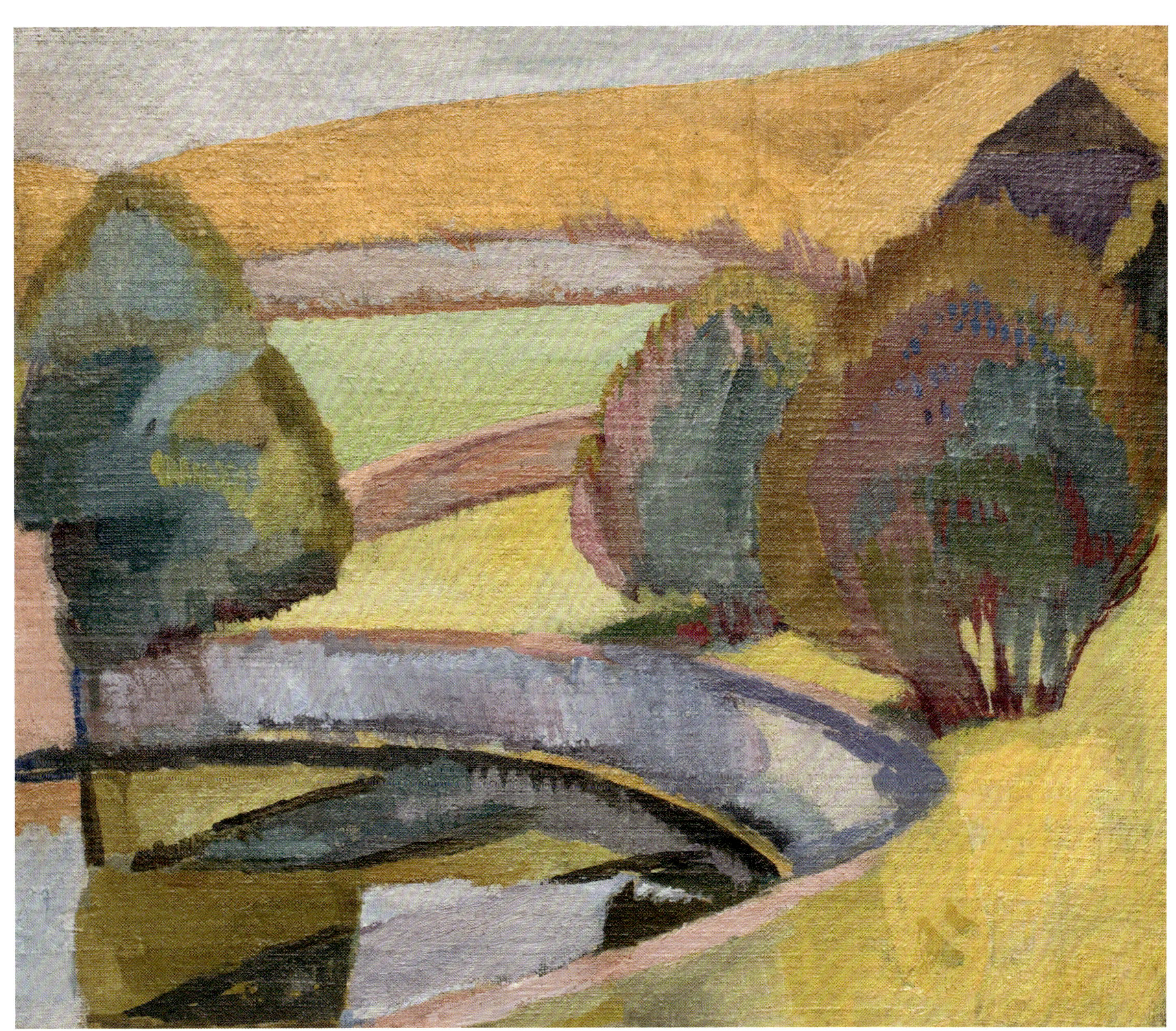

5

Duncan Grant

Still life with Compotier and Glass, c. 1916

Initialled *D.G* lower right
Oil on canvas, 16½ × 12¼ in. (41.9 × 31 cm)
Private Collection

The compotier depicted here remains in Charleston's collection today. It was given to Duncan by Barbara Bagenal (née Hiles), who famously camped in the garden at Charleston a year after this still life was painted.

Painted four years after his inclusion in Roger Fry's *Second Post-Impressionist Exhibition*, the present still life exemplifies the enduring and profound impact of European modernism on Duncan's style.

Manipulating the shallow composition, Duncan deftly delineates the contours of every surface of the compotier and wineglass. The paint is applied in short, sharp brushstrokes reminiscent of the work of Paul Cézanne (fig. 27). The flattened perspective also alludes to cubist tendencies, which Duncan admired at both Post-Impressionist exhibitions; the elevated vantage point here looks down on the table, whilst simultaneously establishing a lower viewpoint of the compotier.

The fluidly applied, iridescent and non-naturalistic colours employed here begin to build in density throughout his later career but are already a hallmark of his paintings during the earlier years of Charleston life. In the early 1920s Clive Bell shrewdly articulated Duncan's developing relationship with colour:

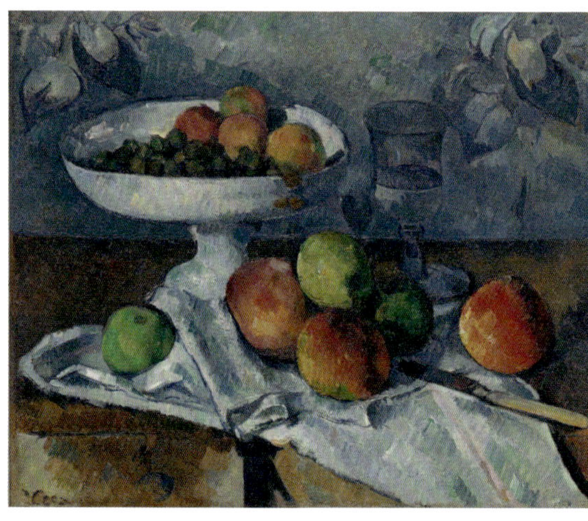

27. Paul Cézanne
Still Life with Fruit Dish, 1879–80
Oil on canvas 18¼ × 21½ in. (46.4 × 54.6 cm)
Museum of Modern Art, New York,
Gift of Mr. and Mrs. David Rockefeller, 69.1991

> *... the very material out of which he builds is coloured in poetry. The thing he has to build is a monument of pure visual art.*[1]

Crystalline and clear, the present painting boldly examines the function of line and colour in humdrum, everyday household objects scattered around their domestic space. ES

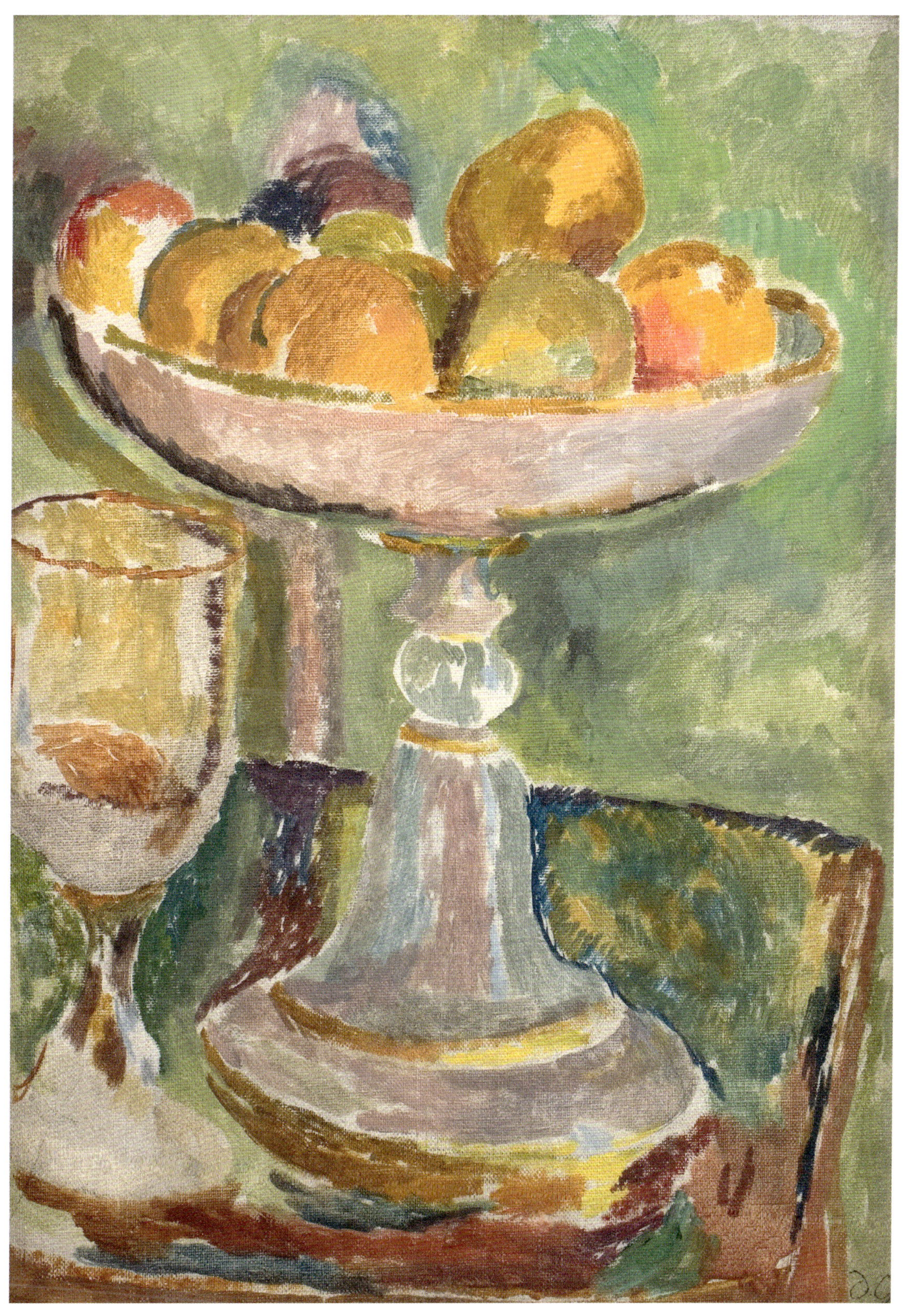

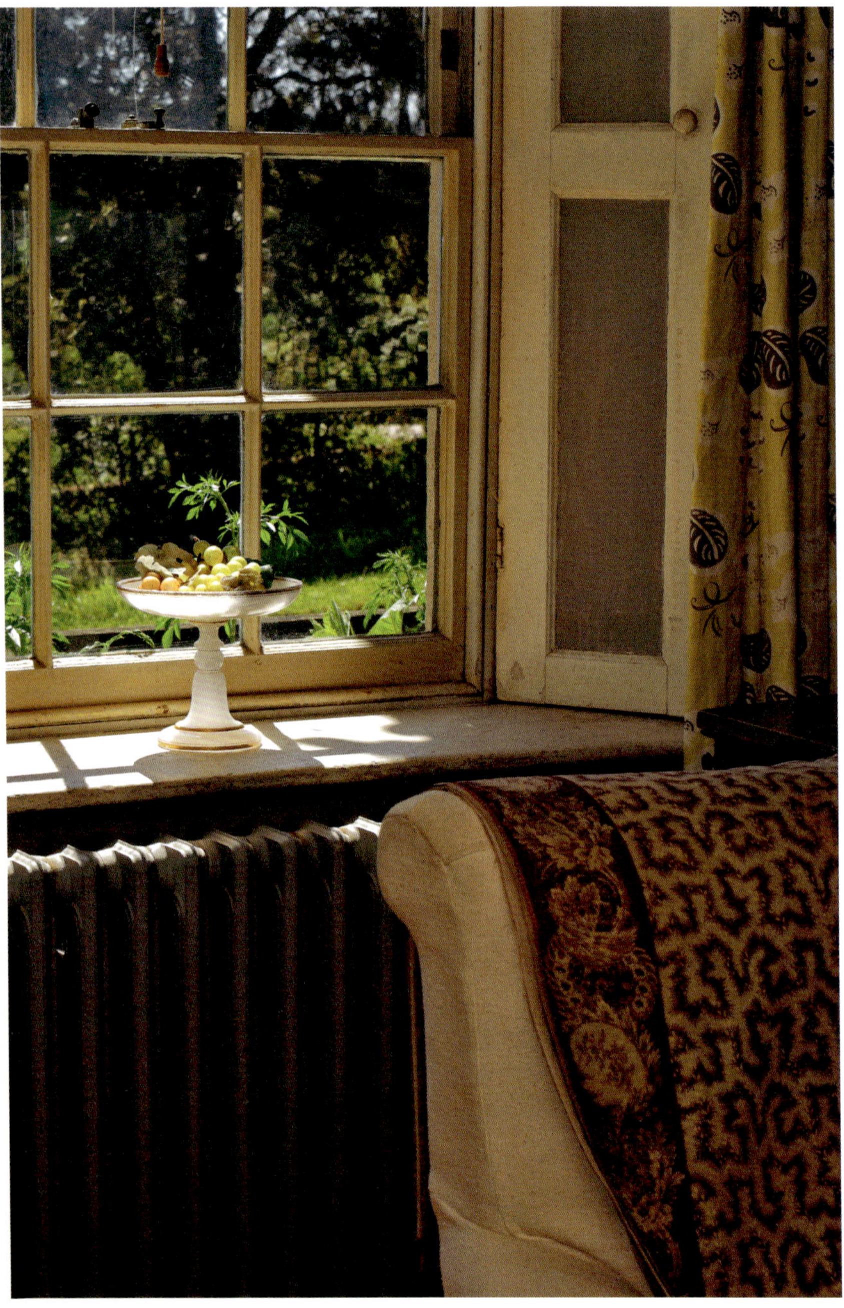

28. Compotier in the window of the Garden Room, Charleston

1 Bell, C. (1922), *Since Cézanne*. Available at https://www.gutenberg.org/files/13395/13395-h/13395-h.htm (accessed 27 May 2021).

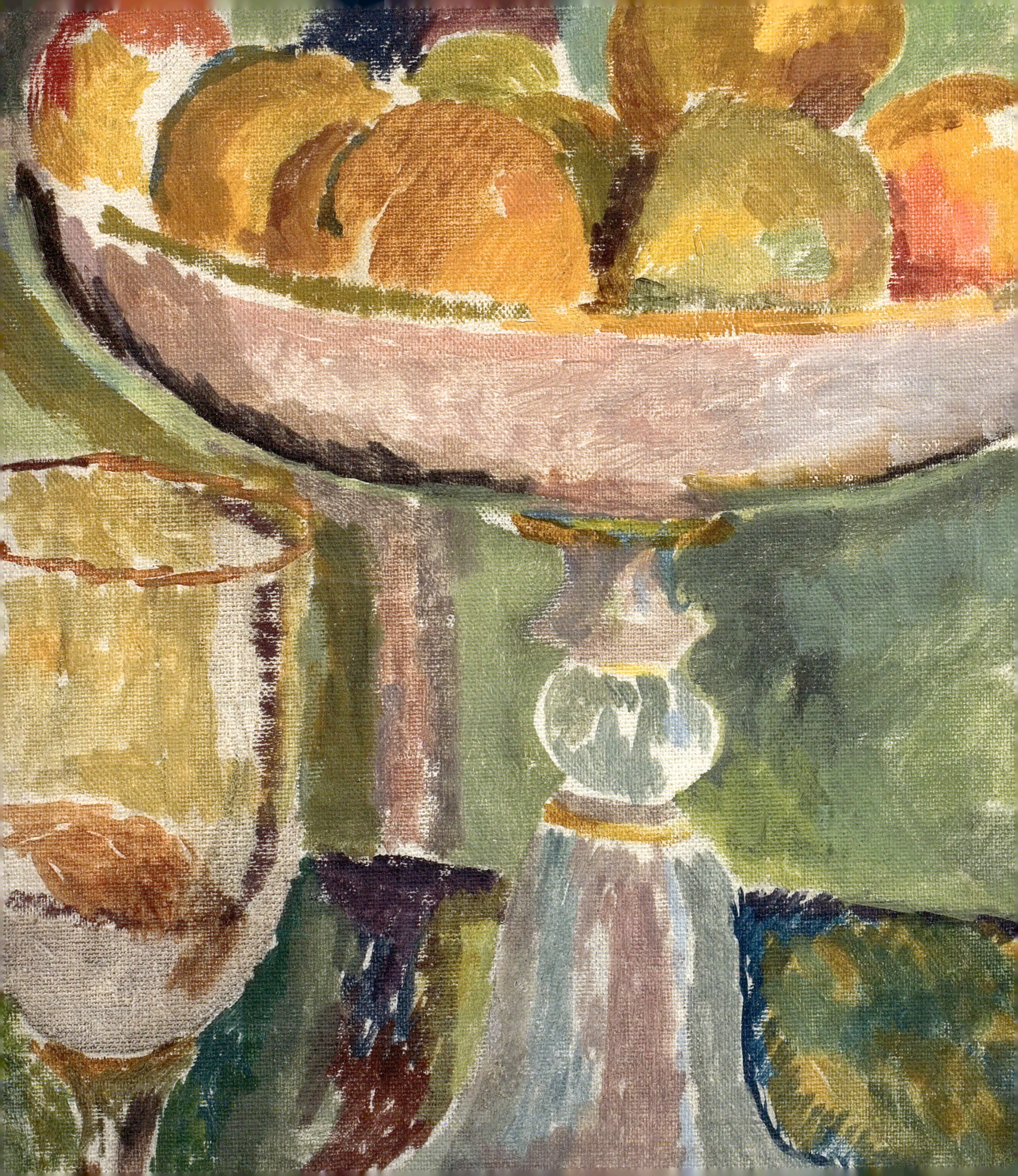

6

Duncan Grant
Linen Chest, c.1917

Oil paint on wooden chest, 20 × 15½ × 35¾ in. (50.8 × 39.5 × 90.8 cm)
The Charleston Trust

Selected literature Naylor, G. (ed.) (1990), *Bloomsbury: The Artists, Authors and Designers by Themselves*. London: Pyramid, pp. 188–89; Nicholson V. (2018), *Charleston: A Bloomsbury House and Garden*. London: White Lion Publishing, pp. 116–17; Shone, R. (1980), *Duncan Grant: Designer*, 1 February–29 February 1980 (exh. cat.). Liverpool: Bluecoat Gallery, p. 16, no. 28; Wolf, H. (2017), *Sussex Modernism: Retreat and Rebellion*, 28 January – 23 April 2017 (exh. cat.). London: Two Temple Place, pp. 20–24

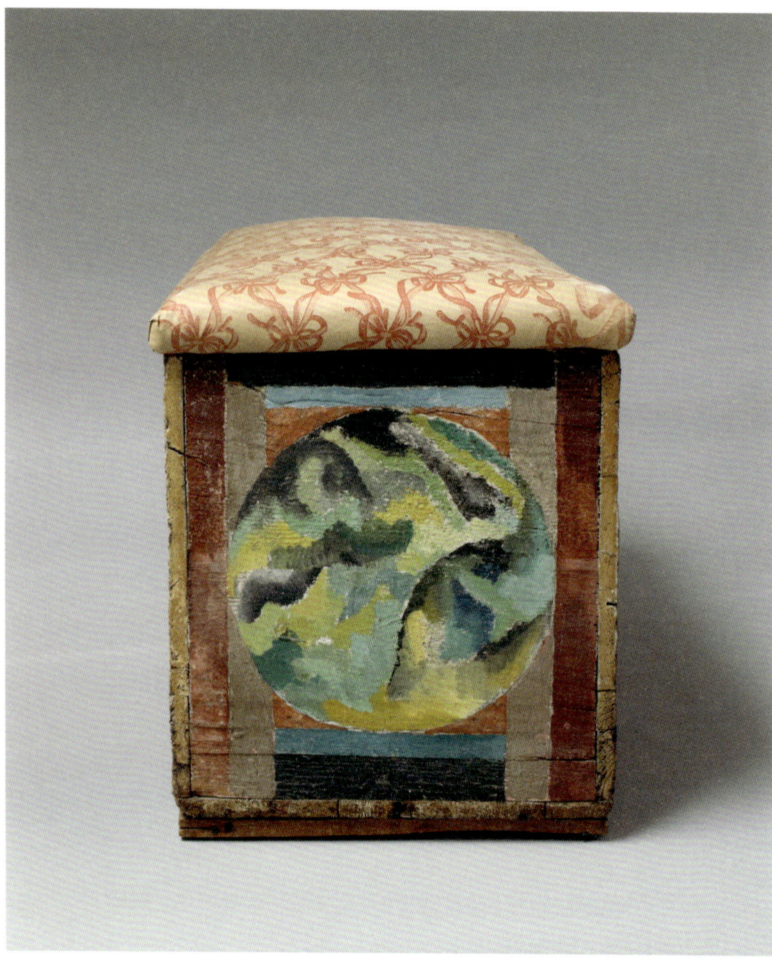

This linen chest was painted by Duncan Grant at Charleston in around 1917 and is amongst his most captivating post-impressionist decorations. The freedom to experiment with colour, form and technique was one of the guiding principles of the Omega Workshops and heavily influenced Duncan and Vanessa's approach to the interior decorations at Charleston.

As a conscientious objector Duncan did not fight during the First World War and instead worked as a labourer on a farm near to Charleston. He started work immediately upon arrival in the countryside, and the transformation of Charleston from an empty house to a busily decorated bohemian home was therefore gradual. Vanessa was the first to start decorating and Duncan assisted when time allowed. Limited funds and wartime conditions dictated the style and type of furnishing in these early years. Some of the furniture was inherited from Vanessa's parents; other pieces came from the Omega Workshops and additional items were picked up at local markets or second-hand furniture shops in Lewes.[1] Some of these finds were then enlivened with painted decoration.

The linen chest is painted on all four sides, with a bold, cubist image of a bather on the front. Briskly painted in vivid colours, it is an unabashed celebration of the male form. Bathers were a theme Duncan explored frequently in the 1910s,

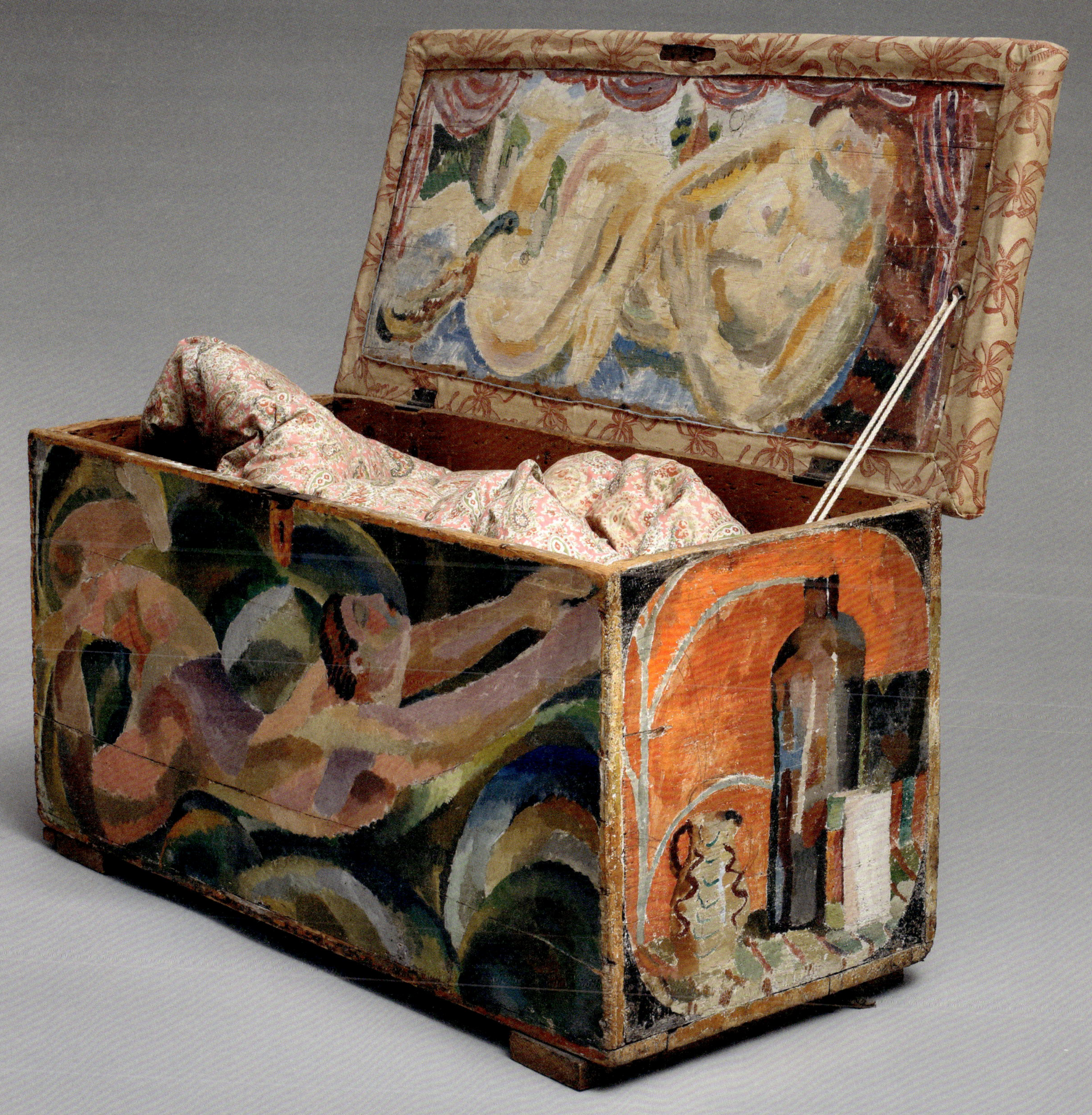

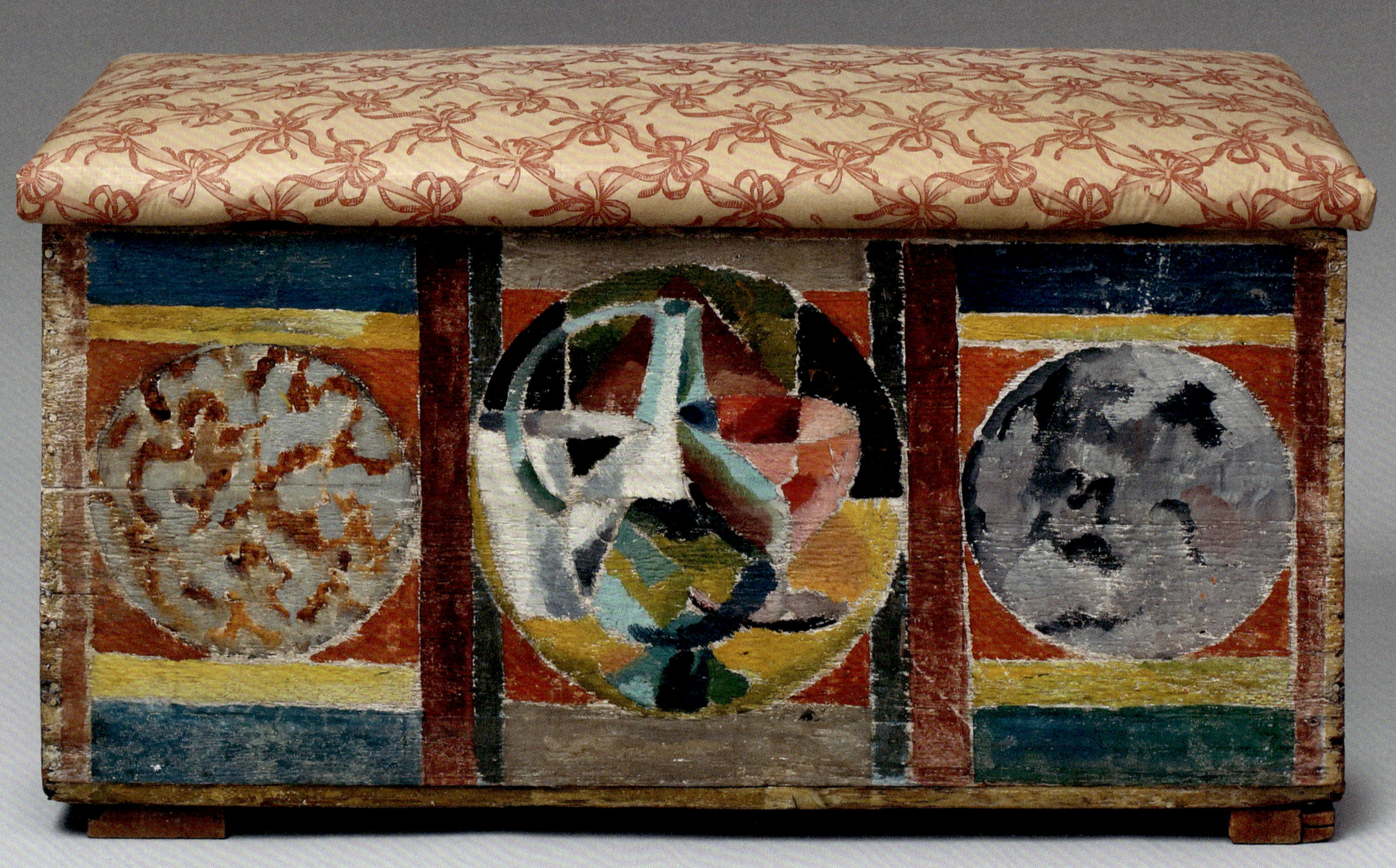

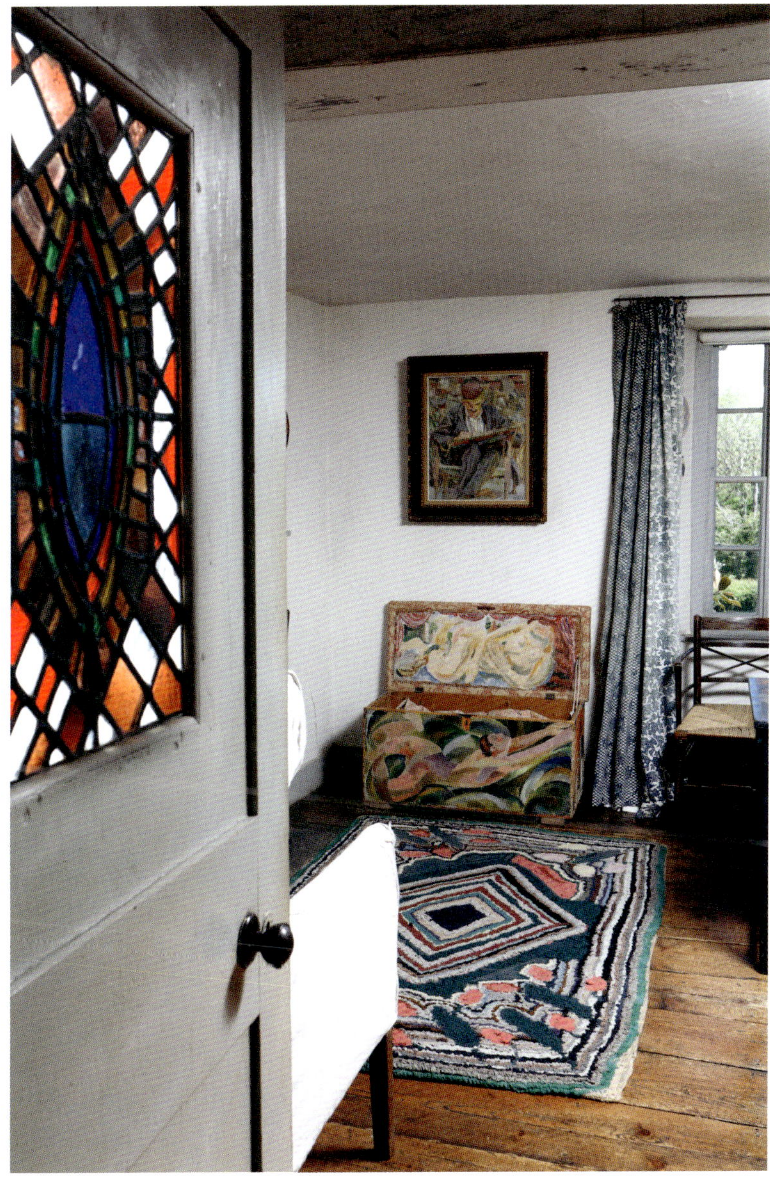

29. The linen chest (cat. 6) in John Maynard Keynes's bedroom, Charleston

perhaps influenced by his trips to the Serpentine in Hyde Park – a men-only swimming area which became a popular haunt within the gay community. Although homosexuality was not decriminalised in the United Kingdom until 1967, Charleston, in its remote rural setting, was a safe haven where Duncan could express his sexuality free from persecution.

On the underside of the chest lid is an image of a reclining female nude representing Leda, who in Greek mythology was seduced by Zeus disguised as a swan. In his depiction, Duncan has replaced the swan with a more docile duck and framed the image with theatrical drapes, as if the figure is on a stage, revealing herself only to those who open the lid. On the reverse of the chest is an abstract image of a jug and two glasses flanked by circular, marble-like motifs set within linear bands of colour. A similar abstract design can be seen on the left side of the chest and on the right is a still life set against a luminous orange background. LH

1 Spalding, F. (1997), *Duncan Grant: A Biography*. London: Chatto & Windus, p. 193.

7

Duncan Grant
Portrait of John Maynard Keynes, 1917

Oil on canvas, 22¼ × 18¼ in. (56.5 × 46.3 cm)
The Charleston Trust

Selected literature Hitchmough, W. (2020), *The Bloomsbury Look*. New Haven: Yale University Press, p. 5, no. 1

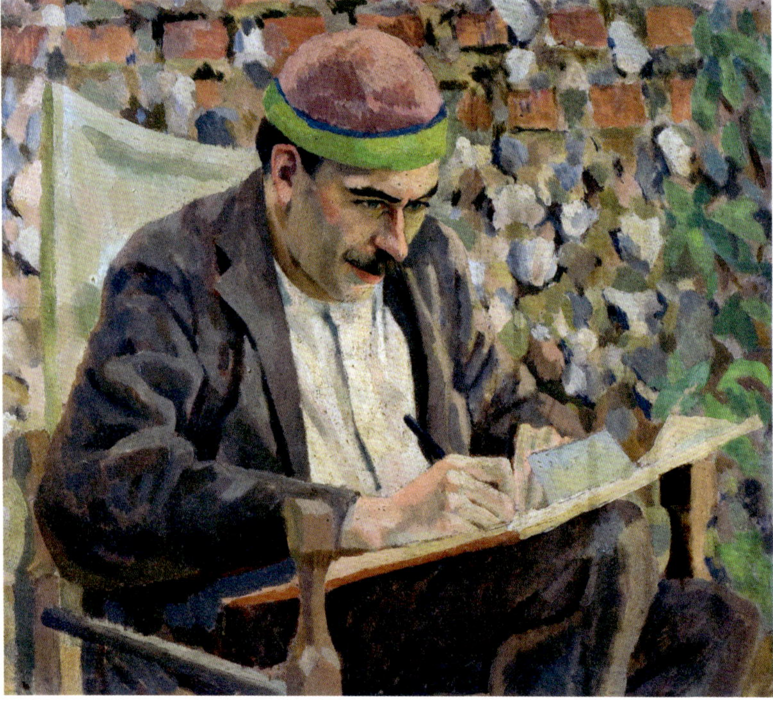

30. Roger Fry
Portrait of John Maynard Keynes, 1917
Oil on canvas, 20½ × 24 in. (52 × 61 cm)
King's College, Cambridge

This portrait of the economist John Maynard Keynes was painted in the walled garden at Charleston during the penultimate year of the First World War. Keynes frequently visited Charleston throughout the war and contributed to its upkeep. He had his own bedroom where he would study and write, and it was here that he wrote part of his most famous book, *The Economic Consequences of the Peace*, published in 1919.

The cubist fragmentation of Keynes's grey suit and the pink brick background partly evokes the work of post-impressionists such as Paul Cézanne. Indicatively, a Cézanne painting was introduced for real at Charleston the following year, when Keynes returned from the Continent with a still life. Keynes, tired and carrying a lot of luggage, was obliged to deposit the painting temporarily in a hedge just up the lane from the farmhouse, where he had been dropped off by the 'government motor'.[1] Duncan and David Garnett rushed to its rescue. It now hangs in the Fitzwilliam Museum, Cambridge.

Here, Keynes is shown seated (reputedly) drafting a telegram to America negotiating a loan to support Britain's war effort. The thought of a Treasury official sitting in the garden of a pacifist household appealing for help funding the war effort might seem odd, but it epitomises the varying perspectives and the open-mindedness which bound the Bloomsbury Group together.

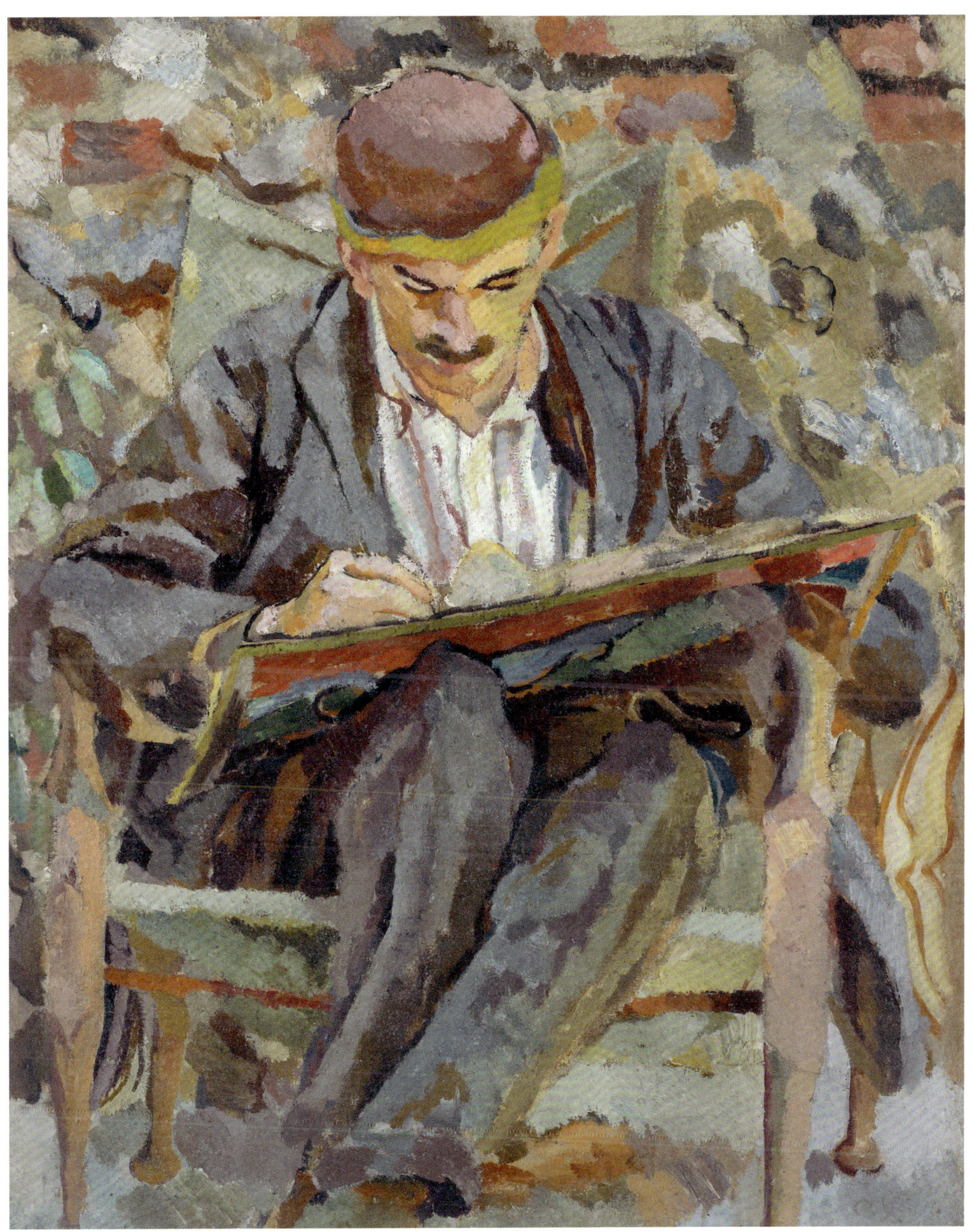

As Keynes wrote the telegram, Duncan and Roger Fry sat and painted him. Duncan's portrait is more painterly than Fry's (fig. 30) and less concerned with likeness than with capturing Keynes's focused mind. It was a side of his character Duncan knew intimately; the two friends had been lovers in the past but now enjoyed a platonic friendship. For Keynes, Charleston was a place of liberation where he could rest, relax and meet friends: 'I shall be back very soon indeed and in great need of Charleston,' he wrote to Vanessa Bell from Paris in 1919.[2] Keynes's arrival at Charleston on Friday evenings, armed with a copy of the *London Evening Standard*, momentarily shattered their rural isolation. Quentin Bell later recalled how it was 'a slightly astonishing thing for it looked so urban and remote in that primitive and countryfied place'.[3] LH

FACING

31. *Portrait of John Maynard Keynes* (cat. 7) above the linen chest (cat. 6) in John Maynard Keynes's bedroom, Charleston

1 Spalding, F. (1998), *Duncan Grant: A Biography*. London: Pimlico, p. 206.
2 Keynes, J.M., to Bell, V., 3 June 1919, King's College, Cambridge (King's/PP/CHA/341/3). Quoted in Hitchmough, W. (2020), *The Bloomsbury Look*. New Haven: Yale University Press, p. 7.
3 Bell, Q. (1995), *Elders and Betters*. London: John Murray, p. 85. Quoted in Hitchmough, W. (2020), *The Bloomsbury Look*. New Haven: Yale University Press, p. 7.

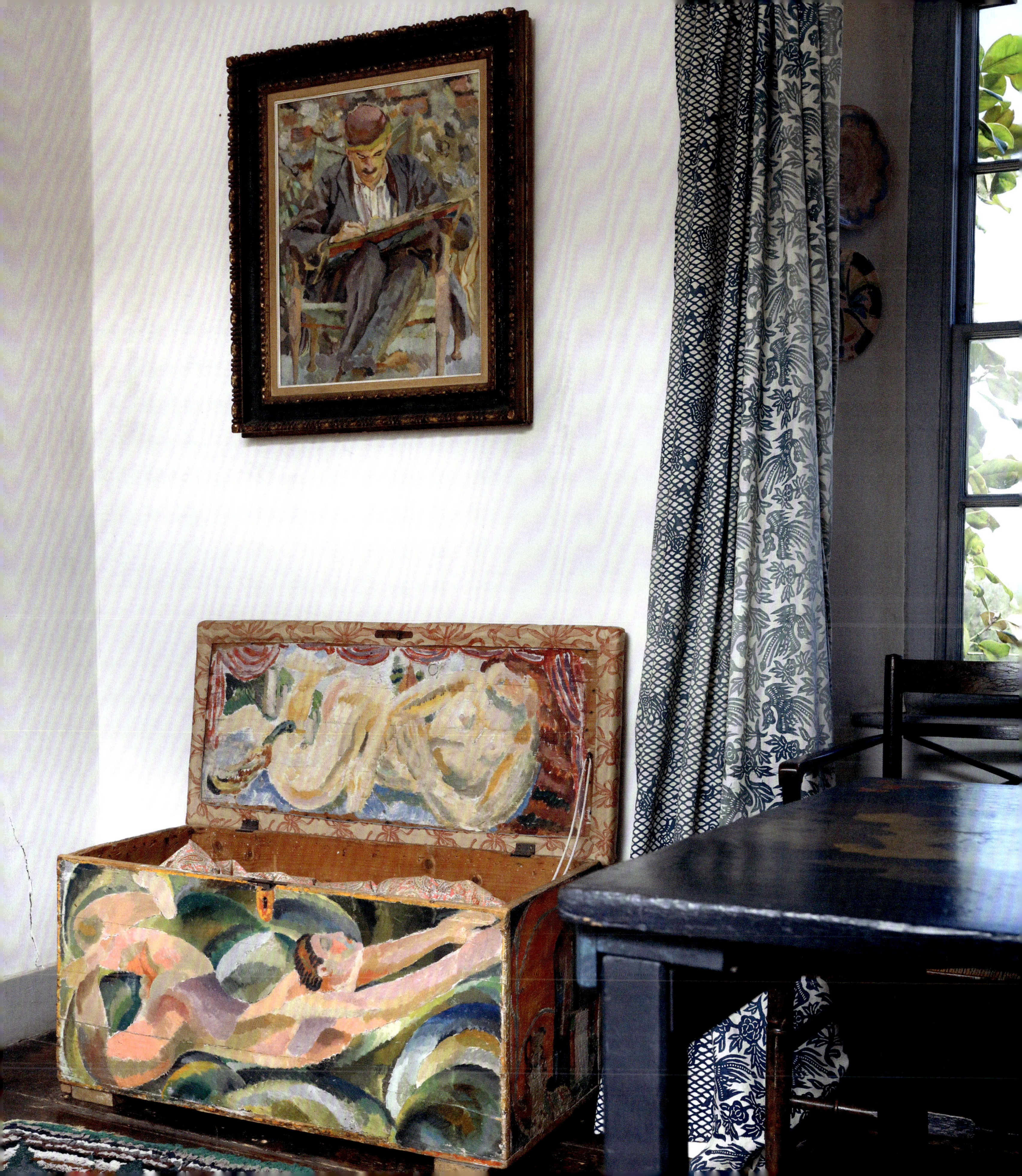

8

Duncan Grant

Still Life with Gourd in a Blue Bowl, c. 1917

Indistinctly signed *D. Grant* lower right
Oil on canvas, 15 × 20 in. (38.1 × 50.8 cm)
Private collection

This arresting still life was painted by Duncan soon after he moved to Charleston with Vanessa and David Garnett in 1916. It is imbued with the same vitality of execution as many of his early post-impressionist works, in which high-key colours and descriptive strokes dominate the compositional character. The result here is a complex yet deeply satisfying arrangement of shape, pattern and design, elevating an otherwise prosaic subject of vegetables and fruit.

As a conscientious objector Duncan worked on a nearby farm as a labourer during the war and had little spare time to paint. Alongside the occasional decorative work for the interior spaces at Charleston (cat. 6) he also painted still lifes during these years. In this he delights in a variety of produce, their shapes and colours mere touchpoints for his imagination. Only a small number of his works from this date survive. The majority were kept by the artist and only sold towards the end of his life.

Duncan and Vanessa rarely signed their early work and as a result there is sometimes confusion over the authorship of their paintings (as well as their interior design works). Such was the case with the present work, which, for many years, was considered to be by Vanessa owing to a misleading inscription on the reverse applied by an unknown hand at a date subsequent to its execution. The later discovery of a pencil signature in the lower right corner has since helped restore this work to Duncan's oeuvre. LH

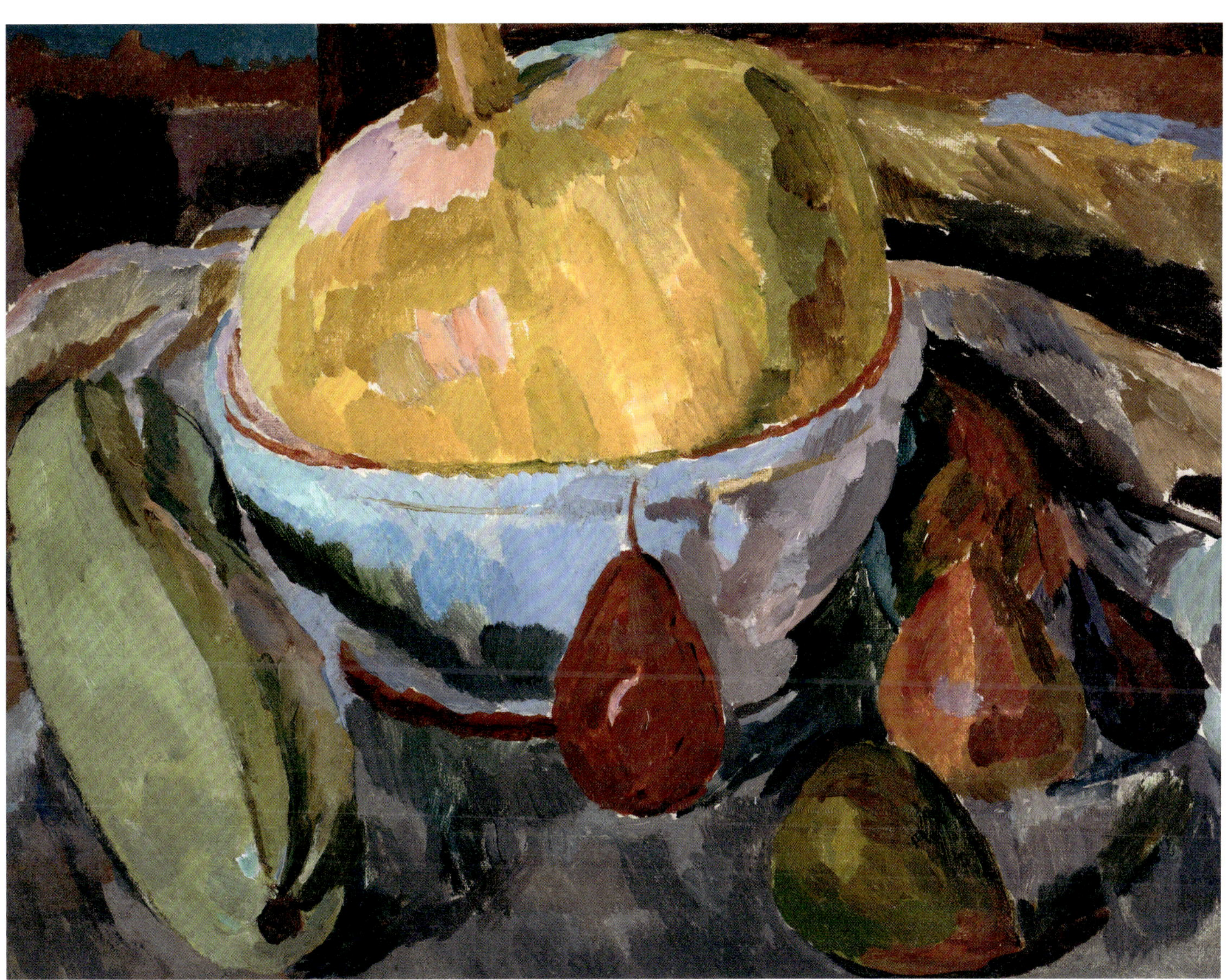

9

Duncan Grant
Kitchen Cupboard Doors, c. 1917–18

Oil on wood, each 16⅞ × 21⅝ in. (43 × 55 cm)
The Charleston Trust

Originally installed at Charleston, these painted cupboard doors typify the occupants' unbridled proclivities to paint not just their surroundings but the dwelling itself. The spontaneous programme of interior works that took place over sixty years can be seen as Charleston's most conspicuous artistic legacy.

Whilst the decoration was gradual (see cat. 6), the process was initiated as soon as Vanessa and Duncan moved to Charleston. These painted panels demonstrate their unrestrained attitude towards interior decoration which obscured the boundary between domestic interior and fine art.

Duncan depicts a stylised still life on each door: one portrays a jug and two glasses and the other a bowl of fruit. Although the Omega Workshops were beginning to fall into decline by this date, Duncan's uncompromising colour palette and design nonetheless continued the company's audacious aesthetic.

Duncan and Vanessa had similar styles when it came to decorative painting – so much so that sometimes even they struggled to remember who had painted what. The confusion was only exacerbated by the ever-evolving decorative process at Charleston. As Virginia Nicholson, granddaughter of Vanessa, pointed out: '... if the table top decorations wore out, they could always just paint some new ones on top.'[1] ES

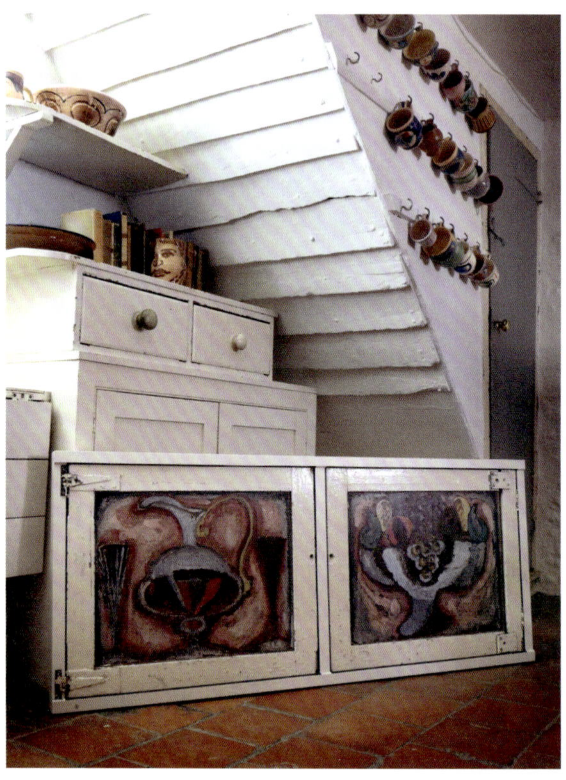

32. The Kitchen, Charleston

1 Nicholson V. (1997) *Charleston: A Bloomsbury House and Garden*. London: Frances Lincoln, p. 9.

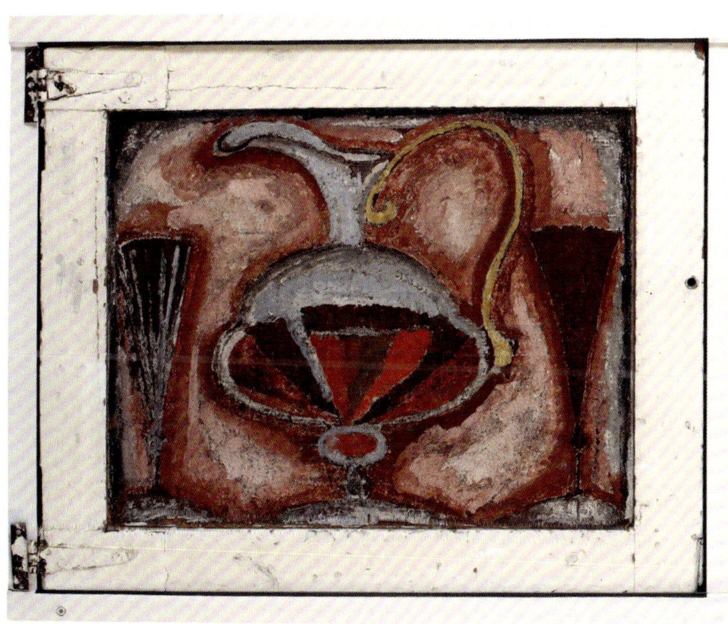
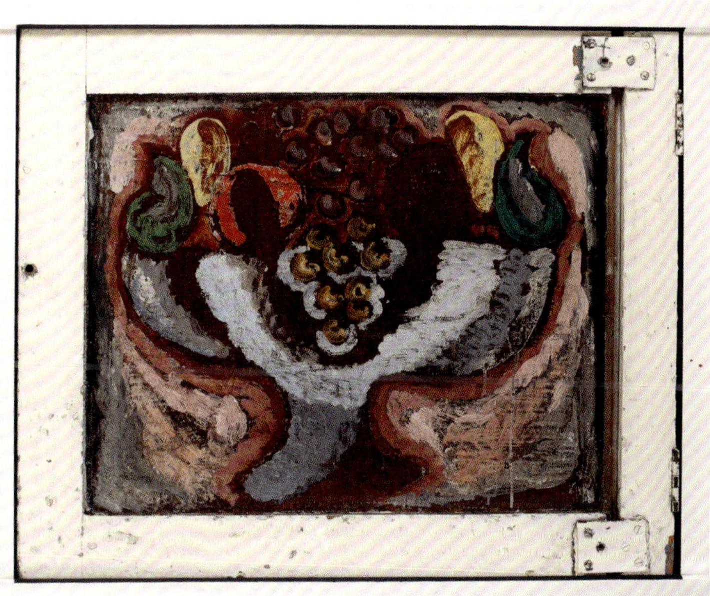

10

Duncan Grant
Portrait of Roger Fry, c. 1919–20

Watercolour on paper, 11¾ × 9 in. (30 × 23 cm)
Peggy Post

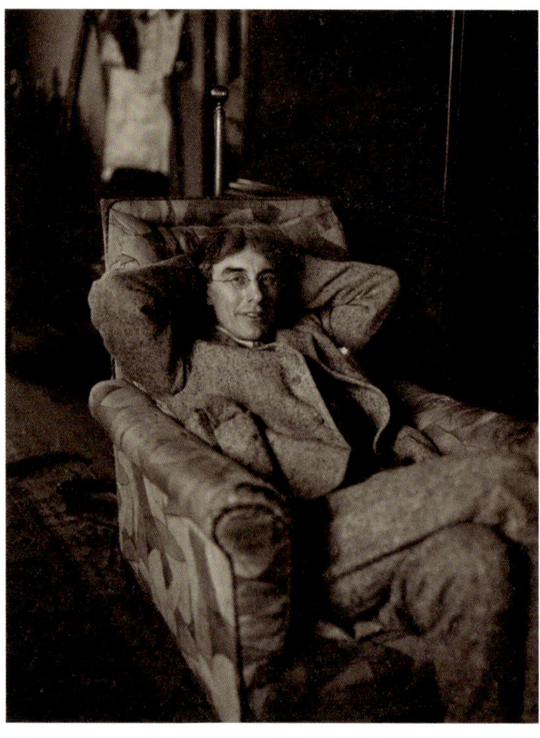

33. Roger Fry
Photograph by Augustus Charles Cooper
National Portrait Gallery Photographs Collection

At Charleston, his imprint is everywhere. It's sometimes forgotten, but the truth is Charleston wouldn't be Charleston without Roger Fry — Virginia Nicholson[1]

Roger Fry (fig. 33) had whipped up a furore in 1910 when he staged *Manet and the Post-Impressionists* at the Grafton Galleries. It included vividly coloured modern works by artists such as Van Gogh, Gauguin and Cézanne and attracted over 25,000 visitors over the course of two months. It challenged established artistic traditions of form and beauty whilst enthusing a younger generation of artists by offering a new and exciting route of artistic expression to explore.

Soon after, an intimate relationship developed between Roger and Vanessa, who had met earlier in 1906. Their intimacy was not to last – Vanessa was drawn instead to Duncan – but their friendship endured, and Roger remained a close friend until his death in 1934. Roger was a regular visitor to Charleston, and his creative imprimatur runs throughout the house and its grounds. His red chairs, designed for the Omega Workshops in 1913, are in the Dining Room downstairs, and several of his paintings – including a copy of an Italian fresco – are hanging on the walls upstairs.

Roger helped design the Studio at Charleston and also the walled garden. His practical mind and hands-on approach helped turn the tired farmhouse into a home. During the first winter at Charleston in 1916, for example, the house was bitterly cold, so Roger built a hearth out of firebricks to direct more heat into the rooms.[2]

The present watercolour portrait was painted by Duncan at Charleston in around 1919. Its radical colouring and loose, lyrical use of line stand in stark contrast to Duncan's portraits at the beginning of the decade. LH

1 Nicholson, V. (2021), 'My Dearest Roger …', *Bonhams Magazine* (no. 67), Summer 2021, p. 18.
2 Ibid.

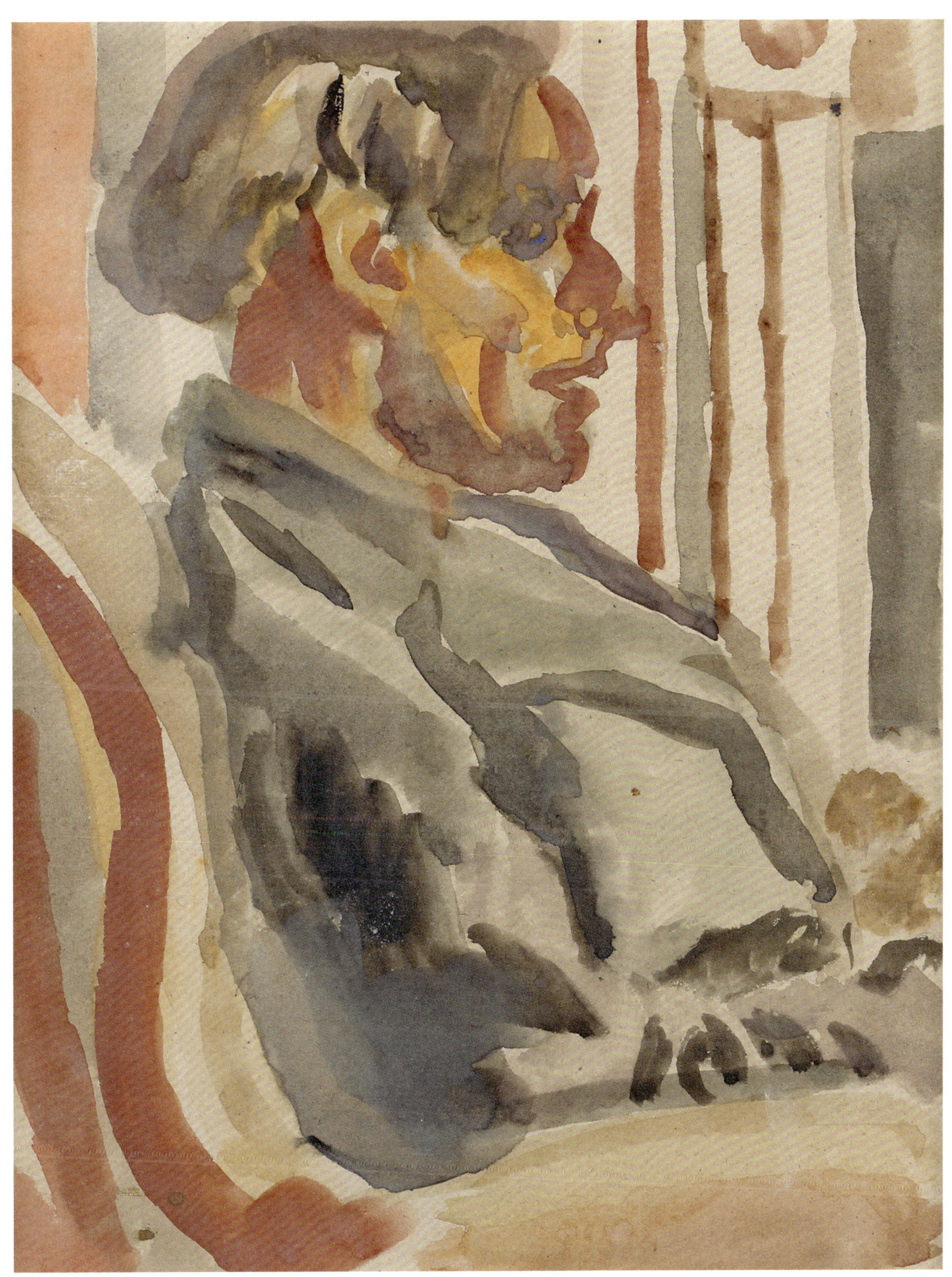

11

Vanessa Bell and Duncan Grant
Studies for *The Muses of Arts and Sciences*, 1920

Oil on canvas, each 33 × 14 in. (83.8 × 35.5 cm)
Private collection

Selected literature Todd, D., and Mortimer, R. (1929), *The New Interior Decoration*. New York: Charles Scribner's Sons, pls. 24 and 25; Keynes, M. (ed.) (1975), 'The Picture Collector', in *Essays on John Maynard Keynes*. Cambridge: Cambridge University Press, p. 286; Shone, R. (1993), *Bloomsbury Portraits*. Oxford: Phaidon, p. 223; *British Modernist Art 1905–1930*, 14 November 1987 – 9 January 1988 (exh. cat.). New York: Hirschl and Adler, 1987, no. 136 (illus.)

After the war, one of Vanessa and Duncan's first mural commissions was for their close friend John Maynard Keynes (cat. 7) who commissioned eight panels for his rooms in Webb's Court at King's College, Cambridge.[1] This was by no means their first commission from the economist: two years earlier Duncan and Vanessa had decorated the sitting room for Keynes at 46 Gordon Square, previously the home of Vanessa and her siblings, Virginia Woolf (née Stephen), Thoby and Adrian Stephen. However, unlike Gordon Square, Keynes's panels are still held in the collection at King's College.

The panels began their life in a temporary studio fashioned from an army hut just outside the walled garden at Charleston. Vanessa expressed some satisfaction with this temporary set-up and reported her progress on the panels in a letter to Roger Fry of 26 August 1920:

> *The hut makes a splendid studio and there are eight divisions all along one side which just take the panels, so it's a perfect place to do them in.*[2]

Comprising a compelling fusion of classical and modernist stylistic references, these studies were painted in preparation for the larger panels and sought to represent a symbolic range of the higher artistic and intellectual aspirations of the Bloomsbury Group. The chosen theme was the arts and sciences, and each of the subjects is portrayed with a specific, although in some cases ambiguous, attribute, as recounted in Vanessa's letter to Fry: 'They are supposed to represent law, science, history etc. though you mightn't think it – in fact we're always changing their arts and sciences'.[3]

Remarkably, despite one having been temporarily separated, these highly significant collaborative studies are now again together as a complete set. ES

---

1 Shone, R. (1993), *Bloomsbury Portraits*. Oxford: Phaidon, p. 223.
2 Bell, V., quoted ibid.
3 Bell, V., quoted in Shone, R. (1976), *Bloomsbury Portraits*. Oxford: Phaidon, p. 234.

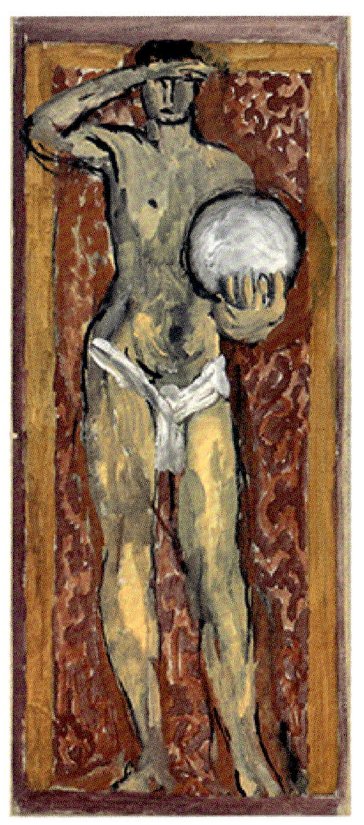
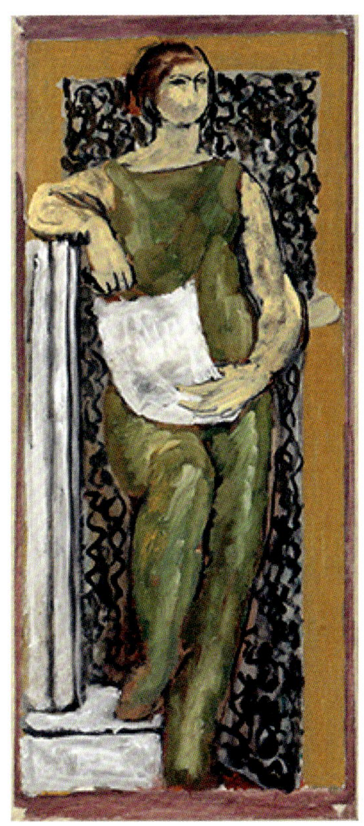
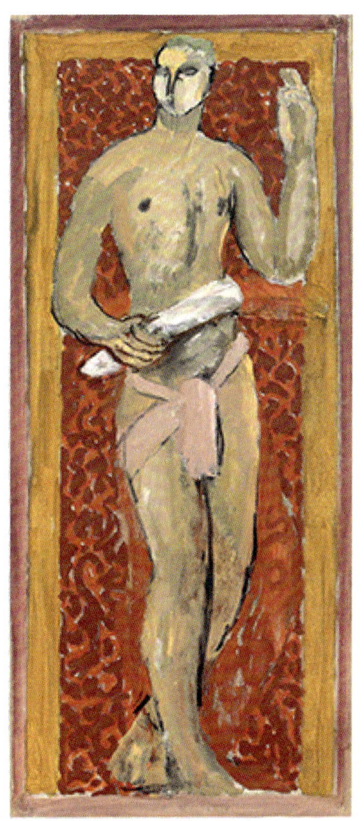
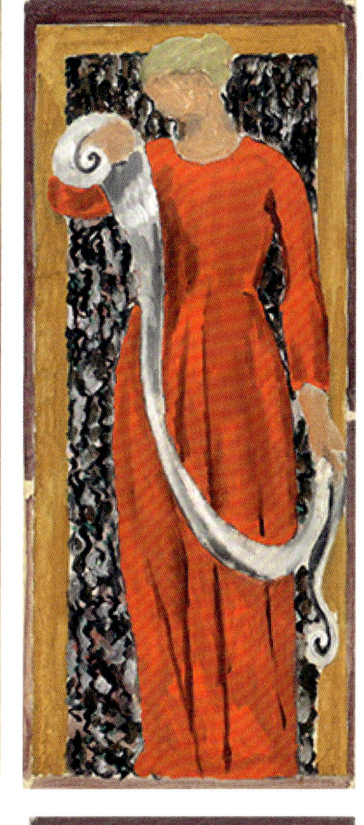
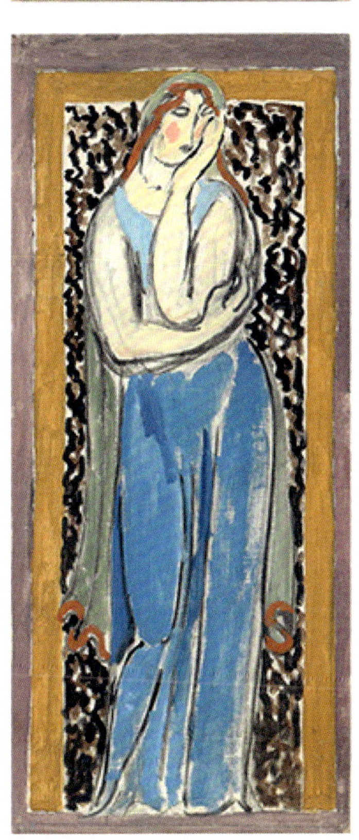
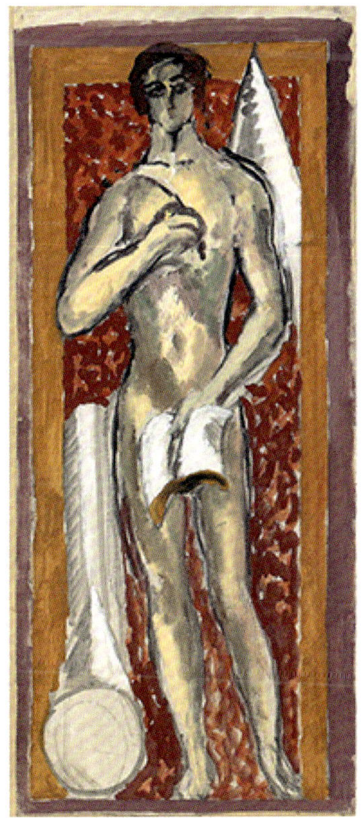
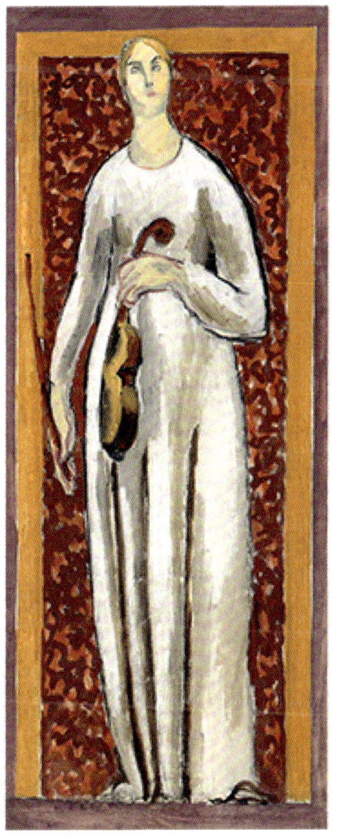
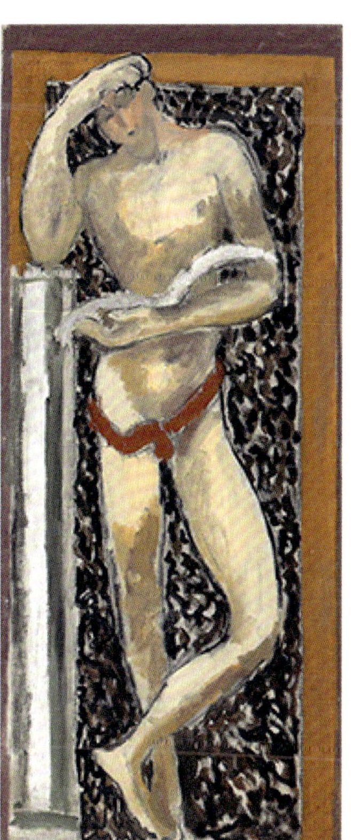

12

Duncan Grant
The Hammock, Charleston, c. 1921–22

Oil on canvas, 32 × 58 in. (81.3 × 147.3 cm)
Private collection

Selected literature Shone, R. (1993), *Bloomsbury Portraits: Vanessa Bell, Duncan Grant and their circle*. London: Phaidon, p. 195, no. 139; Shone, R. (1991), *Duncan Grant & Vanessa Bell: Design and Decoration 1910–1960*, 23 October – 22 November 1991 (exh. cat.). London: Spink, pp. 24, 25, 31, no. 49

This large composition is a lyrical celebration of Charleston, showing a moment of quiescence when art, family and location come together. Duncan has effectively elevated the garden to a riverbank, evoking open-air Parisian depictions from previous decades of life and leisure in happy unison. It is also another reminder of how the component parts of Charleston's surroundings could perform the role of a passive muse to its artistically creative inhabitants.

It is playful and inventive in its composition, as well as tenderly construed. In the hammock at the centre is Vanessa being gently rocked by Quentin; Angelica is to the right, pulling a toy down the garden path towards the viewer; Julian is on a punt on the pond in the top left. In the lower left is Sebastian Sprott, Julian and Quentin's tutor, and in the background a horse and cart. This is Charleston in the aftermath of war – in its role as family home and a refuge of peace, calmness and human interaction.

The Hammock is ambitious in its scale and subject matter and was painted from preparatory oil sketches and drawings (fig. 34). It was undertaken around 1921–22, probably in preparation for another work of the same scale and subject now in the Laing Art Gallery, Newcastle-upon-Tyne. The present work was kept by Duncan and remained at Charleston until his death in 1978.[1] LH & ES

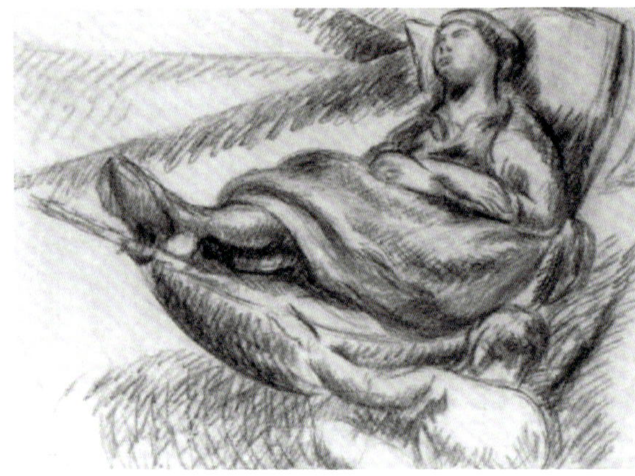

34. Duncan Grant
The Hammock, 1922
Chalk, 18½ × 24¾ in. (47 × 62.9 cm)
Private Collection

1 Clarke, D. (2012), *The Politics of Partnership: Vanessa Bell and Duncan Grant, 1912–1961*. Unpublished PhD thesis, University of Sussex. Available at: http://sro.sussex.ac.uk/id/eprint/46493/1/Clarke,_Darren_K..pdf (accessed 28 June 2021).

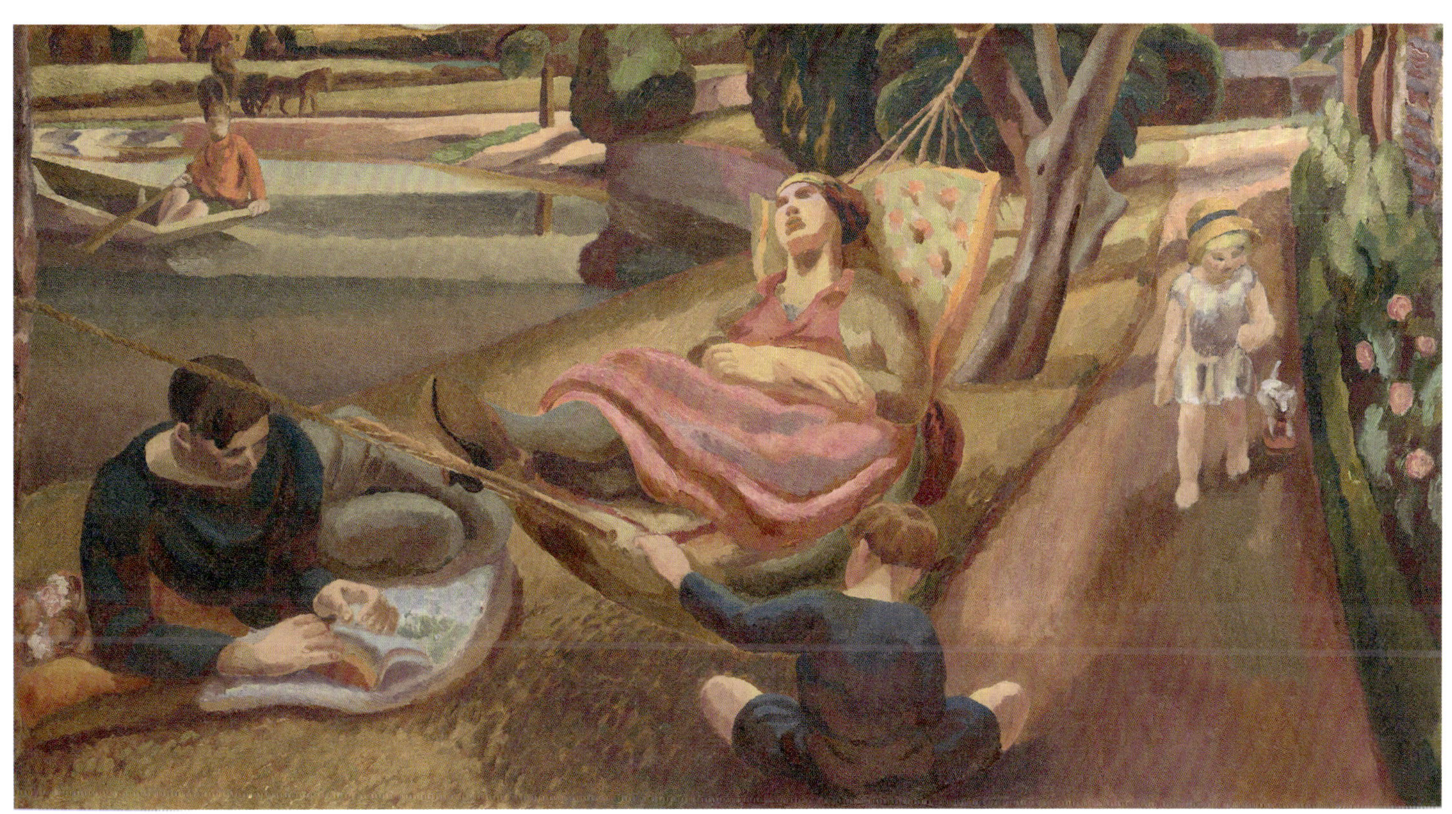

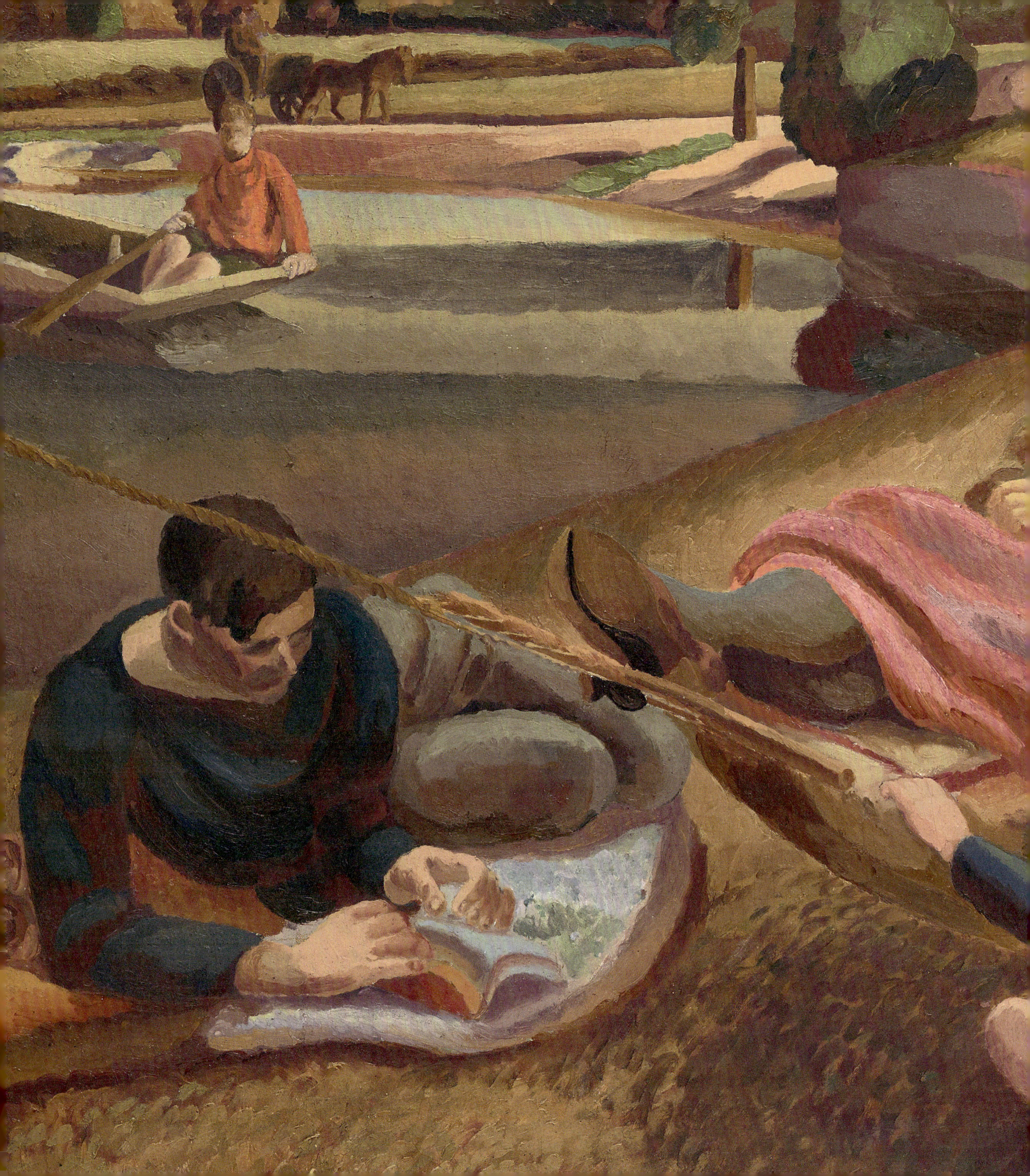

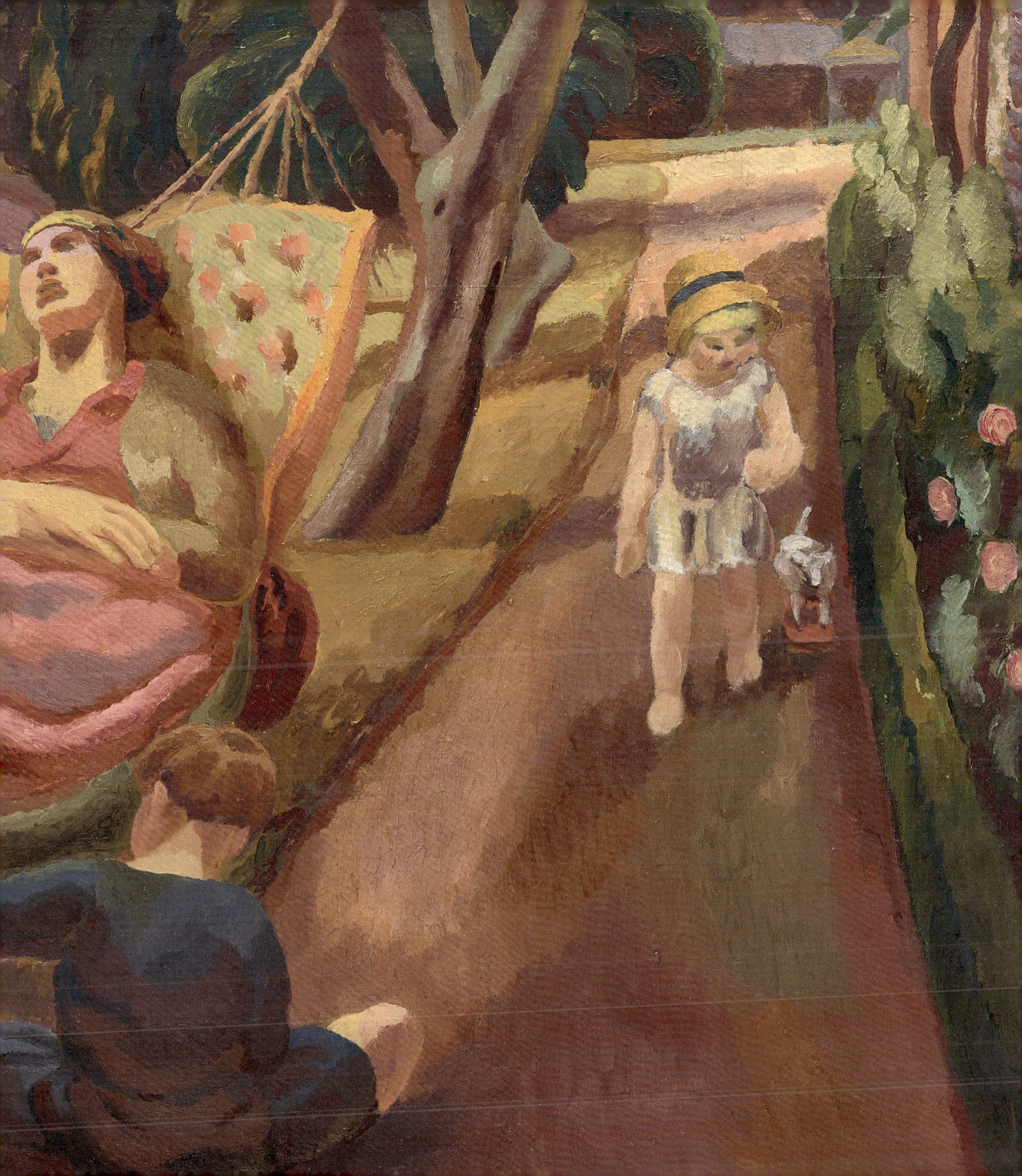

13

Duncan Grant
Angus Davidson at Charleston, c. 1923–28

Oil on canvas, 24⅛ × 29 in. (61 × 73.5 cm)
Private collection

This portrait of Duncan's friend and lover Angus Davidson was painted in the spare bedroom at Charleston. It is a reminder of how the constant flow of visitors to Charleston – many of whom were painted in situ by Duncan and Vanessa – is a component part of its artistic heritage. This work is also an unselfconscious depiction of Charleston's relaxed interior charm: bright cut flowers, colourful rugs, chairs and walls, a modernist painting and a nineteenth-century table strewn with papers and objects fill the horizontal composition, all of them fluently coalesced by Duncan's assured, sweeping strokes.

Angus was one of Duncan's closest and most loyal friends and from 1922 a regular visitor. Initially it was Angus's brother Douglas who caught Duncan's eye; but when Douglas moved to America, Duncan's affections turned to Angus.[1] Described by Frances Spalding as 'a tall, handsome, magnificent figure of a man who inwardly wanted to be a tiny little woman',[2] Angus evidently had a profound effect on Duncan, who told him that he thought he loved him in a way more than he had ever loved anyone before.[3] Although Angus's feelings did not align with Duncan's their relationship endured for several years and they remained lifelong friends. Angus posed for Duncan numerous times during this period and was the subject of one of his most sensual nudes (fig. 35).

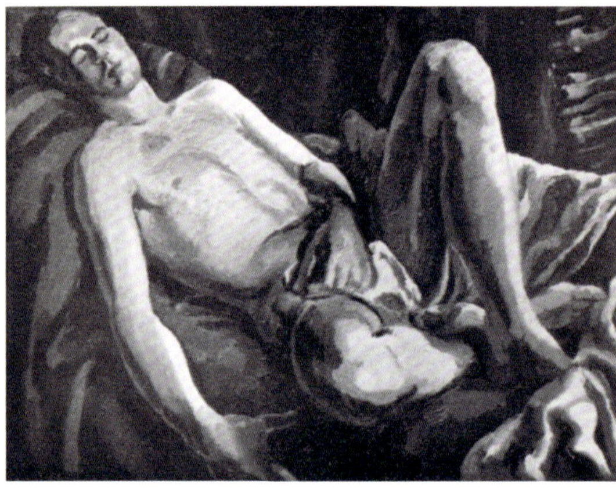

35. Duncan Grant
Nude, 1923
Medium and size unknown
Whereabouts unknown

Well educated and affable, Angus slotted comfortably into the circle of friends who congregated at Charleston. He also became well acquainted with the Woolfs, who appointed him secretary of the Hogarth Press at the end of 1924. His tenure was not a great success, owing largely to his relaxed nature, and he left the press at the end of 1927. LH

---

1 Spalding, F. (1998), *Duncan Grant: A Biography*. London: Pimlico, p. 236.
2 Ibid.
3 Ibid.

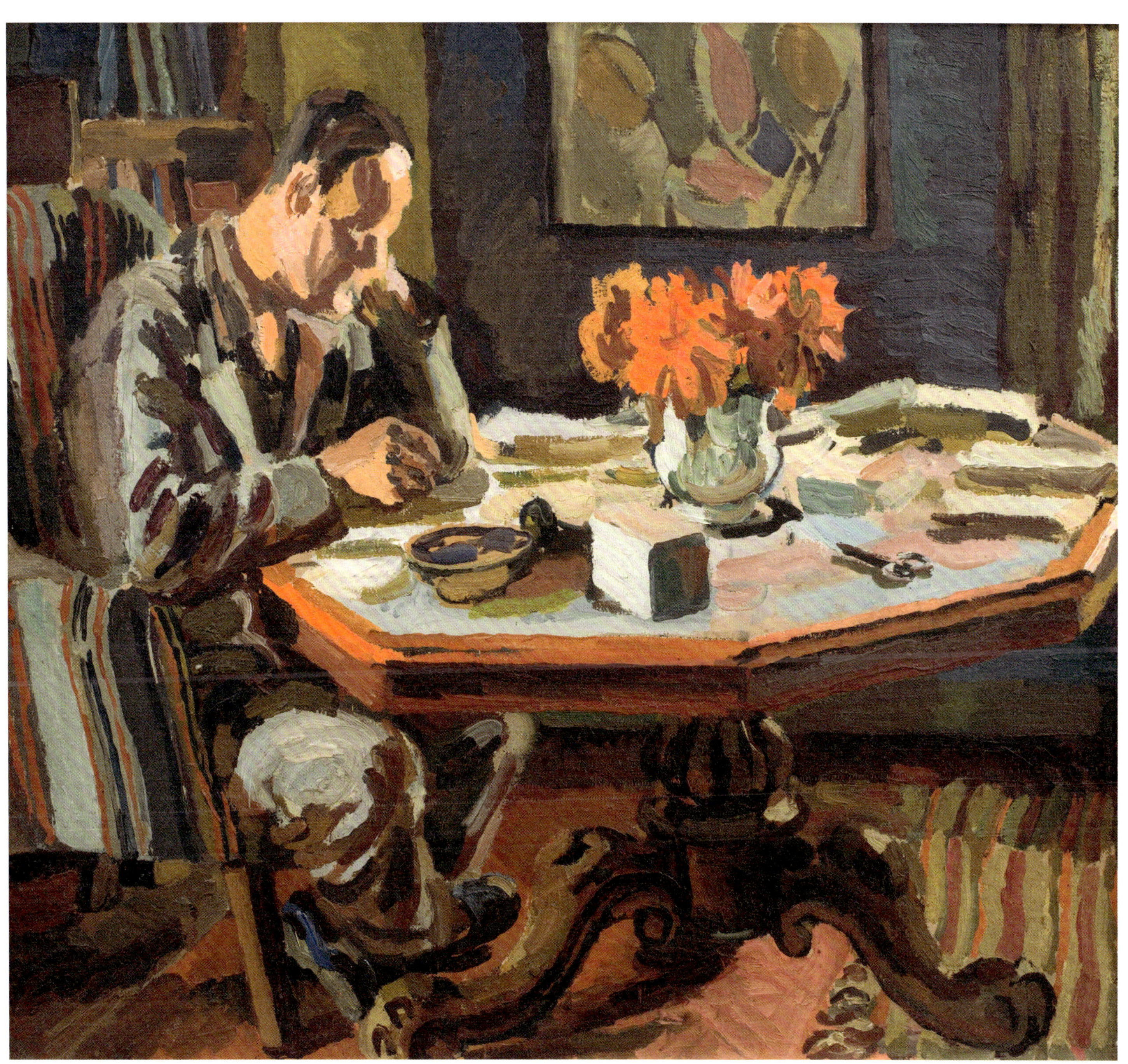

14

Stephen Tomlin
Duncan Grant, 1924

Bronze, 14¾ in. (37.5 cm) high
The Charleston Trust

This likeness of Duncan Grant was sculpted in 1924, eight years after he had moved into Charleston, by Stephen Tomlin, a talented yet tragic friend of the Bloomsbury Group.[1]

Tomlin (known as 'Tommy'), who was bisexual, was good looking, intelligent and an artful conversationalist, and as such fitted perfectly within the Bloomsbury coterie. His remarkable seductive charm was well known, and Virginia Woolf described him as 'the devastation of all hearts'.[2]

Educated at Harrow, Tommy was friends with Angus Davidson (cat. 13) and his brother Douglas, who introduced him to Duncan in the early 1920s.[3]

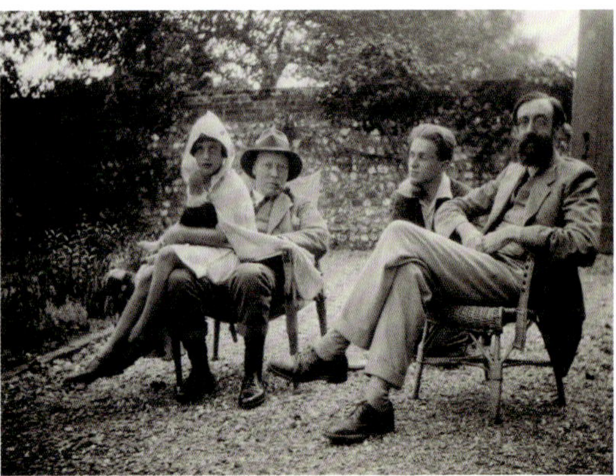

36. Angelica Garnett, Clive Bell, Stephen Tomlin and Lytton Strachey
Photograph by Vanessa Bell, 1926
National Portrait Gallery, London

Like many before him, Duncan was drawn to Tommy, and although the relationship did not last they remained close friends. In 1924, soon after their relationship had cooled, John Maynard Keynes and David Garnett (who also had affairs with Tommy) persuaded Duncan to sit for this bust portrait – 'what they call being immortalised in bronze', Duncan wrote to a friend.[4] It was cast in bronze the following year; one cast was bought by John Maynard Keynes and is now in the National Portrait Gallery, London, and the other, the present work, was acquired by David Garnett.

Tommy was a complex character and suffered from depression for most of his adult life. He temporarily found happiness when he married Julia Strachey (niece of Lytton) in 1927, but his mental health deteriorated and he became increasingly reliant on drugs and alcohol. They separated in 1934 and his decline continued. He died in 1937 aged just thirty-five. LH

---

1 For a more complete overview of Tomlin's life, see Bloch, M., and Fox, S. (2020), *Bloomsbury Stud: The Life of Stephen 'Tommy' Tomlin*, London: M.A.B.
2 Woolf, V. 7 January 1926, *Letter to Vita Sackville-West*, in Nicolson (ed.) (1977) *The Letters of Virginia Woolf, Volume Three*, 1923–1928, London: Hogarth Press, p.226.
3 Spalding, F. (1997), *Duncan Grant: A Biography*. London: Chatto & Windus, p. 253.
4 Grant, D. 18 November 1924. *Letter to Mina Kirstein.*

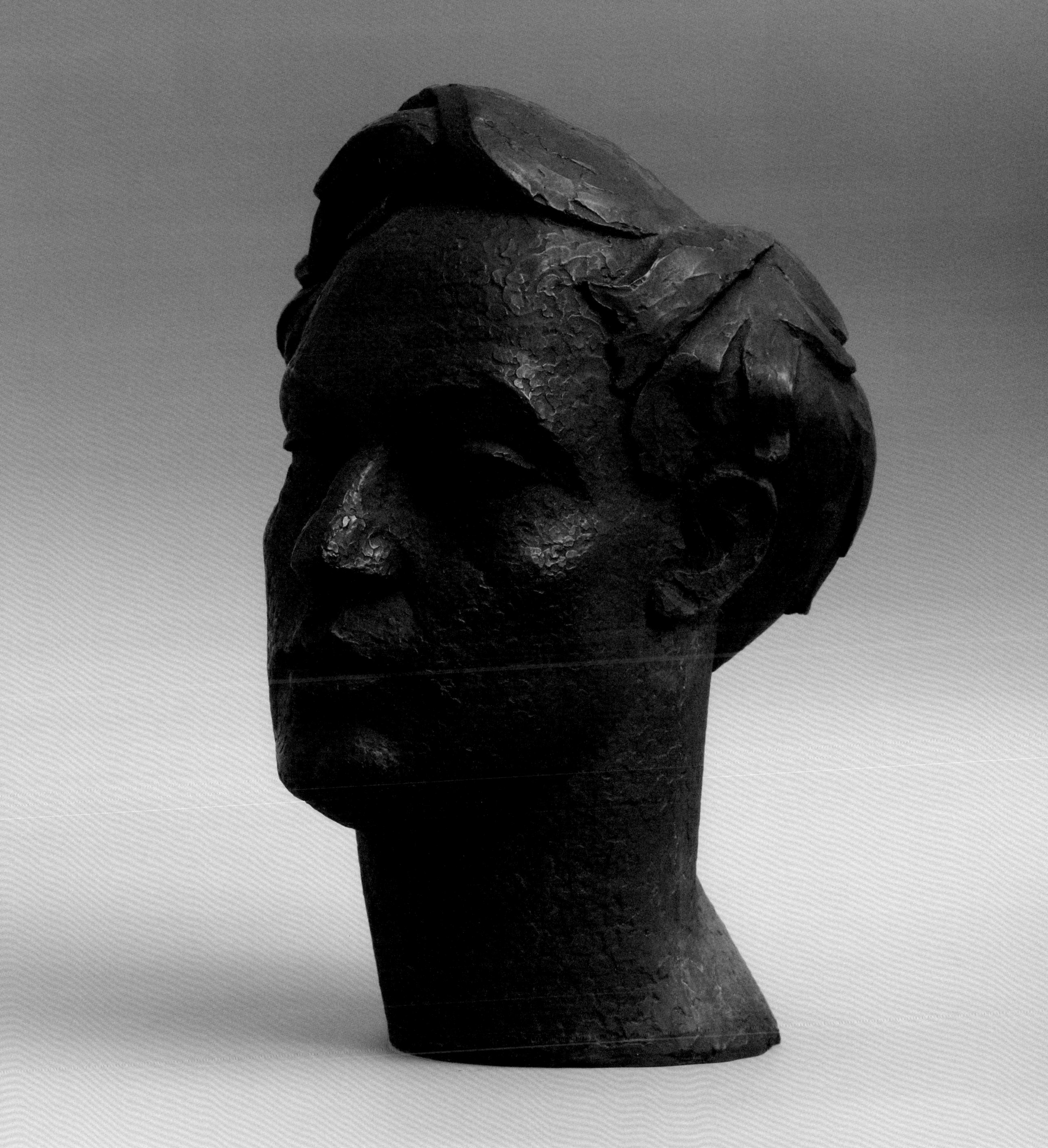

15

Duncan Grant
Julian Bell Reading, 1930

Oil on board, 31½ × 21½ in. (80 × 54.4 cm)
The Charleston Trust

Selected literature Naylor, G. (ed.) (1990), *Bloomsbury: The Artists, Authors and Designers by Themselves*. London: Pyramid, p. 179

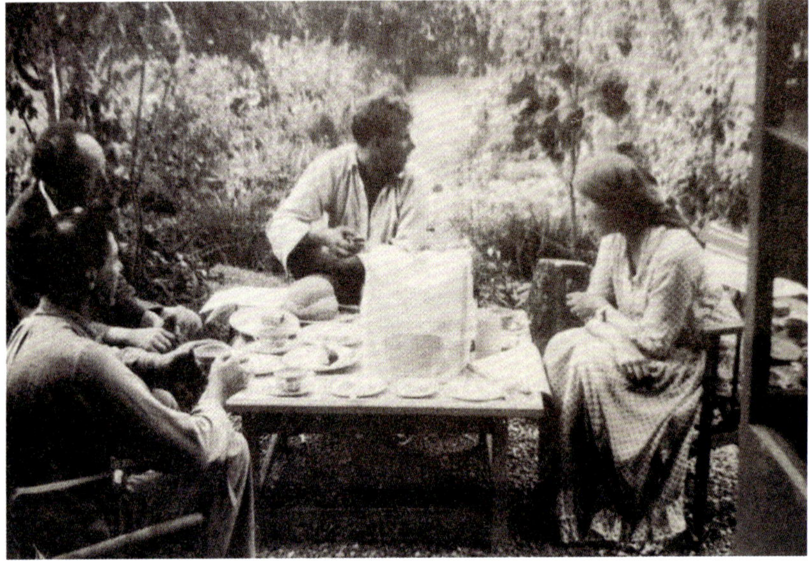

37. Duncan Grant, Clive Bell, Vanessa Bell, and Julian Bell in the garden at Charleston
Photograph by Lettice Ramsey
By permission of her grandson, Stephen Burch

Painted at Charleston by Duncan in 1930, this subtly expressive work represents Julian Bell, son of Clive and Vanessa. Suffused into a garden setting with rhythmic, conspicuous strokes, it alludes to Julian's attachment to nature and to study that were defining parts of his tragically short life.

Julian was born in London in 1908 and moved to Charleston in 1916 when Vanessa, Duncan and David Garnett took the lease of the farmhouse. He was immensely fond of Charleston and enjoyed the freedom – both physical and intellectual – that it allowed. It fostered a love of nature and wildlife which later manifested itself in his poetry, and it was always the place he called home.

Julian's education at Charleston during the war years was unorthodox yet evidently effective. Following boarding school he attended King's College, Cambridge, where he joined the Cambridge Apostles – the intellectual discussion group through which some of the Bloomsbury Group passed. By 1930 Julian had started writing poetry, his education at Cambridge having emboldened his ambition to write whilst reaffirming his desire for independence. In the autumn of that year he returned to Cambridge as a research student with the aim of later being appointed a fellow of his college. This same year, one dominated by reading and writing, the present work was painted. After leaving Cambridge (without a fellowship) Julian

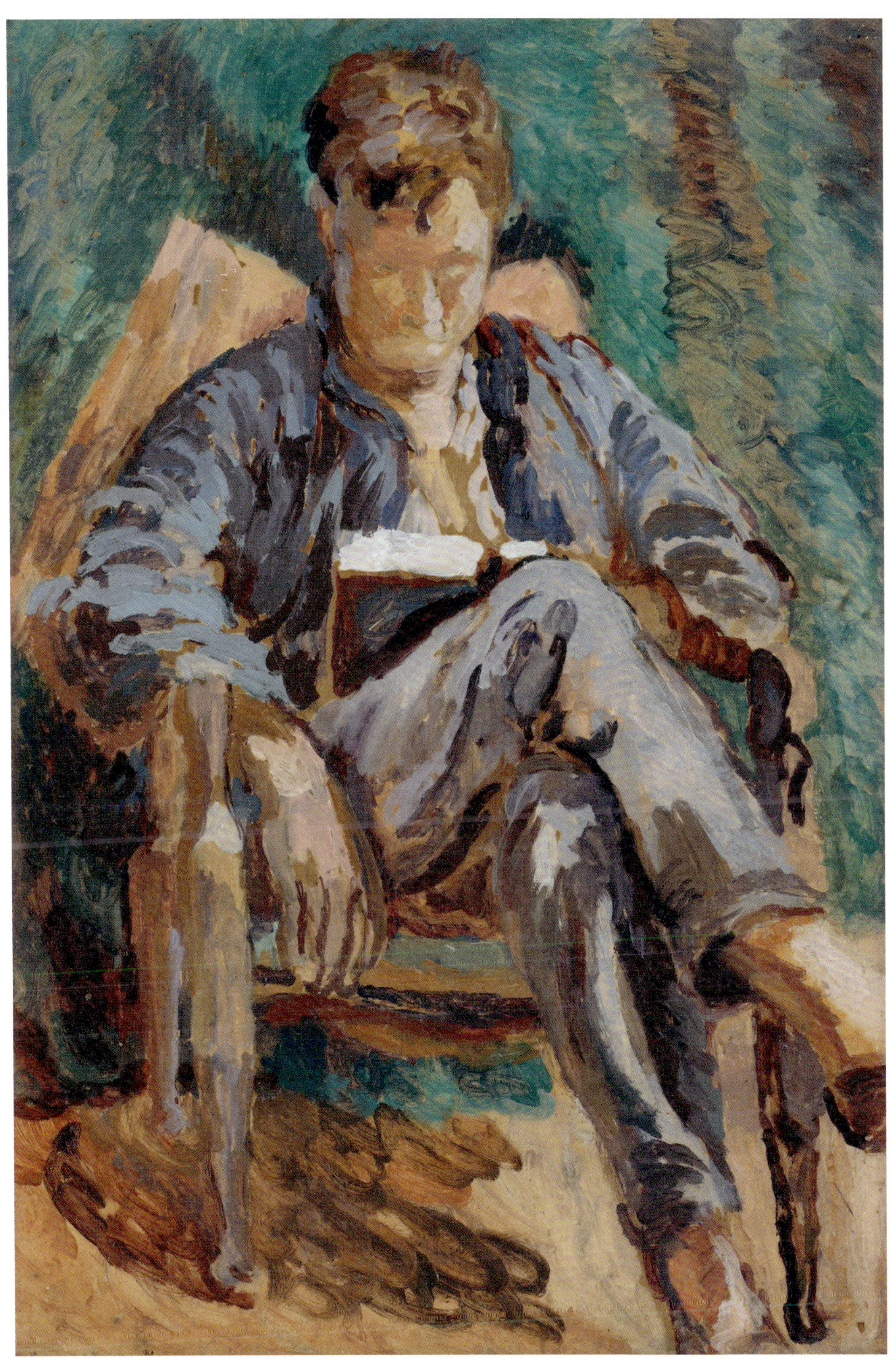

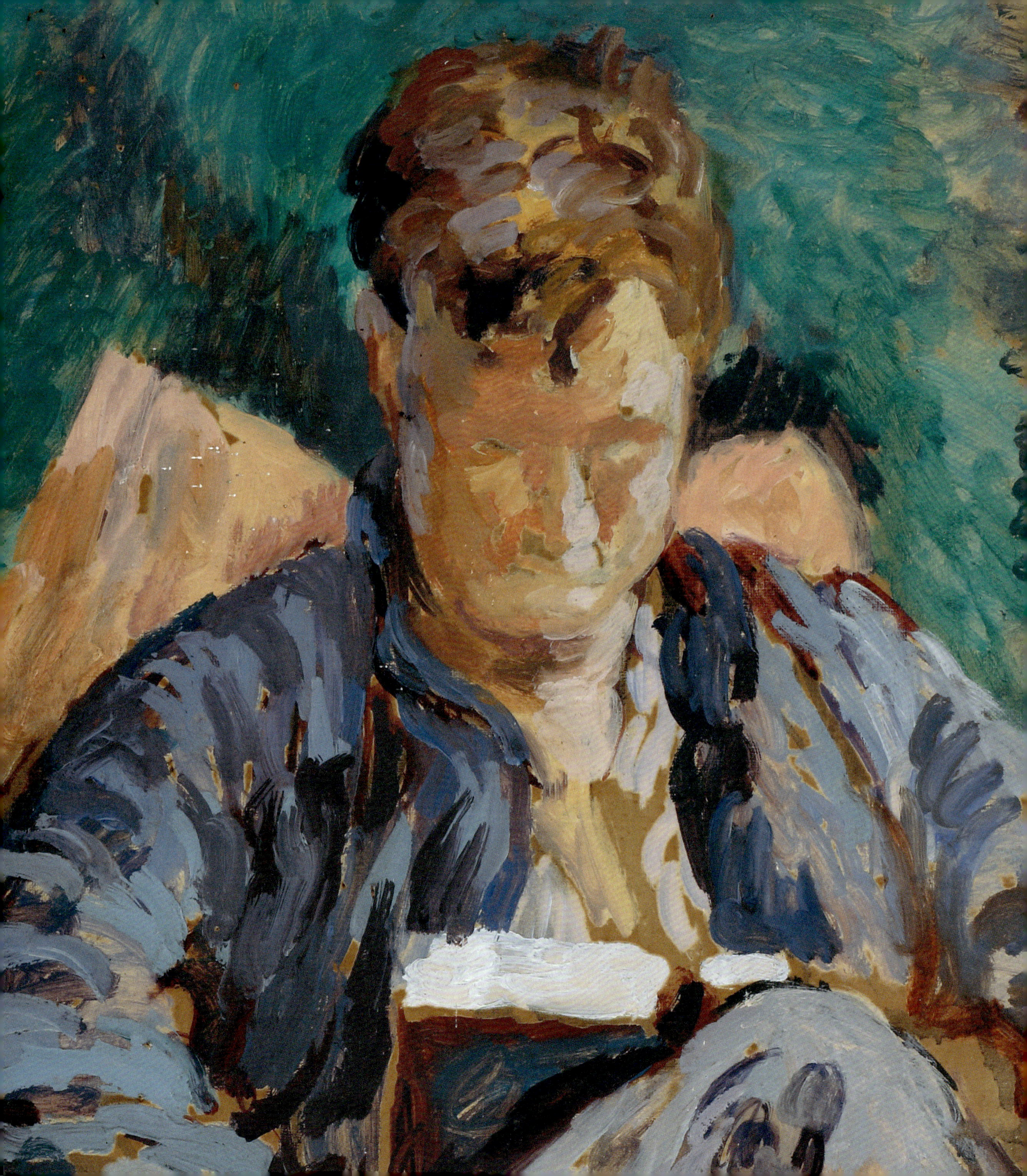

was offered the post of Professor of English at the National University of Wuhan in China and he set off the following month. Vanessa wrote him weekly letters in which she kept him updated on events at home but never concealed the sense of loss that his absence had on her and the household: 'I think of you so much here, you are essential to this place. It belongs to you and you to it.'[1]

In between love affairs – including one involving a married Chinese woman – Julian kept up to date with current affairs and became increasingly concerned with the civil war in Spain. He expressed his desire to enlist in the army of the Spanish Republic, which alarmed Vanessa and Duncan. They encouraged him to return to Charleston before deciding. Although the family were able to dissuade Julian from enrolling as a soldier, he applied to work as an ambulance driver with the Spanish Medical Aid and departed in June 1937. He was killed less than a month later whilst working near the front line. His death had a profound impact on Vanessa, who never fully recovered, and, although Duncan remained strong for the sake of his companion, Julian's death was a hard blow. LH

---

1 Bell, V. 29 March 1936, *Letter to Julian Bell*, in Marler, R. (1993), *Selected Letters of Vanessa Bell*. London: Bloomsbury Publishing, pp. 408–11.

16

Duncan Grant
Still Life with Teapot, 1929

Signed *D. Grant* / 29 lower centre
Oil on canvas, 24⅜ × 20¼ in. (62 × 51.5 cm)
The Charleston Trust

We went over to Charleston yesterday. Although thinking quite well of ourselves, we were not well received by the painters. There they sat like assid[u]ous children at task in a bedroom – Roger, Nessa & Duncan; Roger on chair in foreground; Nessa on sofa; Duncan on bed. In front of them was one jar of flowers, & one arrangement of still live .... For some reason, the talk was not entirely congenial. I suspect myself of pertness and so on ... — Virginia Woolf, 6 August 1923[1]

Virginia Woolf's diary entries offer discerning and entertaining insights into the everyday artistic activities at Charleston.

By the late 1920s, when the present work was painted, still-life painting had become an ingrained, near-obligatory task at Charleston. Depictions of flowers, vases, ceramics and fabric designs drifted from canvases to cupboards in countless variations. The present work by Duncan depicts an arrangement set upon a table dressed with household items, including a teapot, a knife, a wineglass and a bottle on a blue-and-white gingham fabric. In comparison with his earlier works, such as *Compotier* (cat. 5), Duncan pays greater attention to the fullness and mass of the objects depicted in this still life. Much like Vanessa, throughout the 1920s Duncan progressively transitioned from a focus on crystalline colours towards an interest in the density of form. ES

1 Woolf, D. 6 August 1923. 'Diary Entry', in Bell, A. O. (ed.) (1978) *The Diary of Virginia Woolf: Volume II 1920–1924*. London: Hogarth Press, p.260.

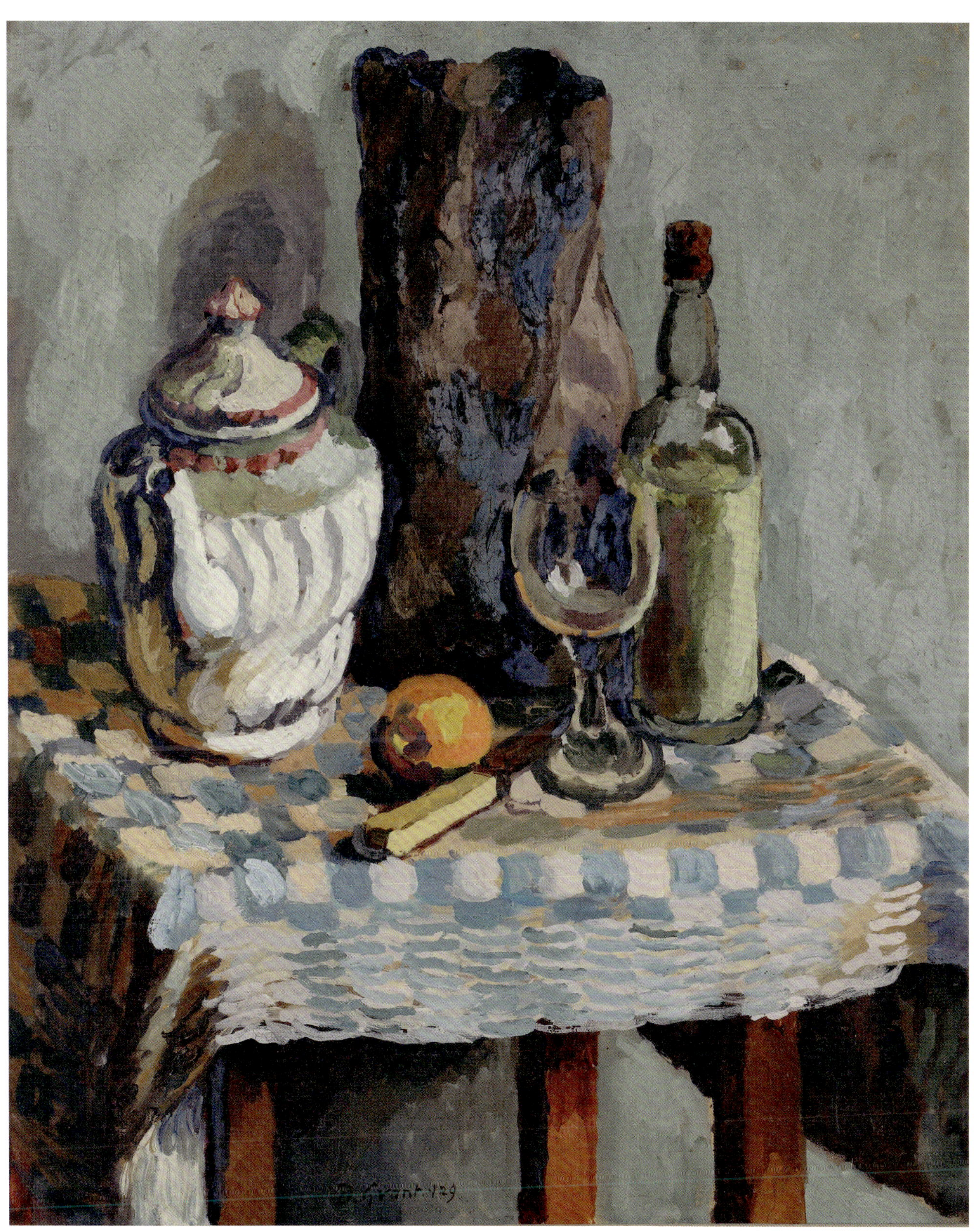

17

Duncan Grant

The Cat, Opussyquinusque, c. 1932

Oil on board, 9 × 12¼ in. (23 × 31 cm)
The Charleston Trust

Selected literature Naylor, G. (ed.) (1990), *Bloomsbury: The Artists, Authors and Designers by Themselves*. London: Pyramid, p. 194

This masterfully fluent painting of a cat was exhibited by Grant at the Venice Biennale in 1932. Employing vigorous, post impressionist-style strokes upon an open light ground, it is a striking example of Grant's capacity to combine the figurative with the decorative. The cat's outlines and face are caught up in continuous rhythmic pattern; its naturalistic form and individuality do not suffer for this, and the cat's single open eye connects meaningfully with the viewer.

Duncan's fondness for felines predates Charleston and one of his early designs for the Omega Workshops was a chair seat decorated with an abstracted image of a cat lying on a cabbage, playing with a butterfly.[1] Vanessa and Duncan had numerous cats whilst living at Charleston and they played an important role in making the house a home (fig. 38). Sleeping cats can occasionally be spotted in the corner of interior scenes and they regularly appear in Duncan and Vanessa's sketchbooks (see fig. 1, p. 9). LH

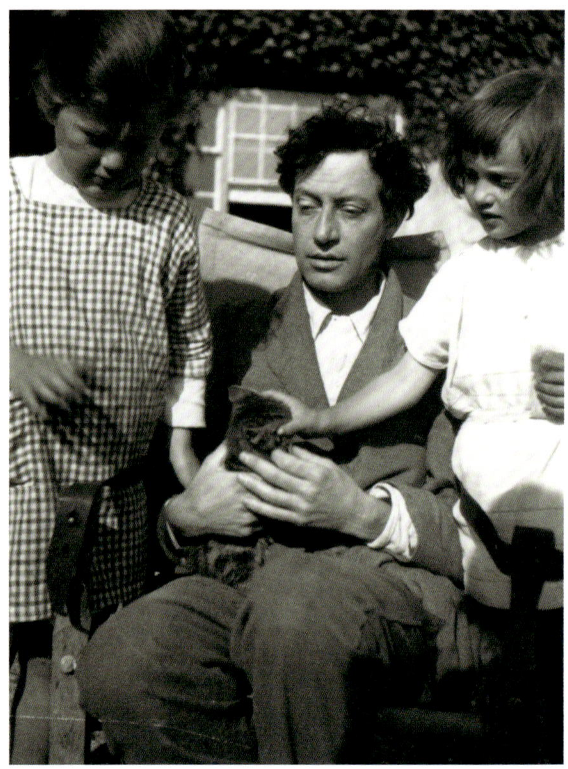

38. Photograph of Duncan Grant with his daughter Angelica Bell (right) and her cousin Judith Stephen, in the garden at Charleston, 1922–24
Tate Archive

---

1 Duncan Grant, *Cat on a Cabbage*, c. 1913, The Charleston Trust.

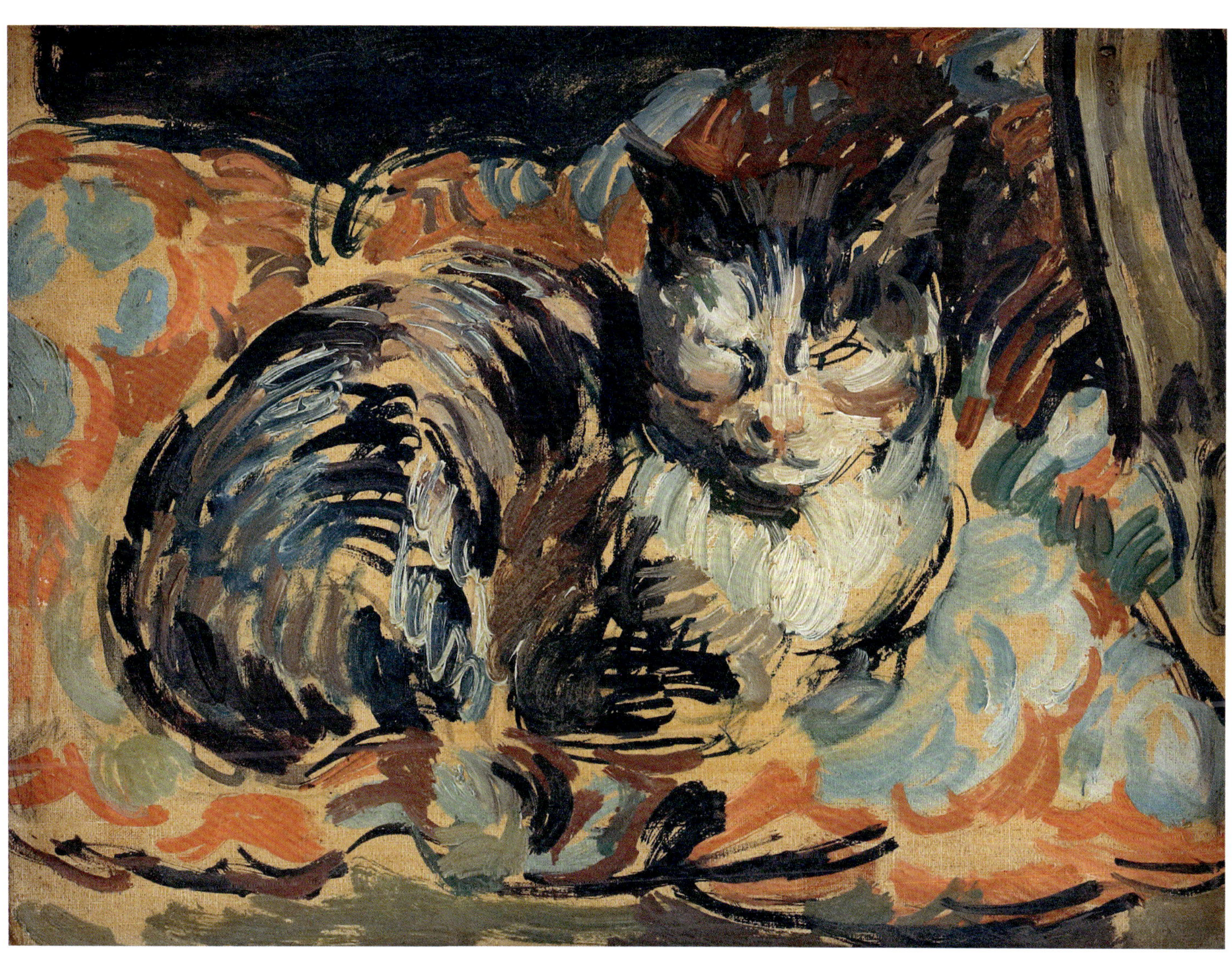

18

Vanessa Bell
The Granary, Charleston, 1932

Signed *V. Bell* 32 lower left
Oil on canvas, 19⅞ × 15⅞ in. (50.5 × 40.5 cm)
Philip Mould & Company

Prior to the arrival of Vanessa, Duncan and David Garnett, Charleston Farmhouse was part of a working farm. Vanessa and Duncan strongly related to this history throughout their time in Sussex. In particular they explored the picturesque possibilities of the surrounding vernacular farm buildings in all seasons, and from multiple perspectives, including their interiors. Requiring no more than a few paces from the front door to capture, these edifices of antiquity and rural continuity palpably express their attachment to their homestead (cat. nos. 24, 25, 26).

During the interwar years Vanessa gradually began to reevaluate her earlier preoccupation with colour. Writing to Roger Fry in 1923, she reflected that her concentration on colour predisposed her 'to destroy the solidity of objects' and she wondered if she could somehow 'get more of that sort of intensity of colour without losing the solidity of the objects and space'.[1] Vanessa's reduced palette in the present work begets a tactile suggestion of volume, whilst simultaneously maintaining tonal luminosity. Her deftly layered strokes of dark paint, which build up the structure of the barn, differ from the softer elasticity inherent in her colour deployment when she first moved to Charleston.

A year and a half after she raised the issue of solidity to Roger Fry, at a talk Vanessa alluded to her new-found attentiveness to form as opposed to colour, stating that 'the fascination of form for the artist is so absorbing'.[2] A manifestation of this new focus is discernible in this rich and highly figurative view of Charleston's granary. ES

1 Bell, V. 19 September 1923. *Letter to Roger Fry*, in Marler, R. (1993), *Selected Letters of Vanessa Bell*. London: Bloomsbury Publishing, p. 272.
2 Bell, V. (at a talk given at Leighton Park School in January 1925), quoted in Tickner, L. (2000), *Modern Life and Modern Subjects*. New Haven: Yale University Press, p. 126.

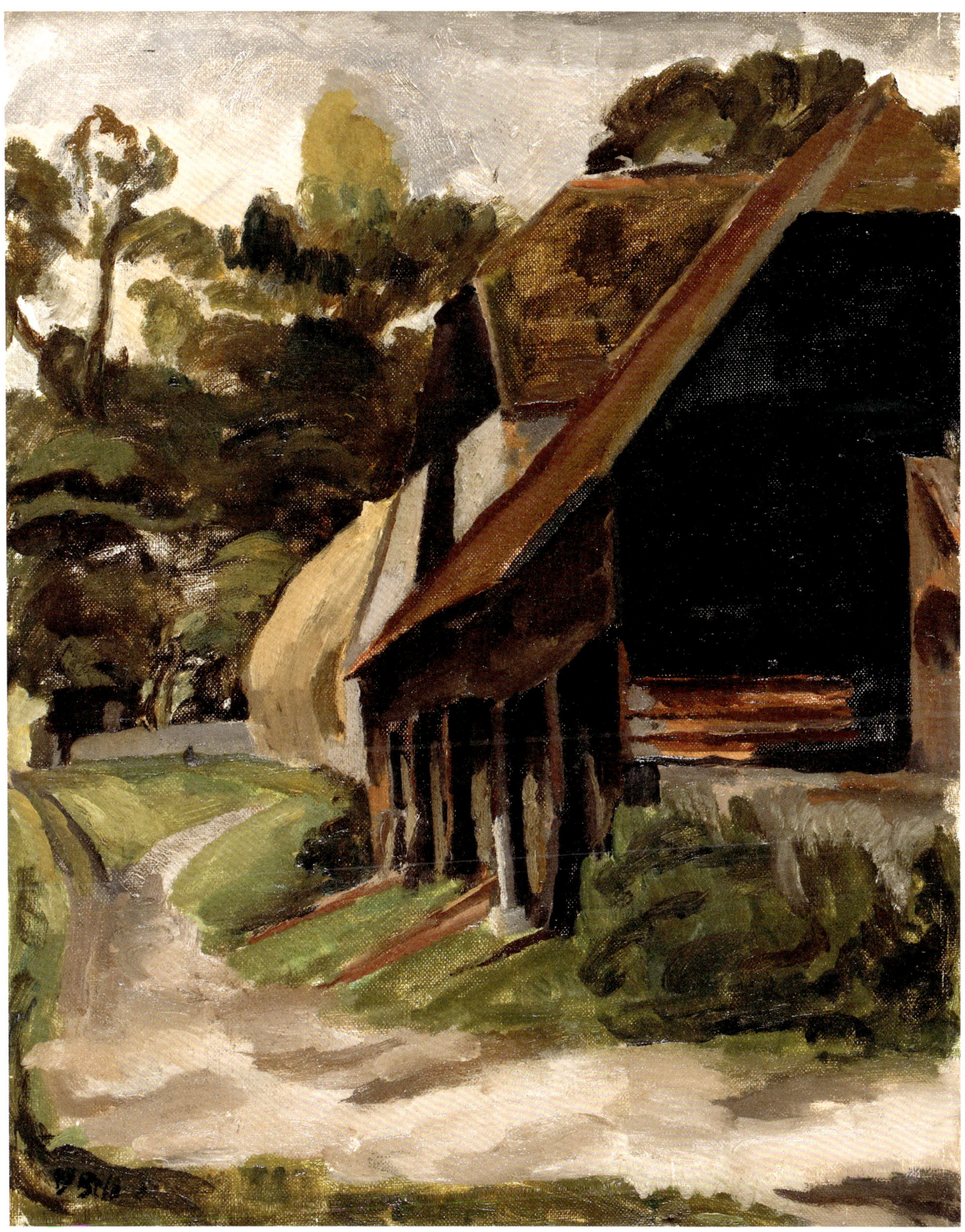

19

Vanessa Bell
Firle Place, 1933

Signed *V Bell* 1933 lower right
Oil on board, 20 × 29 in. (50.8 × 73.2 cm)
Private collection

This deft portrayal of house and landscape was painted by Vanessa Bell in 1933 and shows Firle Place, the home of the Gage family. The gestural brushstrokes and evident swiftness of execution suggest a work produced in the open, directly observing the subject and surrounding light effects.

Charleston sits within the three hundred-acre Firle Estate and was leased from the Gages by Duncan, Vanessa and David Garnett from 1916. Over time Duncan and Vanessa became well acquainted with their landlords, and their friendship improved in 1931 when Henry Gage, the 6th Viscount, married Imogen Grenfell, who was particularly fond of Duncan.[1] They would sometimes visit Firle and on occasion would host the Gages in the garden at Charleston. Not all of their guests were familiar with their landlord, however, and on one occasion Roger Fry mistook Lord Gage for the plumber and directed him to the bathroom.[2]

Towards the end of his life Duncan became friends with with Lord Gage's elder son, John, and in 1967 he painted his portrait at Charleston (fig. 39). It is one of Duncan's more characterful and engaging portraits from his later years and a testament to a relationship that existed between the two families in this rural corner of East Sussex over half a century. LH

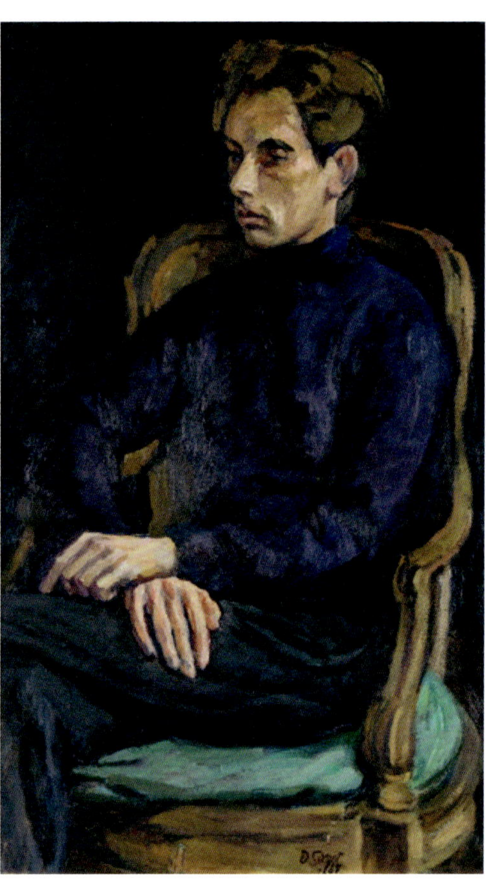

39. Duncan Grant
Portrait of the Hon. John Gage, later 7th Viscount Gage, 1967
Oil on millboard, 25½ × 14½ in. (64.8 × 36.8 cm)
Firle Place

1 Spalding, F. (1998), *Duncan Grant: A Biography*. London: Pimlico, p. 352.
2 Ibid., pp. 352–53.

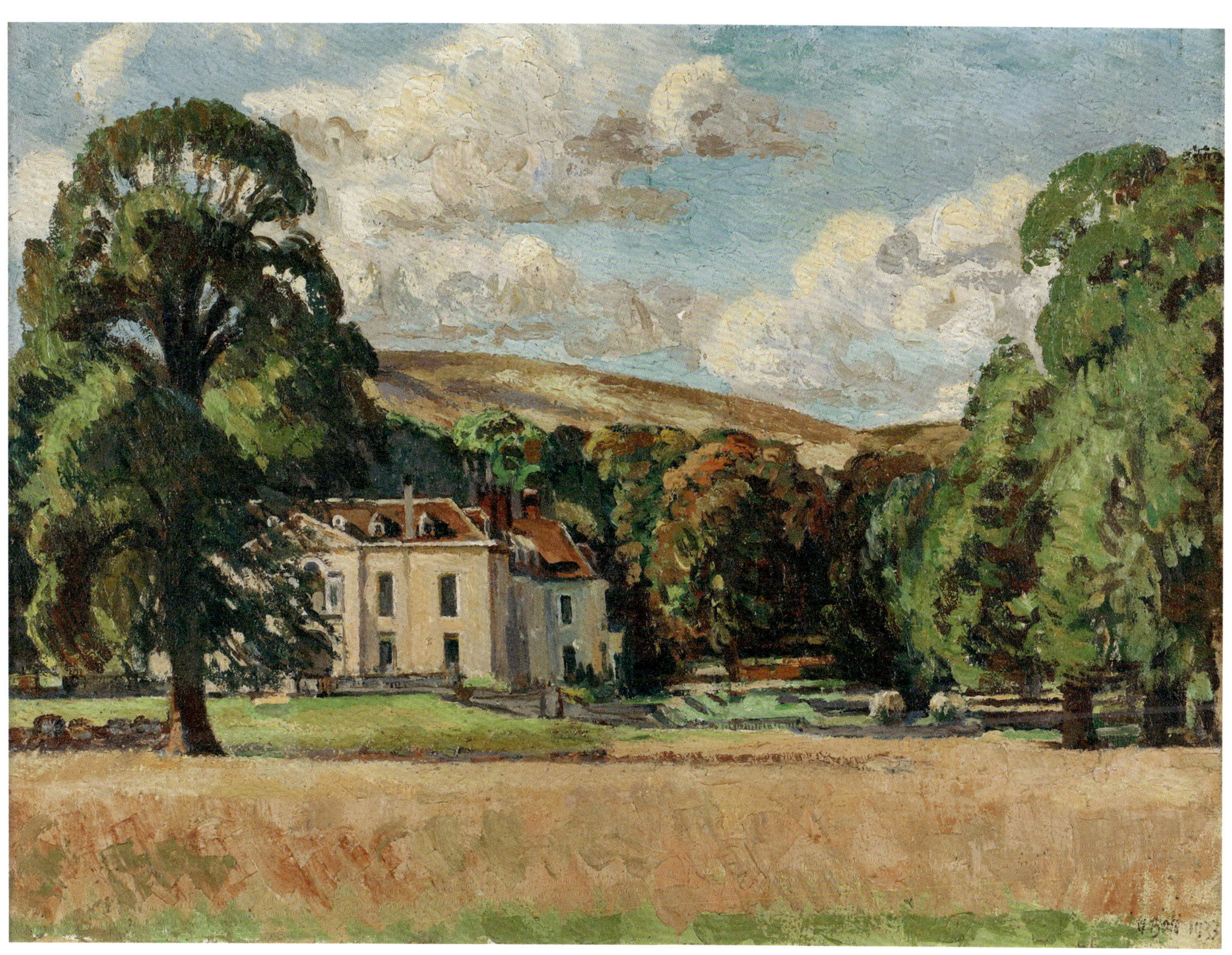

20

Duncan Grant
Barns and Pond at Charleston, c. 1934

Watercolour and pencil on paper, 24¼ × 31⅛ in. (61.5 × 79 cm)
The Bloomsbury Workshop, London

With liquid spontaneity, Duncan has produced a chromatic rural idyll denoting the combined themes of leisure and work at Charleston that characterised the interwar years. Although a watercolour study for a larger oil entitled *Farm in Sussex* (fig. 40), it is notably freer than the final oil painting, evoking Grant's early twentieth-century post-impressionist boldness to which, as an artist of innumerable parts, he could effortlessly revert.

The union of work and rural freedom began to constitute a substantial trope in both Duncan and Vanessa's respective oeuvres. The granary – the lower of the two buildings depicted here – is depicted in numerous paintings in this exhibition. It was demolished in the 1970s – a dismay for Duncan given his enduring attachment to the farm and its agricultural legacy.[1]

Of the three figures in the foreground, two have been identified as Angelica and her friend Judith Bagenal. Charleston's surrounding farmland during this time offered endless entertainment for the children who visited. Barns and haybales made for an excellent alternative playground – as long as the farmer remained unaware of any troublesome activity.[2] Duncan captures this childlike enchantment and charm in the present watercolour. ES

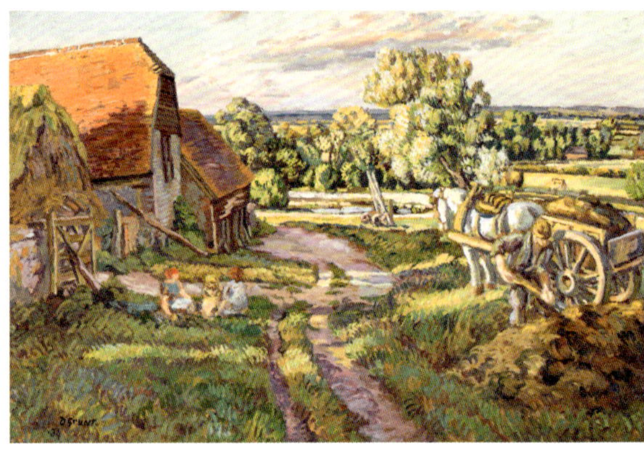

40. Duncan Grant
Farm in Sussex, 1934
Oil on canvas, 33½ × 50¼ in. (85 × 127.7 cm)
Walker Art Gallery, Liverpool

1 Shone, R. (2008), *20th Century British Art including Works from the Collection of Bannon & Barnabas McHenry*, lot 1, London, 17 December 2008.
2 *Duncan Grant at Charleston* (1969). Directed by Christopher Mason [Film]. Sussex: The Charleston Trust.

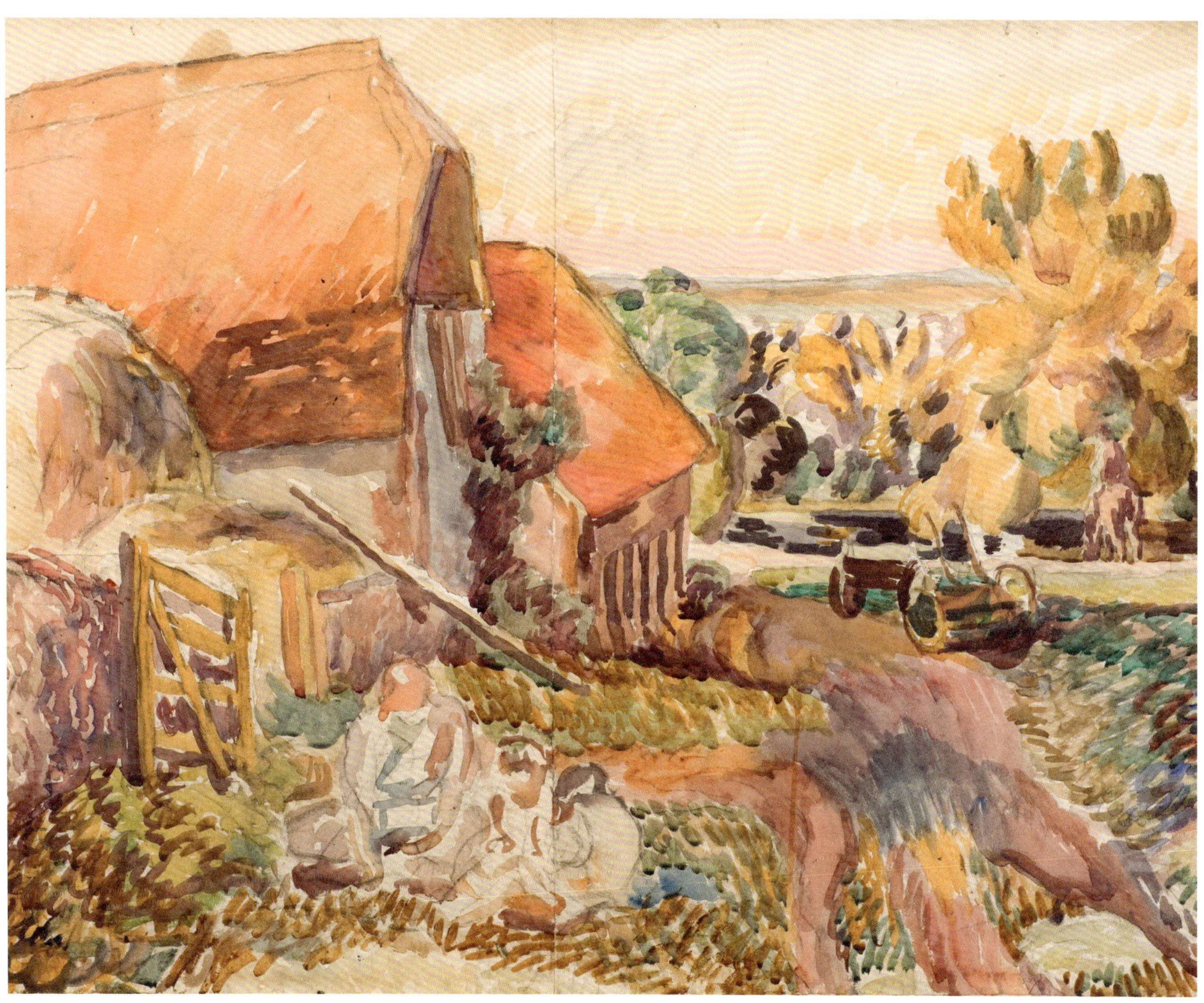

21

Vanessa Bell
Interior with the Artist's Daughter, c. 1935–36

Signed *V. Bell* lower right
Oil on canvas, 28½ × 23⅝ in. (72.4 × 60.1 cm)
The Charleston Trust

Selected literature Milroy, S., and Dejardin, I.A.C. (eds.) (2017), *Vanessa Bell*, 8 February – 4 June 2017 (exh. cat.). Dulwich Picture Gallery. London: Philip Wilson Publishers, pp. 133–35

At Charleston, Vanessa and Duncan's daughter, Angelica, was immersed in a world with no creative constraints. The highly interconnected and innovative group of individuals which Angelica found herself within was a well-established collaborative unit. David Garnett, her future husband, recalled in his memoir that even 'the question of her name became the subject of continual debate .... All Bloomsbury sent for suggestions'.[1]

This cast of strong characters maintained a scarcity of boundaries and surplus of freedom which later instilled in Angelica a sense of displacement, which she was to articulate in her autobiography *Deceived with Kindness*. Whilst the 'elders' went about their day 'in their own dreamlike fashion' – to use Angelica's words – she found comfort in the studio at Charleston:

> *The Studio was the citadel of the house, the sanctuary in which I spent the most treasured hours of my life.*[2]

In the present painting, Angelica is depicted by Vanessa in the studio. Absorbed in reading, she certainly appears content and seemingly unaware of her viewer. She seems equally engrossed in her surroundings; rows of books line the back wall, adding depth to the composition. Vanessa adds further perspective in the foreground through a still-life arrangement consisting of a vase of flowers and artichoke leaves alongside an open book and sewing materials on a bold floral fabric.

In this instance, Vanessa fuses decorative design and fine art through the prominent presence of Duncan's textile designs. The two armchairs depicted here are covered in Duncan's designs for Alan Walton Ltd, which were used for the upholstery in the music room at the Lefevre Gallery.
ES

---

1 Garnett, G. quoted in Clarke, D. 'Darren Clarke talks to Henrietta Garnett about her Mother's Life', *Charleston Press* (No. 1), 8 September 2018 –6 January 2019, p. 66.
2 Garnett, A. (1984) *Deceived with Kindness*. Oxford: Oxford University Press, p. 97.

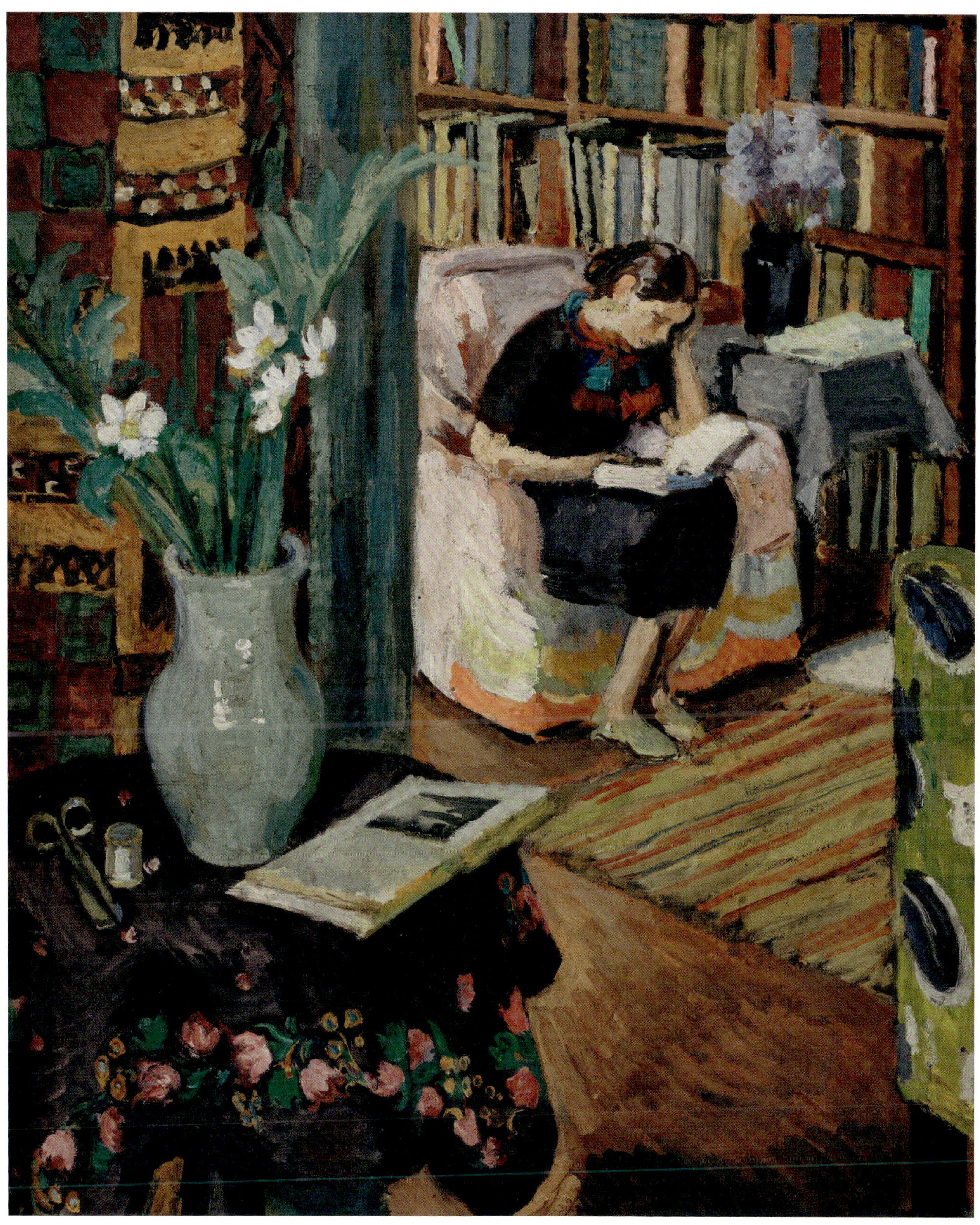

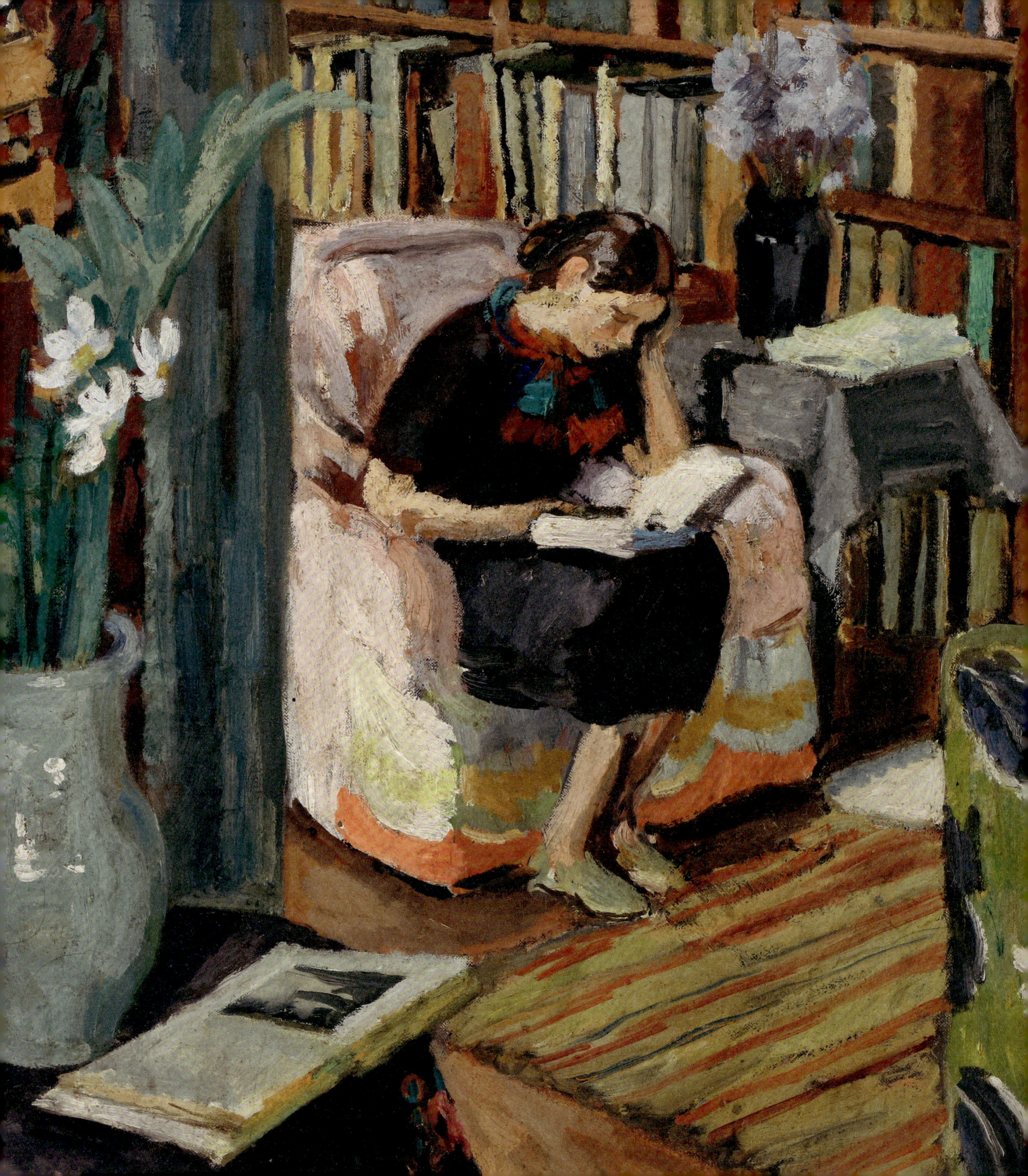

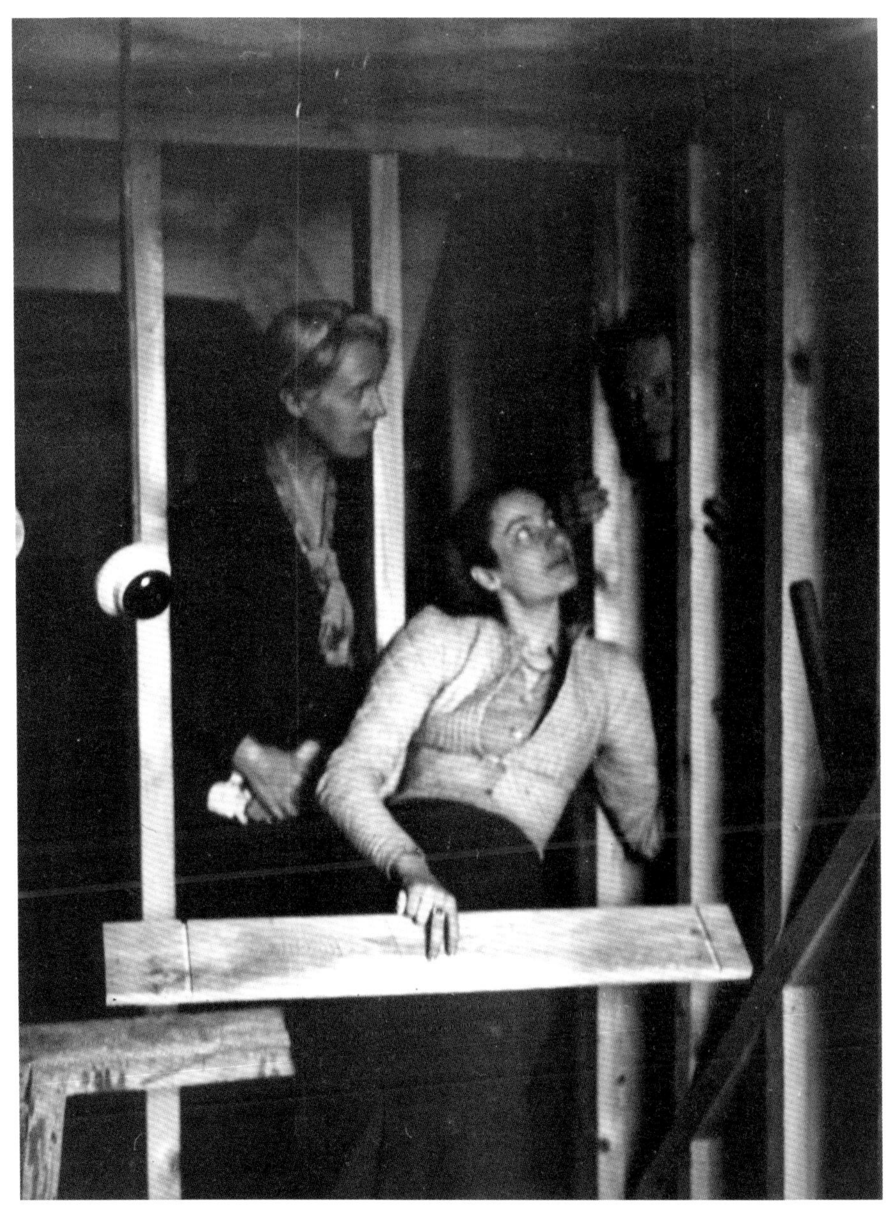

41. Vanessa Bell, Angelica Garnett and Duncan Grant
The Charleston Trust

22

Vanessa Bell

The Weaver: Angelica Bell weaving in the studio at Charleston, 1937

Signed *V. Bell* / 1937 lower left
Oil on canvas, 11⅜ × 15½ in. (29 × 39.5 cm)
The Charleston Trust

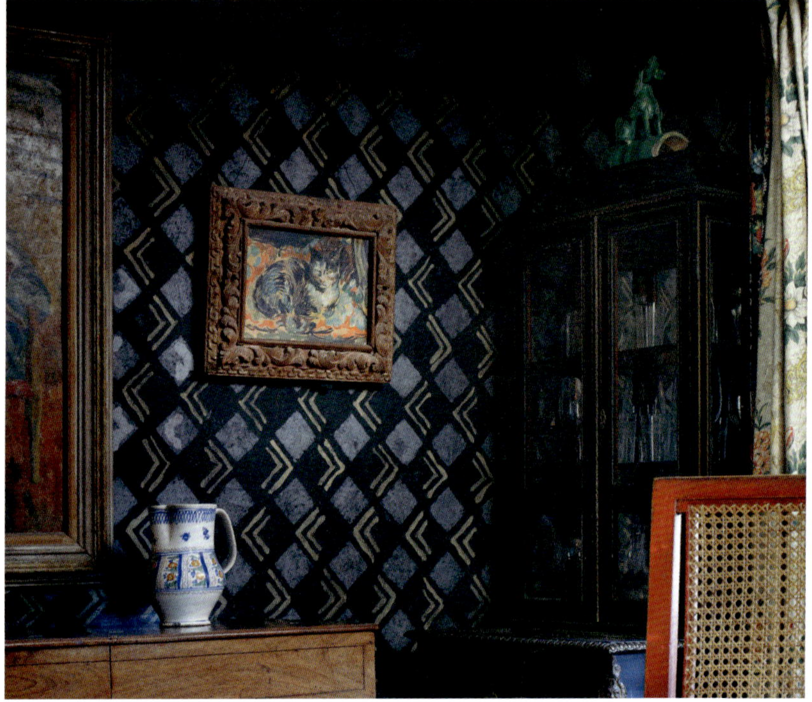

42. The Dining Room, Charleston

Upon their arrival at Charleston, Vanessa and Duncan captured in paint their visitors, friends and family in moments of focused creative activity. This portrait of Angelica weaving at her loom epitomises Charleston as a place of creation, collaboration and innovation.

Sewing, weaving, painting and singing all came naturally to the youngest member of the Charleston household. So much so indeed that it has been retrospectively asserted that Angelica was cursed with being 'too gifted' at everything and anything she turned to, to the point she was never able to settle on one art.[1]

Much like her portrait of Angelica reading (cat. 21), Vanessa's portrait depicts Angelica immersed in concentrated activity. Sarah Milroy, co-curator of the first major retrospective of Vanessa Bell, asserts that Vanessa 'seems to have experienced her children more as creative peers than as dependants'.[2] The children were indeed encouraged to contribute towards the ongoing decoration of the house, and this painting embodies Vanessa's delight in industrious intergenerational collaboration, which Charleston facilitated through its numerous studios and expansive wall space. For example, the iconic 'wallpaper' mural (fig. 42) in the dining room at Charleston was designed by Duncan and Vanessa but executed with the help of both Angelica and Quentin in 1939. ES

1 Garnett, H. (2018), 'Darren Clarke Talks to Henrietta Garnett about her Mother's Life', *Charleston Press* (no. 1), 8 September 2018 – 6 January 2019, p. 66.
2 Milroy, S., 'Some Rough Eloquence', in Milroy, S. (ed.) (2017), *Vanessa Bell*. London: Philip Wilson Publishers, p. 29.

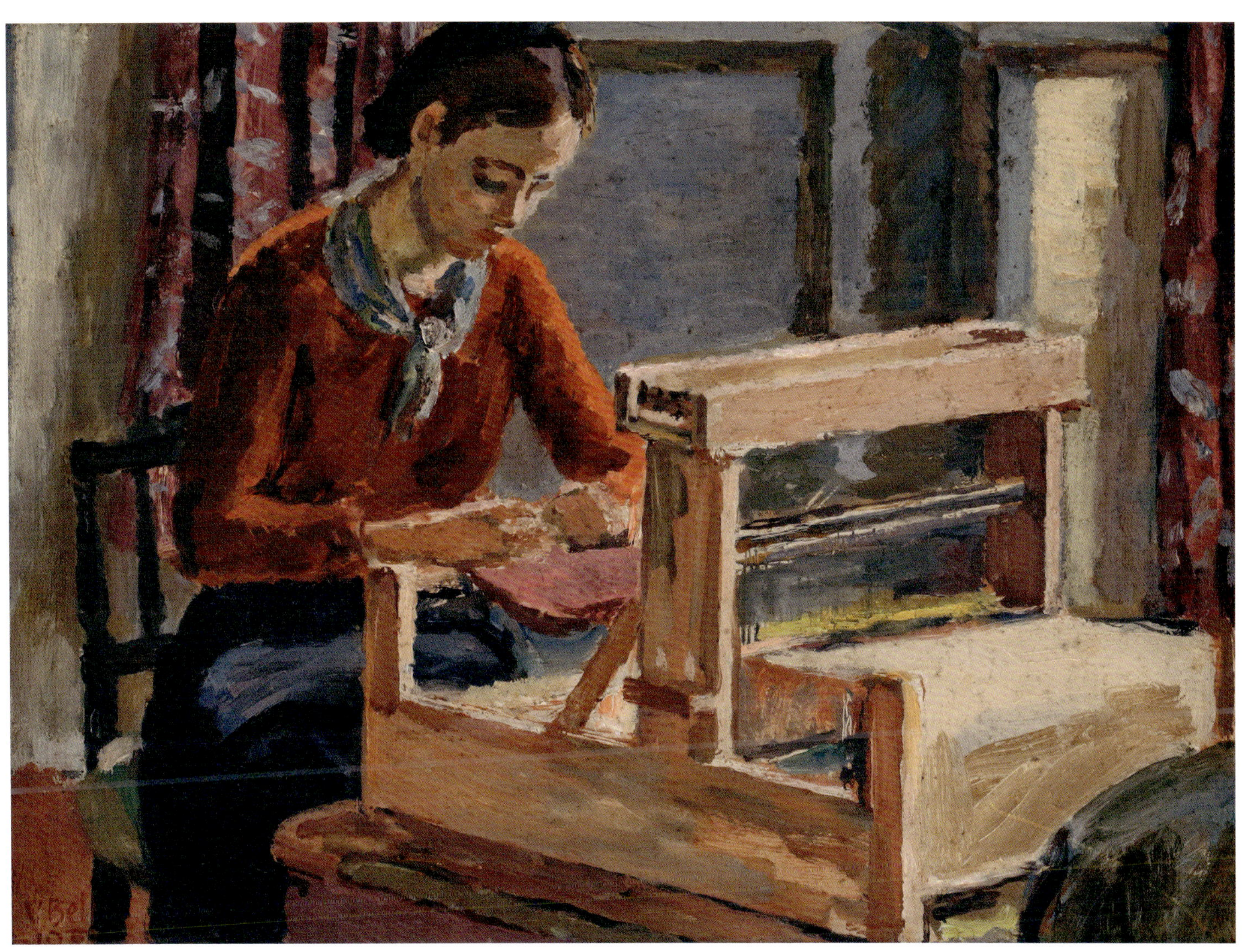

23

Vanessa Bell

Apples and Vinegar Bottle, 1937

Signed *V Bell* 1937 lower left
Oil on canvas, 14⅝ × 17⅜ in. (37 × 44 cm)
The Bloomsbury Workshop, London

Selected literature Górska, B. (ed.) (2010), *British Bohemia*, 14 September 2010 – 9 January 2011 (exh. cat.). Krakow: International Culture Centre, p. 97

This still life is likely to have been one of the first paintings executed by Vanessa in the months after the death of her son Julian in July 1937; the presence of apples and quinces is a seasonal indication that the composition was likely created in late summer or the Autumn of that year.

Vanessa and Julian had an immensely strong bond. In 1935, just under two years before he died, and two years before this painting was executed, Julian wrote to his mother:

> *The other thing, which doesn't really need to be said between us, is that I love you more than anyone else, and always have done so, ever since I can remember. Also, that if I've managed to have a happy life I owe it more to you than anyone else – after you, perhaps to Roger and Bloomsbury and Cambridge.*[1]

In light of Vanessa's attachment to Julian, a certain soberness may be construable in this still life. The fruit could be seen as suggestive of a summer that is at its end, and the configuration of the ceramic vinegar bottle with the dripping brushstroke from its head is painted with communicable feeling. This bottle, which Vanessa purchased on one of her summer trips to Italy, also highlights the transition in Vanessa's lifestyle before and after Julian's death – from European travels every summer towards an increasingly secluded, domestic life anchored at Charleston, partly perpetuated by the onset of the Second World War.

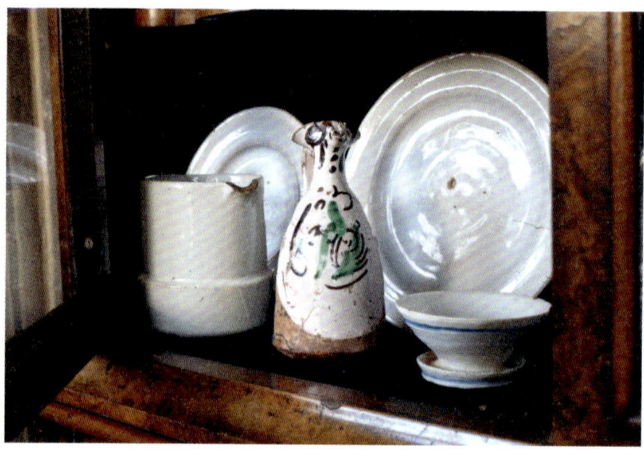

43. The vinegar bottle is still in the collection at Charleston, in the Studio

Of particular note in this work, and arguably adding to its expression, are the conspicuous strokes of tactile impasto and Italianate hues. Vanessa's reduced palette indicates the return to a slightly subtler crystallisation of colour that she employed throughout the post-war years. ES

1 Bell, J. 26 September 1935. *Letter to Vanessa Bell*, in Naylor, G. (ed.) (1990), *Bloomsbury: The Artists, Authors and Designers by Themselves*. London: Pyramid, p. 156.

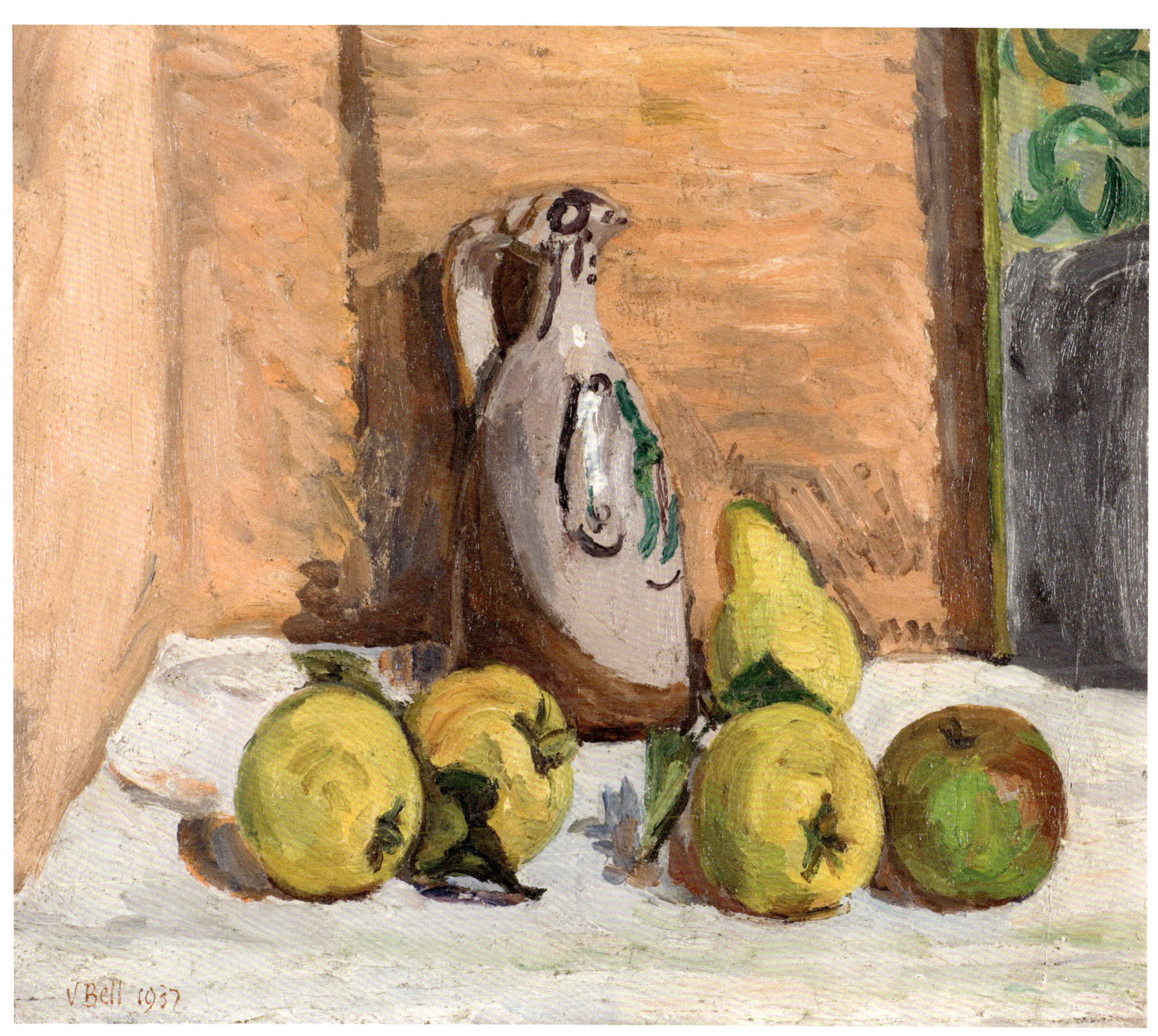
V Bell 1937

24

Vanessa Bell

The Barn at Charleston, Winter, c. 1940

Signed *V. Bell* lower left
Oil on canvas, 23⅞ × 20 in. (60.7 × 50.8 cm)
Philip Mould & Company

Selected literature *The Charleston Newsletter*, no. 23, June 1989, reproduced in colour, Annex 2, p. 58

Bell values removedness, but she sets it pictorial challenges
— Julian Bell[1]

Julian Bell's perceptive comment regarding his grandmother's art could be used to help describe the essence of the present winter landscape. At the composition's centre sits a barn – the granary – an expression of the agricultural humanity that had shaped the farmhouse's surroundings over many centuries. Acknowledging the influential snow scenes of Monet, Vanessa has agilely tempered the snowfall with strokes of light green upon the background and a pool of light-blue shadow to suggest the beginnings of a thaw. The result is an affectingly poetic wartime depiction of a Charleston winter.

As discussed in reference to Vanessa Bell's *Apples and Vinegar Bottle* (cat. 23), Vanessa's later years were clouded by the death of her son Julian in the Spanish Civil War. Their close relationship was instantly recognisable, and after his death Vanessa became gradually isolated, content to embrace the now ingrained domestic and somewhat circumscribed studio routine of Charleston.[2] In 1939, Vanessa moved from the studio she had previously shared with Duncan into an attic studio at the top of the house.

Her later paintings often appear to offer a form of escape for the artist. As expressed in this exhibition, prior to this date paintings of Charleston by Duncan and Vanessa were generally governed by bright and warm palettes, which depict Sussex in the height of summer – clouds reflected in the pond and dappled light bouncing off the surrounding trees. Winter, however, offered contrasting artistic possibilities. The present painting was probably painted during the winter of 1940–41, which was notable for its heavy snowfall. ES

---

1 Bell, J. (2017), 'Landscapes Near and Far'. In Milroy, S. and Dejardin, I. A. C. (eds.), *Vanessa Bell*. London: Philip Wilson Publishers, p. 154.
2 Shone, R. (1999), *The Art of Bloomsbury*, 4 November 1999 – 30 January 2000 (exh. cat.). London: Tate Gallery, p. 206.

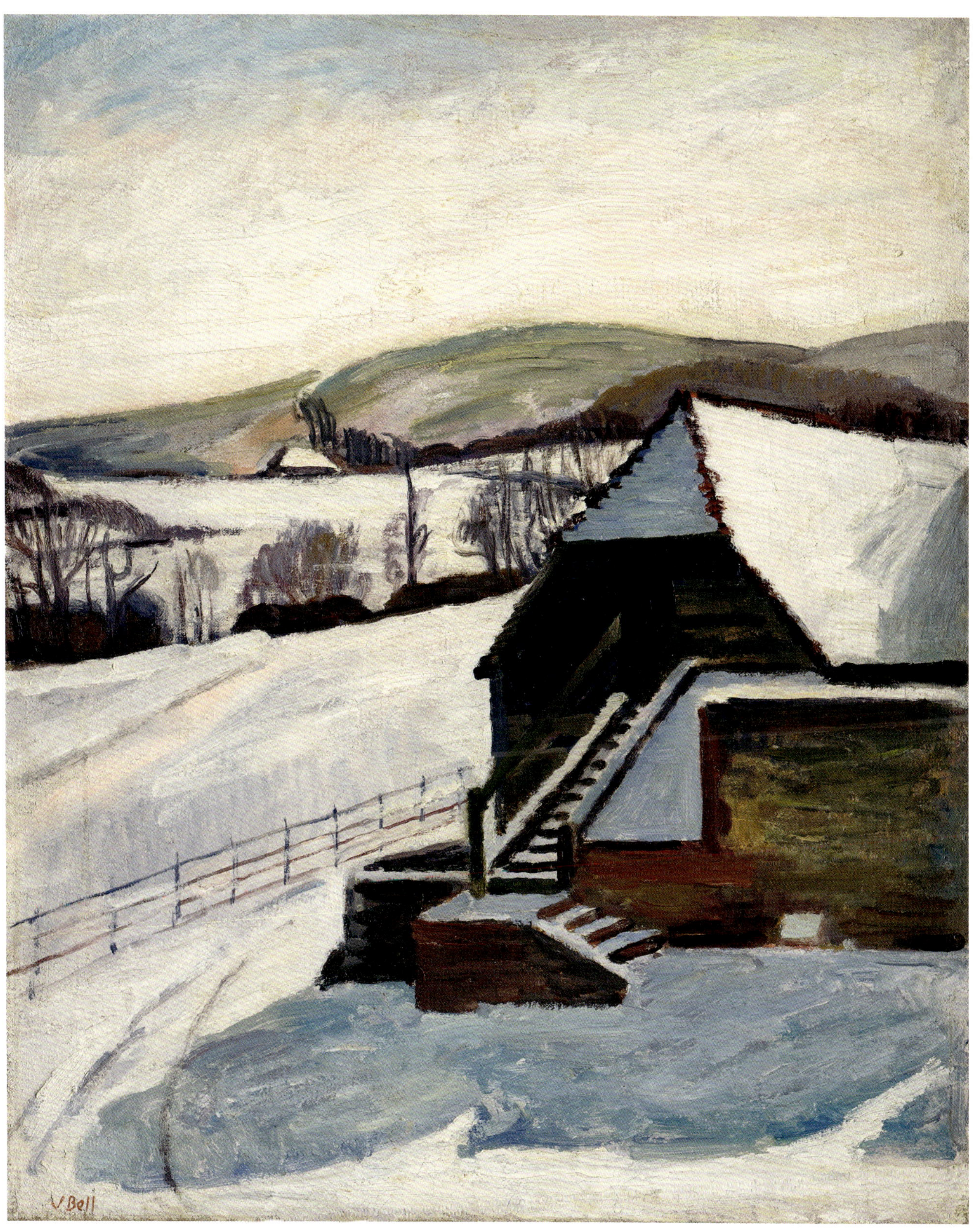
V.Bell

25

Duncan Grant

The Threshing Barn, Charleston, 1942

Signed *D Grant. /42* lower left
Oil on canvas, 47⅝ × 23¾ in. (120.9 × 60.5 cm)
Philip Mould & Company

Painted in the winter of 1942, this atmospheric composition has recently been identified as an interior view of the threshing barn at Charleston. On a canvas of the size and scale he often utilised for full-length nudes, Duncan skilfully captures the barn's impressive perpendicular scale and subdued tonal drama. The vigorously applied warm earth colours are relieved by the piercing yellow light in a manner reminiscent of old master depictions of Nativity scenes.

The present work is one of the larger paintings of this type of subject undertaken by Duncan during the Second World War. It allows a revealing glimpse into the more confined life at Charleston farmhouse during the wartime years. The barns were an omnipresent source of artistic subject matter that required no travel. Duncan and Vanessa responded profoundly to the continuity of these structures – the honesty of their design, the quality of building materials and their unashamed functionality.

The threshing barn stands adjacent to the farmhouse. The open barn door in the distance originally led to the former farmyard, which has now been replaced by a milking parlour. The construction of the barn, based on a medieval prototype, is highly distinctive: its L-shape, with two connecting chambers, is a special characteristic of barns in this part of Sussex. ES

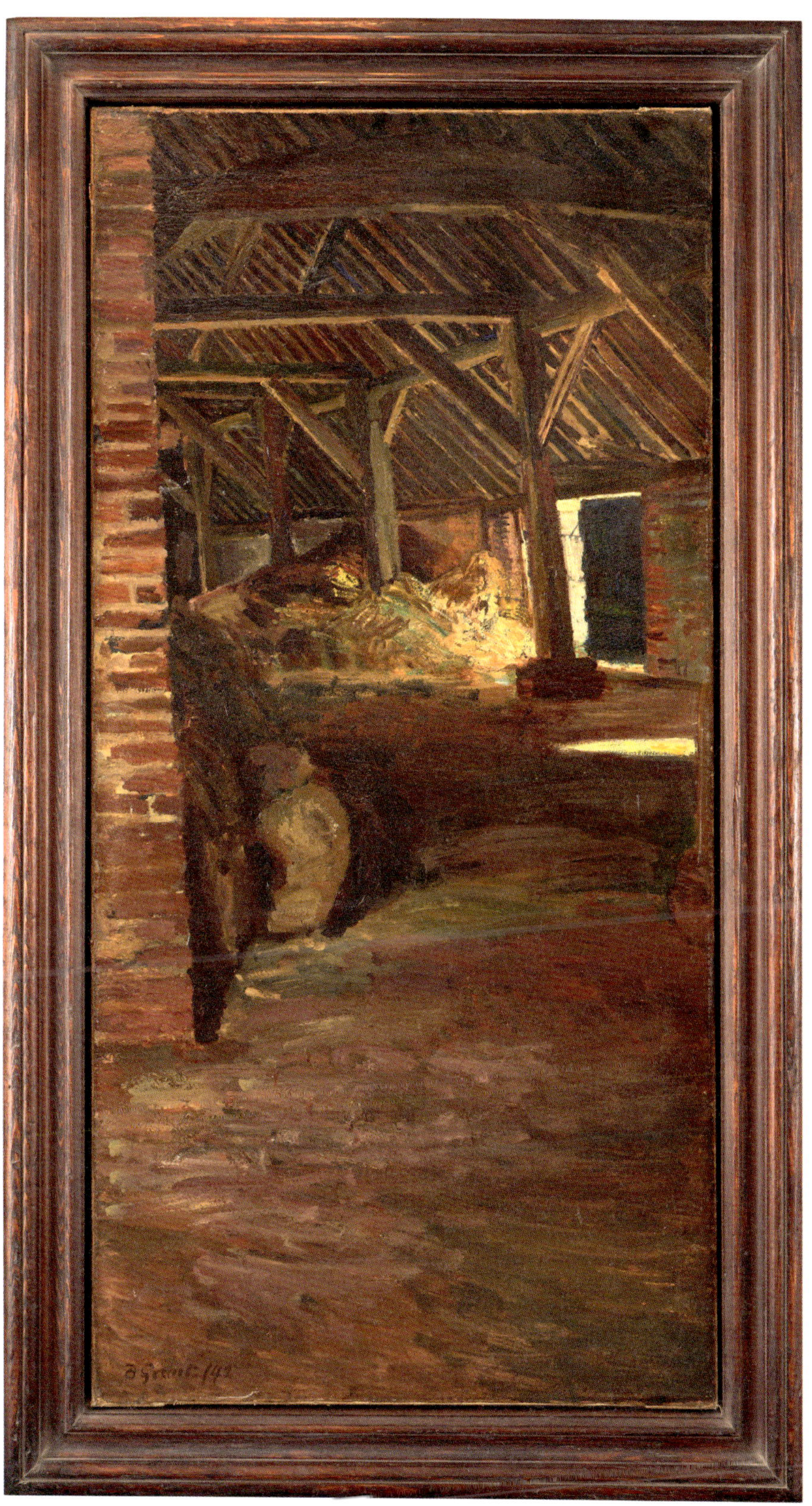

26

Duncan Grant
The Farmyard at Charleston, 1942

Signed *D Grant. /42* lower right
Oil on canvas, 25 × 29⅞ in. (63.5 × 76 cm)
Philip Mould & Company

At the outbreak of the Second World War, Vanessa and Duncan moved back to Charleston permanently.

Agricultural activity abounded around them at Charleston, and Duncan and Vanessa sketched, drew and painted its manifestations. Numerous sketchbooks held at Charleston are filled with studies of the farm, from the buildings to the livestock (fig. 44). This continual stream of inspiration upon their doorstep, evolving and shifting with each season, was one they turned into an artistic gift – and the present work is a notably successful and descriptive example.

Sheep farming was the main agricultural activity in the area, and Duncan has subtly elevated a prosaic subject with artistic distinction. The sheep are expertly choreographed to create a composition of rhythm and balance. Repetitive daubs of paint reflect the tactile, rustic surfaces. Delighting in, and no doubt enhancing, the russet and blue hues of the roof and the patterned flint wall beneath, an otherwise unpromising composition is marshalled into a work of highly satisfying agricultural genre.

The lambs present in the foreground suggest that this painting was begun in the spring of 1942.

ES

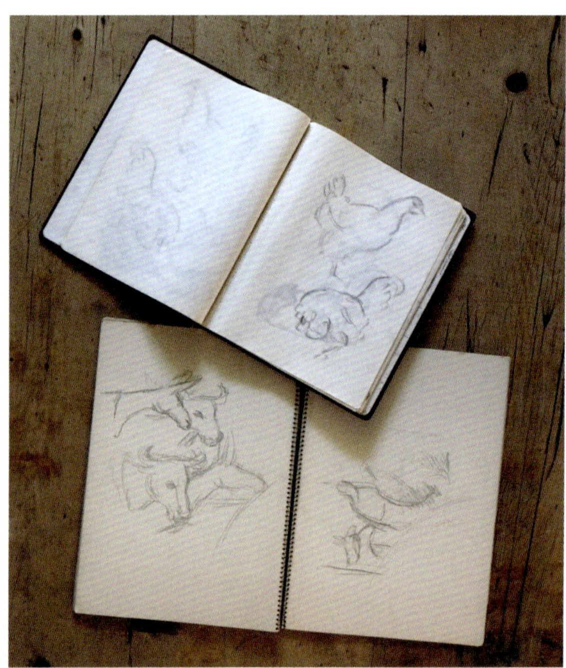

44. Duncan Grant and Vanessa Bell sketchbooks
The Charleston Trust

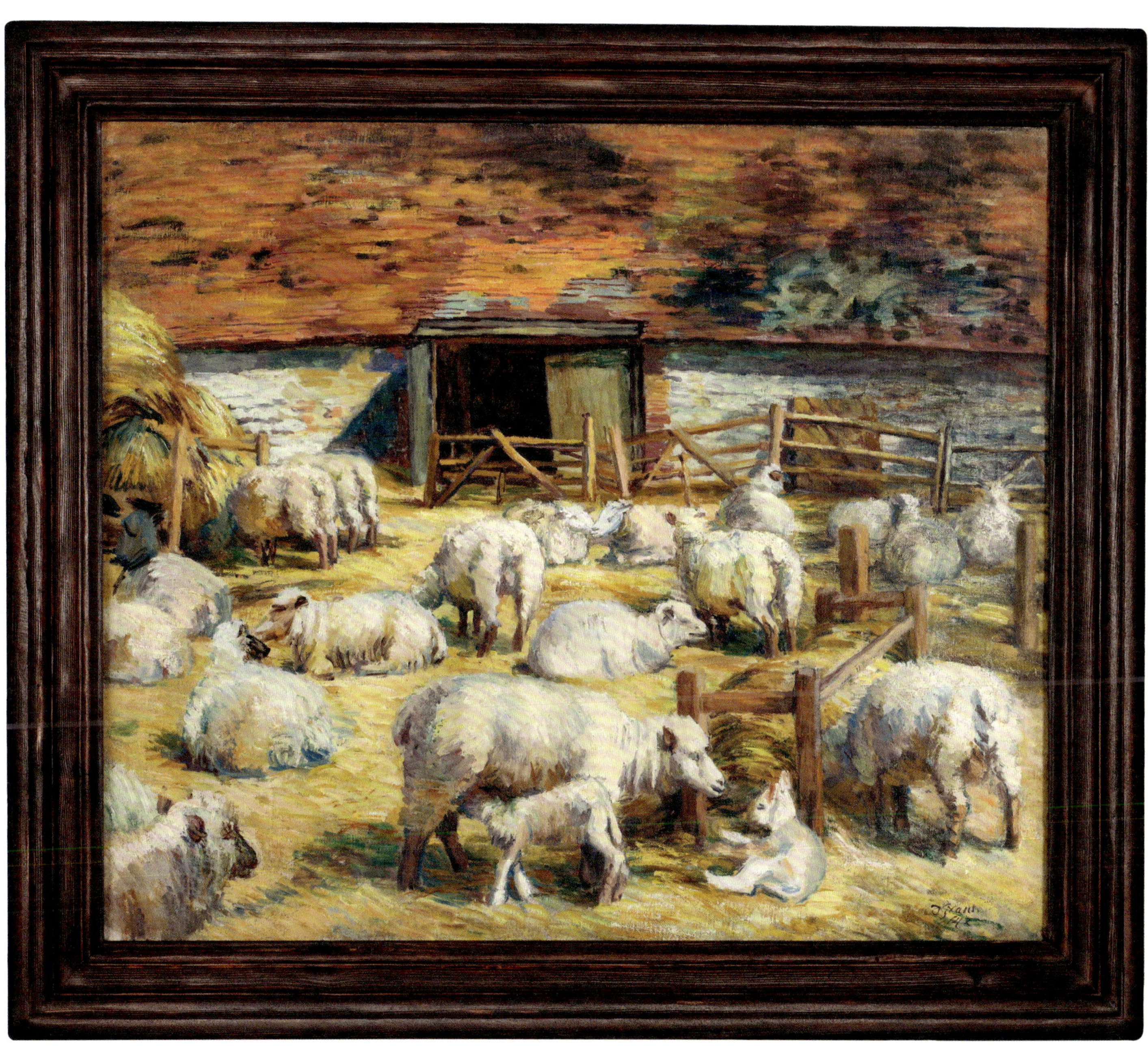

27

Vanessa Bell
Study for *The Annunciation*, 1943

Oil on plaster board, 44⅛ × 36⅛ in. (112 × 91.6 cm)
The Charleston Trust

Three and a half miles from Charleston, at the height of the Second World War, Berwick Church became the venue for Vanessa and Duncan, together with Quentin and Angelica, to execute wall paintings in a far more formalised sense than they had ever attempted at Charleston. It also granted them scope to create something of the impact of pre-Reformation painted interiors encountered on their travels to the Continent.

A connection with the church had previously been established through Sir Charles H. Reilly, the next-door neighbour of Duncan's aunt. Charles was also a great friend of Bishop George Bell of Chichester, who advocated the return of the pre-Reformation practice of patronage by the Church of local artists in his 1929 enthronement address. Duncan and Vanessa were endorsed as artists who could rise to this challenge.

Sketches were subsequently drawn up for the approval of the bishop and later the Berwick Church parish. Vanessa created studies for *The Annunciation* and *The Nativity* for the walls of the nave and Duncan sketched *Christ in Glory* for the chancel arch, whilst Quentin and Angelica also planned decorations. After heated debate amongst the parishioners it was agreed that Duncan's depiction of Christ should become less revealing.[1] Even Vanessa retrospectively admitted 'Duncan inclined to make him [Christ] too nude and attractive in his Christ of Glory'.[2]

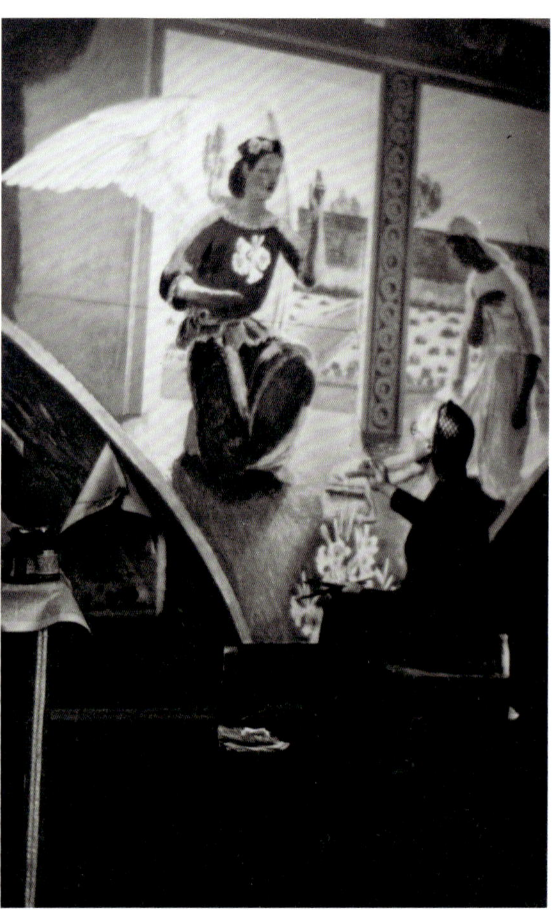

45. Vanessa Bell painting *The Annunciation* mural for Berwick Church. The ornamentation of the pillar and the curtains were removed from the final mural
Tate Archive

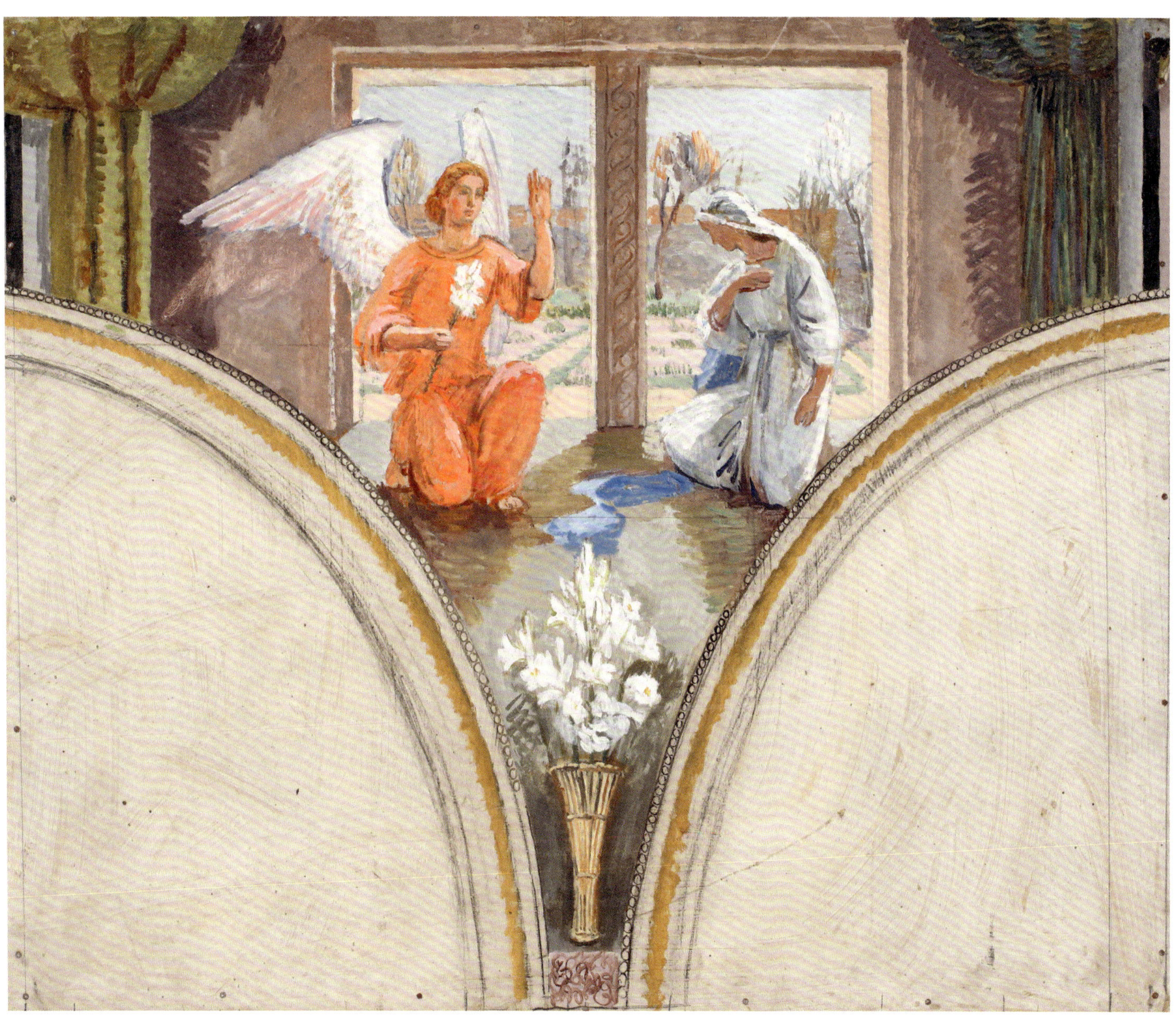

FACING

47. Vanessa Bell
The Annunciation
Berwick Church, East Sussex

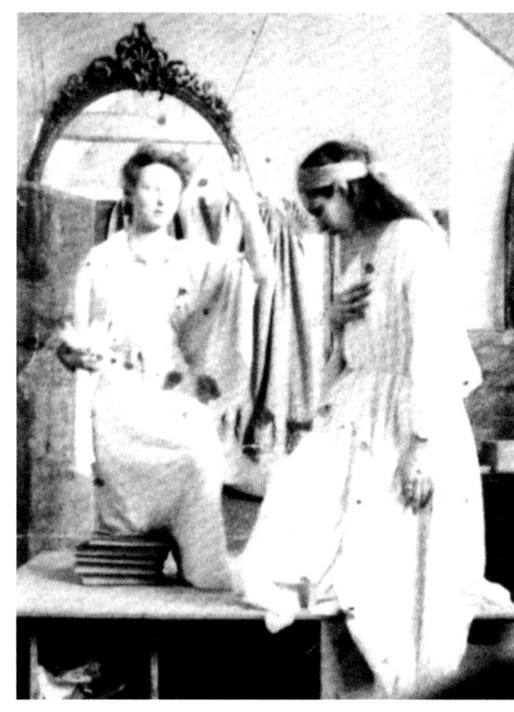

46. Chattie and Angelica Bell posing for *The Annunciation* mural in Berwick Church
Tate Archive

This is a study for *The Annunciation* on the south wall of the nave. The Virgin Mary kneels before the Angel Gabriel with a walled garden in the background. With its flint wall and smart flower beds, it takes inspiration from the view of the garden at Charleston, as seen from Vanessa's studio at the top of the house. The figures themselves also embody Charlestonian roots: Angelica was the life model for the Virgin Mary whilst her friend Chattie Salaman modelled for the Angel Gabriel (fig. 46).

Vanessa seemed to take the challenge in her stride, writing a couple of years after the installation of the artworks:

> *It has certainly been an odd experience coming into touch with a real live Bishop .... The odd thing is that it seems to be as easy as anything to get the right religious emotion into one's works ... on the whole it's quite easy to hit off a good holy atmosphere.*[3]

In a letter to the bishop, the eminent art historian Kenneth Clark lauded Vanessa's work for Berwick Church: 'I am delighted by the two panels by Mrs. Bell. They seem to me amongst the very best things she has ever done.'[4] Since then, the church's interior has been praised by many, including Sir Nicholas Serota, Chair of Arts Council England and former Director of the Tate, who deemed it to be 'of national and even international importance', stating, 'it is, critically, the only example in the country of the complete decoration of the interior of an ancient rural parish church by twentieth-century artists of repute'.[5] ES

---

1 *Archive Journeys: Bloomsbury*. Available at: https://www.tate.org.uk/archivejourneys/bloomsburyhtml/art_together_berwick.htm (accessed: 15 April 2021).
2 Bell, V. 11 March 1945. *Letter to Jane Bussy*, in Marler, R. (1993), *Selected Letters of Vanessa Bell*, London: Bloomsbury Publishing, p. 489.
3 Ibid.
4 Clark, K., quoted in Shone, R. (1969), *The Berwick Church Paintings* (exh. cat.). Eastbourne: Towner Art Gallery.
5 Serota, S., quoted in (2018) *The Vision of Bishop Bell*. Available at: https://www.berwickchurch.org.uk/bishop-bell.html (accessed: 16 April 2021).

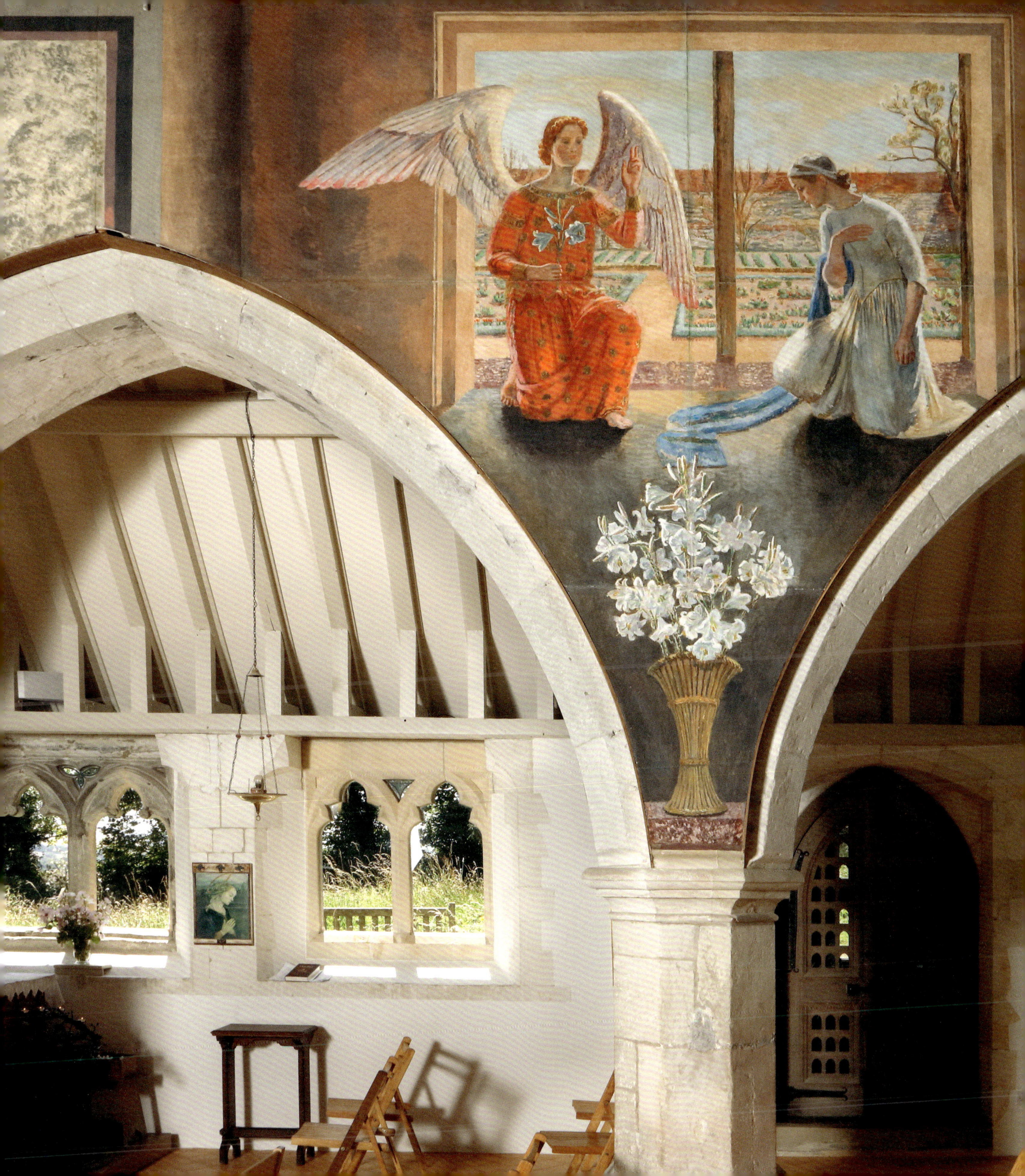

28

Duncan Grant
The Pond, Winter, c. 1943

Signed *D Grant* lower right
Oil on canvas board, 16¼ × 20¼ in. (41.2 × 51.4 cm)
Philip Mould & Company

Much like the barns, the pond at Charleston offered endless inspiration for Duncan and Vanessa's artistic ingenuity. It was one of the first outdoor spaces painted by Vanessa on arriving at Charleston in 1916 (cat. 4). The changes of season, and how this patch of still water responded, became a transforming natural muse (cat. nos. 12, 31, 32).

When the outbreak of the Second World War seemed imminent Duncan and Vanessa let their London studios to friends, packed their canvases and furniture into trucks and moved to Charleston permanently. They were joined by Clive Bell, who had his own study and library in Vanessa's old bedroom that housed his vast collection of books.[1] In between moments of panic and wartime anxieties life was relatively relaxed at Charleston at this time, with each resident contributing to its upkeep. 'Everything here is calm and luxurious,' Angelica wrote to David Garnett in July 1940.[2]

Conditions at Charleston were less pleasant in the winter months, however, and despite the recent installation of modern radiators and electricity, the house was cold and uncomfortable. Snow, wind and rain frequently battered the house during the wartime years, with one notable fatality being the gazebo on the pond, which had been constructed by Duncan in the mid-1930s.

Vigorously painted using a combination of brush and palette knife on a prepared panel, as with Vanessa's barn in snow (cat. 24), the present work indicates an awareness of Claude Monet's natural landscapes. LH

1 Spalding, F. (1998), *Duncan Grant: A Biography*, London: Pimlico, p. 368.
2 Bell, A., to Garnett, D. 27 July 1940. King's College, Cambridge. Quoted ibid., p. 370.

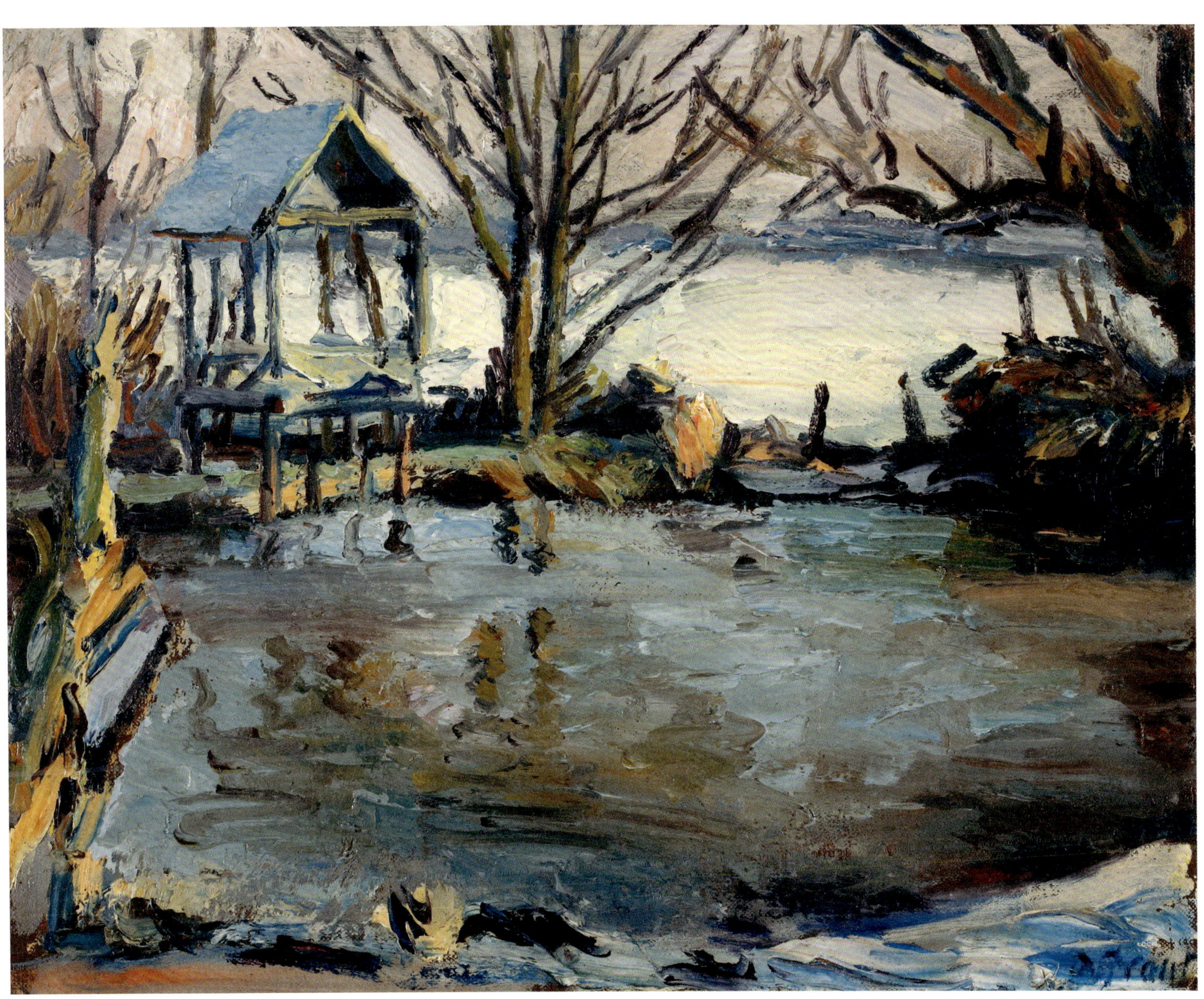

29

Duncan Grant
The Pig's Carcass, 1944

Signed *D Grant. /44* lower right
Oil on canvas, 18 × 22 ½ in. (45.6 × 57.2 cm)
Philip Mould & Company

Although titled *The Pig's Carcass* when exhibited at the Leicester Galleries in 1945, this work actually depicts a veal carcass. Duncan's focus on this domestic scene in many ways reflects his transition from a life of interwar metropolitan freedom and foreign travel to the protective world of Charleston. Possibly aware of a similar subject memorably portrayed by Rembrandt (*Slaughtered Ox*, 1655), Duncan tackles the subject with a flurry of post-impressionist-inspired brushstrokes and vibrant colour.

Though it has been suggested that the figure in the background could be Vanessa, it is more likely to be based on the housekeeper, Grace Higgens, who was the longest-serving member of the domestic staff at Charleston. She tended to the household's needs for over fifty years and is also the subject of Vanessa's *Grace Higgens in the Kitchen* (cat. 30), which usually hangs in the corridor outside Duncan's bedroom at Charleston. Duncan referred to her as 'the angel of Charleston' on account of her charming and vivacious character.

Duncan's interpretation of the kitchen at Charleston differs considerably from Vanessa's more illustrative and domestic composition, although the central wooden table displaying the ingredients is a focal point for both artists. The large carcass is a surprising subject matter considering that food was strictly rationed during the war. The government's 'Dig for Victory' campaign encouraged wartime self-sufficiency, and it is possible that cattle were reared on the farm at Charleston. Such a luxury at a time of restriction *surely* called for celebration, and this canvas certainly memorialises what would have been a moment of indulgence and excitement. ES

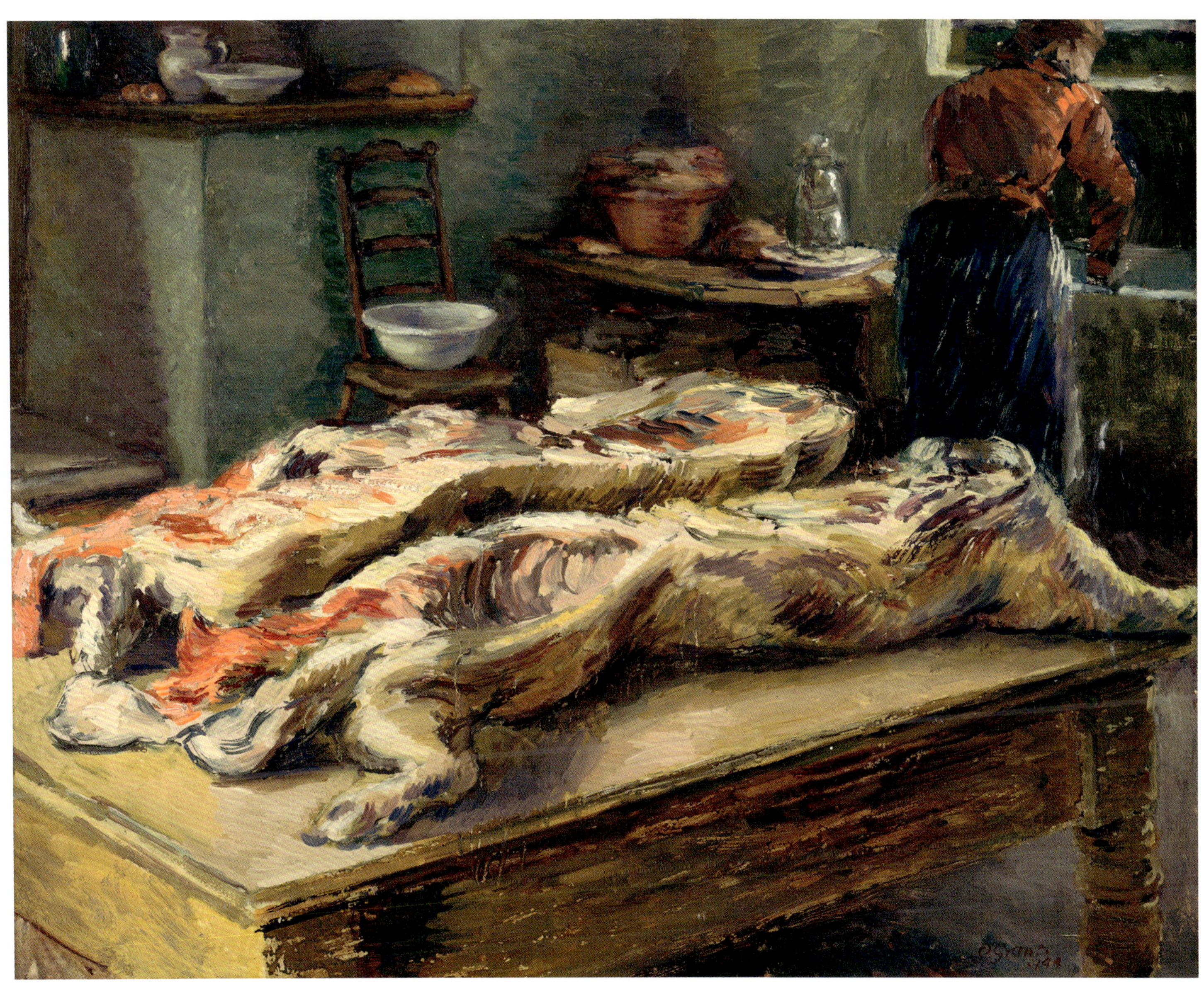

30

Vanessa Bell
Grace Higgens in the Kitchen, c. 1943–45

Initialled *VB* lower left
Oil on canvas, 34⅜ × 47⅛ in. (87.3 × 119.5 cm)
The Charleston Trust

Selected literature Nicholson, V. (2018), *Charleston: A Bloomsbury House and Garden*. London: White Lion, pp. 52–53

When Vanessa, Duncan and David Garnett first moved into Charleston there was no running water, electricity or heating. Four domestic staff moved with them to assist with the day-to-day running of the house, and the kitchen soon became a space operated predominantly by the staff. By the time this work was painted, the kitchen had firmly become the domain of Grace Higgens (née Germany) who worked at Charleston from 1920 to 1970. She tended to the household's needs for fifty years, serving as housemaid, nurse, cook and finally housekeeper.

Vanessa captures Grace preparing a meal in a composition that evokes pictorial illustration in the clear delineation of the subject and its component parts. Various fruit and vegetables adorn the kitchen table, all likely to have been grown at Charleston; the apples, carrots and other root vegetables suggest that this was painted in the autumn, when these would be harvested.

Just out of the composition to the left are the stairs which led to Grace's living quarters on the floor above. According to Virginia Nicholson, granddaughter of Vanessa and Clive Bell, this attic room was referred to as 'High Holborn' in reference to the London thoroughfare just south of Bloomsbury.[1]

As well as living at Charleston, Grace accompanied Vanessa and Duncan on their family

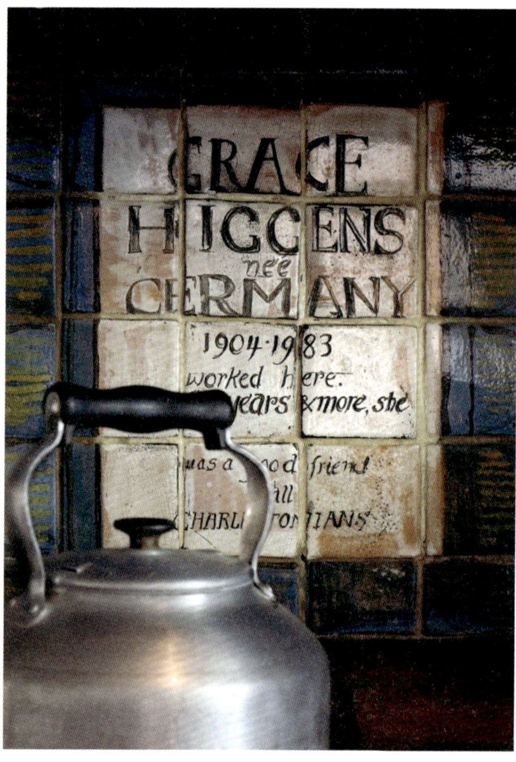

48. Grace Higgins memorial plaque, behind the stove in the Kitchen at Charleston

holidays and would often pick up new cooking techniques and recipes. The garlic hanging in the background is an indication of the influence of French cuisine inspired by their trips to France before the Second World War.

When Grace died in 1983, Quentin Bell designed a plaque commemorating her vital role in the running of the house which is still nestled above the Aga today (fig. 48). This painting, which usually hangs in the corridor outside Duncan's bedroom at Charleston, was found in Vanessa Bell's studio after she died in 1961. ES

---

1 Nicholson, V. (2018), *Charleston: A Bloomsbury House and Garden*. London: White Lion, p. 50.

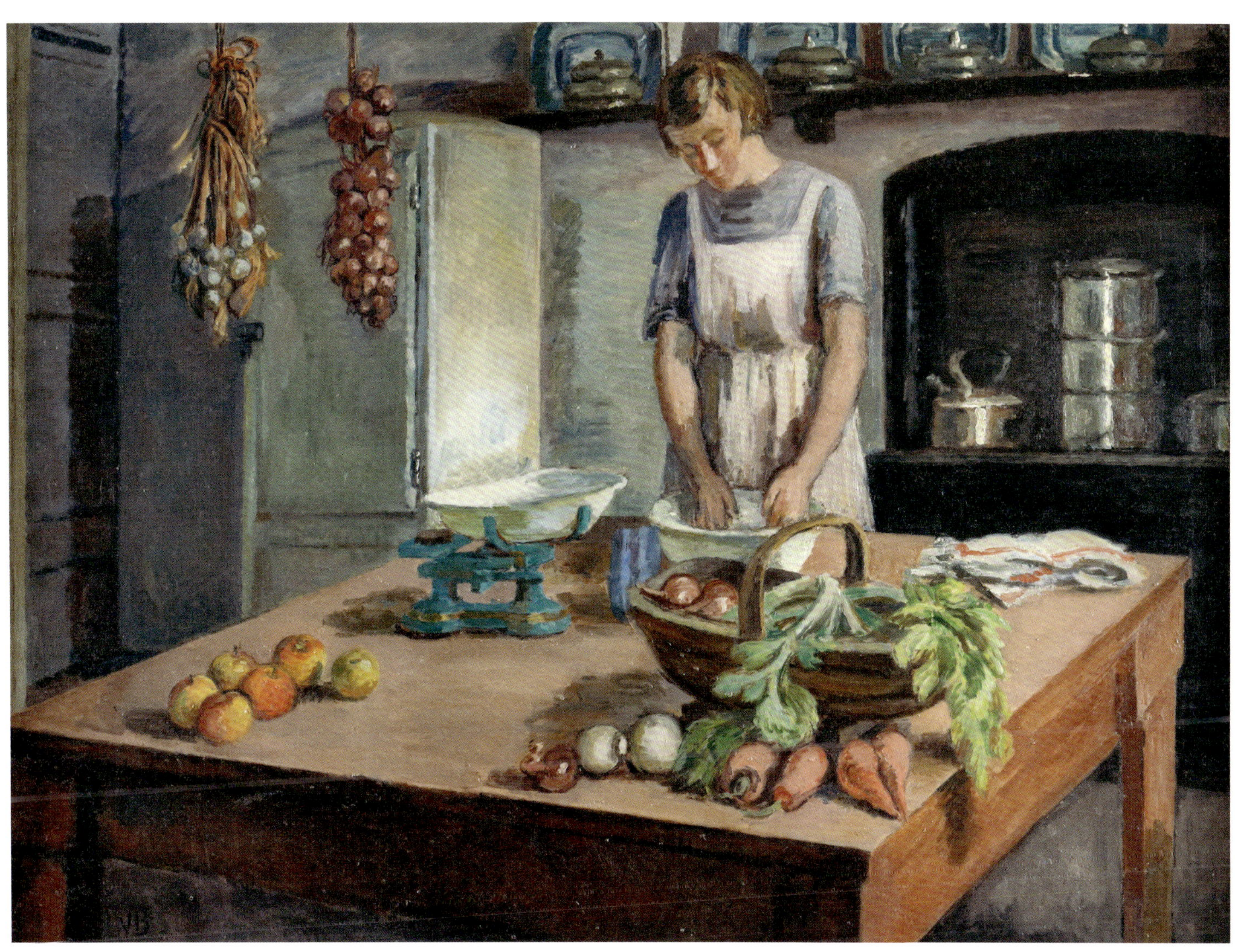

31

Duncan Grant

The Barn at Charleston, c. 1945

Signed *D Grant* lower right
Oil on board, 21¼ × 28 in. (54 × 71 cm)
Philip Mould & Company

By the date that this landscape was painted the war had been raging for over five years. This view, which Duncan revisited numerous times, is a testament to the confinement imposed throughout the wartime years and the correspondingly growing role that Charleston played as muse for Duncan and Vanessa. This painting relates to a larger work by Duncan painted in c. 1944, the composition almost identical apart from the lack of the two figures and dog present in the middle distance of this painting.

However, even prior to the war this view clearly resonated with Duncan, as well as the torrent of visitors who stayed at Charleston, such as Roger Fry, who painted the same view in 1918 (fig. 49).

The barn depicted was originally intended for the threshing and storage of grain; the large openings on either side of the building allowed harvest wagons to enter the threshing floor in the centre, and the grain was stored in the sections on either side of the barn.[1] Here the barn is celebrated for both its functional *and* aesthetic triumphs. Paintings of Charleston by both Duncan and Vanessa are generally governed by bright, warm palettes and the present painting is no exception. The forceful, painterly gestures of the early post-impressionists are echoed in the vigorous horizontal strokes of the barn and the briskly painted dappled light reflected in the pond. Grafting reality and imagination, Duncan here manipulates colour as a means of adjusting mood.

This idyllic composition is a testament to the serene lifestyle constructed at Charleston and the familiar experiences of day-to-day life that followed.

ES

49. Roger Fry
The Farm Pond, Charleston, 1918
Oil on canvas, 22 × 30 in. (55.8 × 76.2 cm)
The Hepworth Wakefield

1 Waterfield, G. *The Barn at Charleston*. Available at: https://www.charleston.org.uk/the-barn-at-charleston/ (accessed on 4 December 2020).

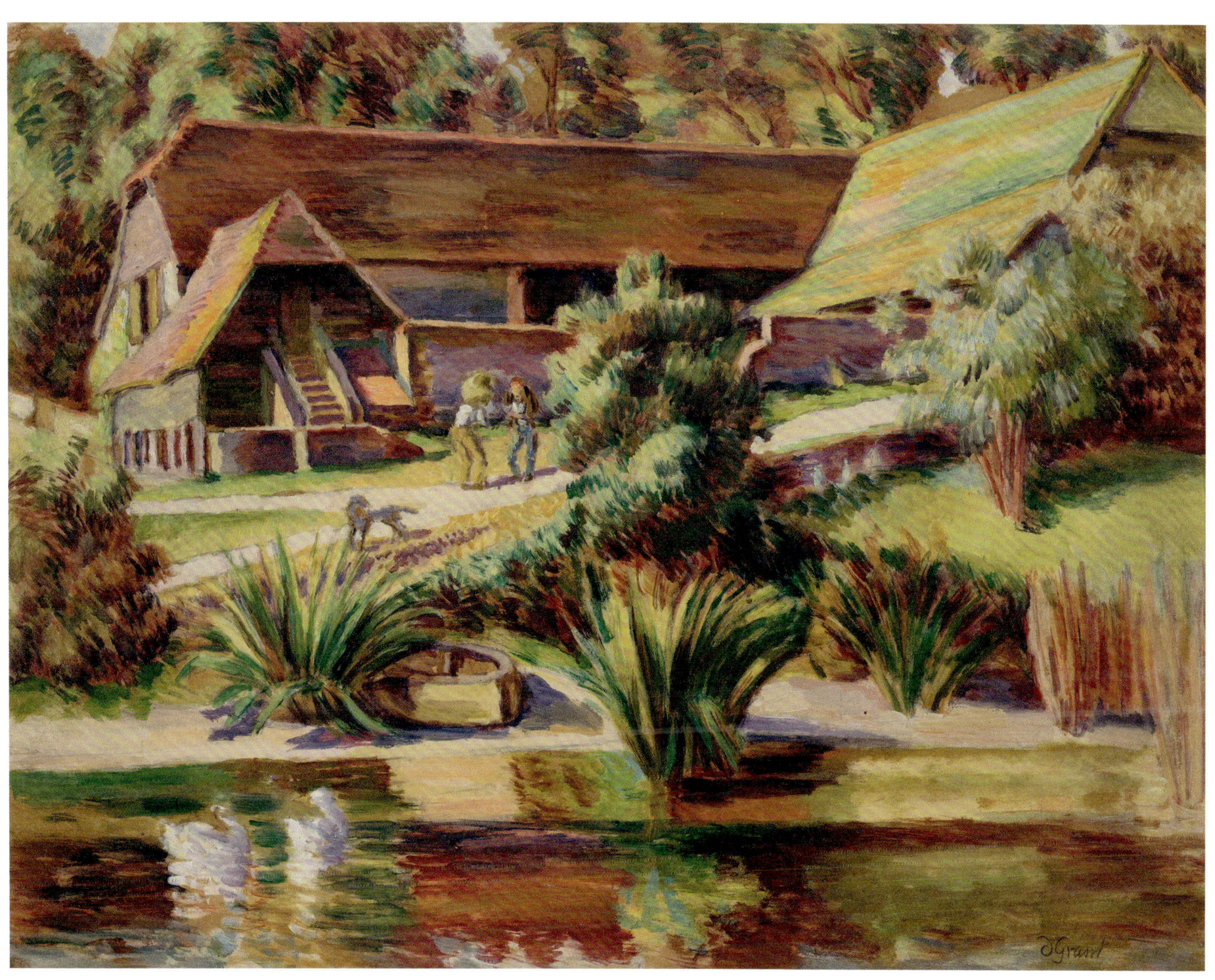
D Grant

32

Vanessa Bell
Charleston, c. 1950

Oil on canvas
24¼ × 20⅛ in. (61.5 × 51 cm)

Selected literature Shone, R. (1976), *Bloomsbury Portraits: Vanessa Bell, Duncan Grant and their circle*. Oxford: Phaidon, p. 162, fig. 100; Nicholson, V. (2018), *Charleston: A Bloomsbury House and Garden*. London: White Lion Publishing, p. 112

In the years following the Second World War the popularity of Vanessa and Duncan's art waned. A new wave of young artists rose to prominence and 'Bloomsbury' was no longer in vogue. In the post-war years Charleston remained with its tenants, and a generation of grandchildren now filled the rooms and explored the joys of its rural surroundings.

Vanessa painted this view of Charleston in around 1950 and it is her only known painting of the front of the house.[1] Its execution is mellow and restrained as befits her later style. Clive Bell is depicted wandering down the path adjacent to the pond in the foreground, in which a watery mirror image of the painting's upper half is rendered. Clive based himself at Charleston from 1939 and died in 1964, three years after Vanessa. Duncan lived at Charleston with Grace Higgens (cat. 30) and her husband until his health deteriorated, at which point he moved to the home of his friend, Paul Roche, where he died in 1978.

Vanessa did not live long enough to witness the resurgence of interest in Bloomsbury, which came about towards the end of Duncan's life. Over the last fifty years, art historians, curators and dealers have exhibited, written about and reassessed the art of Bloomsbury. In so doing they have introduced a new generation to the work of Vanessa, Duncan and their peers. At the centre of this exciting and ongoing process of rediscovery remains Charleston, the unassuming farmhouse tucked within the Sussex Downs. Saved by the vision and attachment of laudable fundraisers, Charleston is, and will continue to be, remembered as the home and muse to one of Britain's most exciting and progressive group of artists and innovators. LH & ES

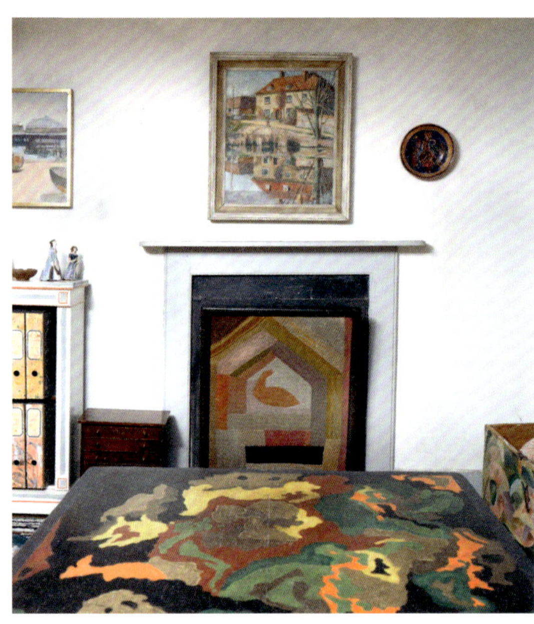

50. John Maynard Keynes's bedroom, Charleston

1 Nicholson, V. (2018), *Charleston: A Bloomsbury House and Garden*. London: White Lion Publishing, p. 112.

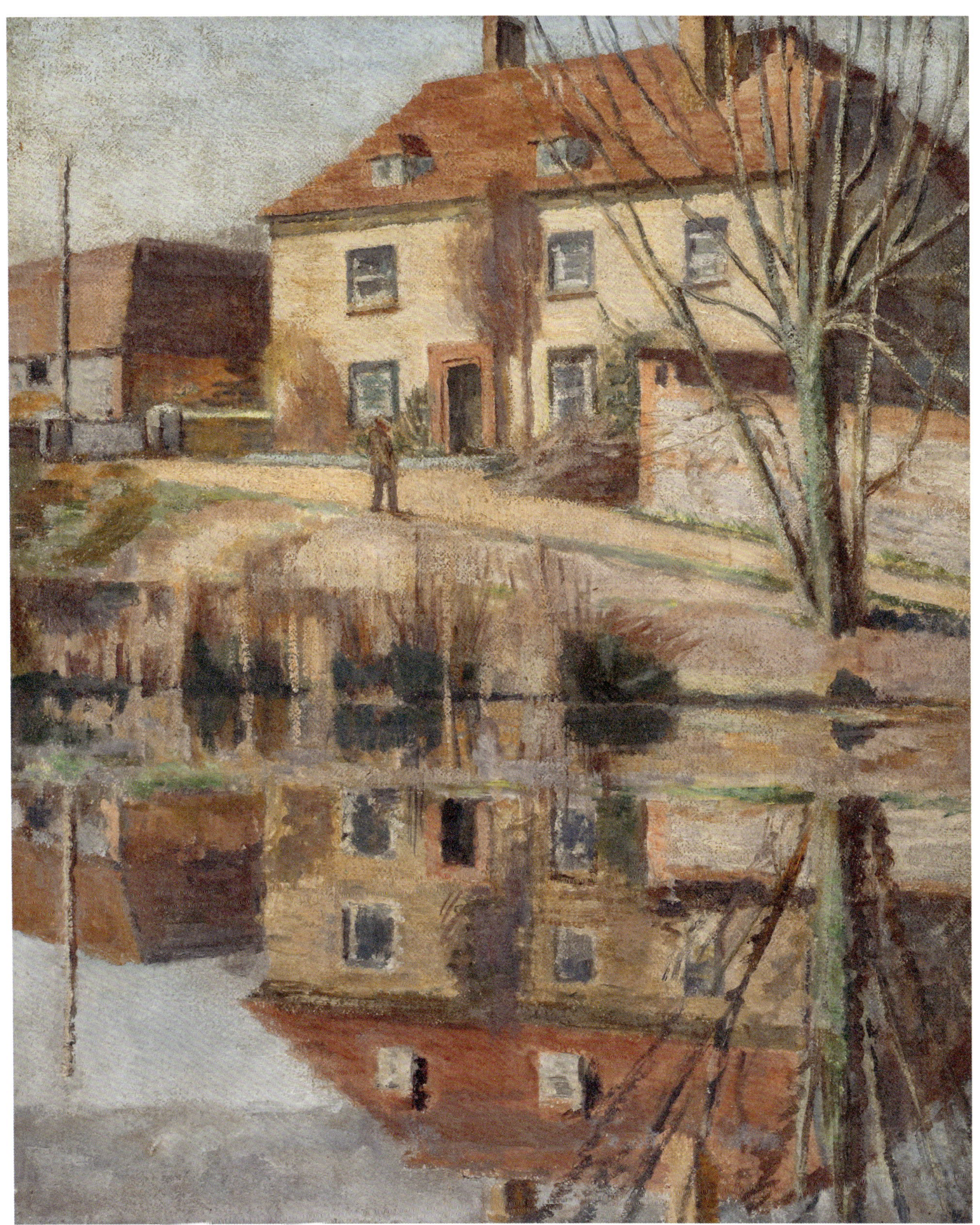

Index

Illustrated pages are in bold. References to Duncan Grant and Vanessa Bell are too numerous to list.

Photographic Credits

Cat. nos. 1, 4, 18, 19, 21, 22, 24, 27, 30, 32 Artwork © Estate of Vanessa Bell. All rights reserved, DACS 2021, Photo © Philip Mould & Company

Cat. nos. 2, 5, 13 Artwork © Estate of Duncan Grant. All rights reserved, DACS 2021, Photo © Piano Nobile

Cat. nos. 3, 6, 7, 9, 10, 12, 15, 16, 17, 25, 26, 28, 29, 31 Artwork © Estate of Duncan Grant. All rights reserved, DACS 2021, Photo © Philip Mould & Company

Cat. 8 Artwork © Estate of Duncan Grant. All rights reserved, DACS 2021, Photo Courtesy of Justin Piperger

Cat. 11 Artwork © Estate of Vanessa Bell. All rights reserved, DACS 2021/ © Estate of Duncan Grant. All rights reserved, DACS 2021, Photo © Philip Mould & Company

Cat. 14 Photo © Philip Mould & Company

Cat. 20 Artwork © Estate of Duncan Grant. All rights reserved, DACS 2021, Photo Courtesy of Tony Bradshaw

Cat. 23 Artwork © Estate of Vanessa Bell. All rights reserved, DACS 2021, Photo Courtesy of Tony Bradshaw

Fig. 1 Artwork © Estate of Vanessa Bell. All rights reserved, DACS 2021/ © Estate of Duncan Grant. All rights reserved, DACS 2021, Photo © Philip Mould & Company

Figs. 2, 6, 20, 38, 45, 46 Photo © Tate

Figs. 3, 4, 9, 10, 11, 15, 16, 18, 19 © Lee Robins

Fig. 5 © Penelope Fewster

Figs. 7, 33 © National Portrait Gallery, London

Fig. 8 © Estate of Vanessa Bell. All rights reserved, DACS 2021, Photo Courtesy of National Portrait Gallery, London

Figs. 12, 13, 14 © The Charleston Trust

Figs. 17, 34, 35 © Estate of Duncan Grant. All rights reserved, DACS 2021

Fig. 21 © Estate of Vanessa Bell. All rights reserved, DACS 2021

Figs. 22, 41 © Estate of Vanessa Bell. All rights reserved, DACS 2021, © The Charleston Trust

Fig. 23 © Estate of Vanessa Bell. All rights reserved, DACS 2021, Photo © Tate

Fig. 24 © Estate of Vanessa Bell. All rights reserved, DACS 2021, Photo Courtesy of Piano Nobile, Robert Travers (Works of Art) Ltd

Figs. 25, 26, 28, 29, 31, 32, 42, 43, 48, 50 © Philip Mould & Company

Fig. 27 © 2021 The Museum of Modern Art, New York/Scala, Florence

Fig. 30 By permission of the Provost and Scholars of King's College, Cambridge

Fig. 36 © Estate of Vanessa Bell. All rights reserved, DACS 2021, Photo Courtesy of National Portrait Gallery, London

Fig. 37 By permission of Stephen Burch, grandson of Lettice Ramsey

Fig. 39 © Estate of Duncan Grant. All rights reserved, DACS 2021, Courtesy National Museums Liverpool, Walker Art Gallery

Fig. 40 © Estate of Duncan Grant. All rights reserved, DACS 2021, Courtesy of The Firle Estate

Fig. 44 Artwork © Estate of Duncan Grant. All rights reserved, DACS 2021/ © Estate of Vanessa Bell. All rights reserved, DACS 2021, Photo © Philip Mould & Company

Fig. 47 Photo © Philip Mould & Company, Artwork © Estate of Vanessa Bell. All rights reserved, DACS 2021

Fig. 49 Courtesy of The Hepworth Wakefield